CW00855500

FUTURE HARVESTS

THE NEXT AGRICULTURAL REVOLUTION

CHRISTOPHE PELLETIER

Updated Edition. July 2011

First Edition: August 2010

Copyright © 2010-2011 Christophe Pelletier
All rights reserved.

ISBN: 1452851921
ISBN-13: 9781452851921

"An empty stomach is not a good political advisor."
ALBERT EINSTEIN

TO ALL

the men and women

committed

to take on

the challenge

CONTENTS

Preface

Food is not only one of the most enjoyable things in life, when prepared well. It is essential to our survival.

By developing agriculture some 10,000 years ago, our ancestors created an important milestone. They moved away from hunting and gathering, and took the first steps towards more food security. Agriculture has evolved dramatically since then. Farmers have been able to domesticate more and more plants and animals to provide for their needs and the needs of their communities. They invented new tools, developed new techniques and learned how to improve and increase production. This has not always been easy and the history of humanity is paved with periods of famines.

It has been a continuing challenge to grow enough food to meet the needs of the growing population. In the 19th century, Malthus was already expressing his concerns about the growth of the population and he foresaw risks of not being able to produce enough. Malthus's theory made sense in the context of his time. However, he did not foresee the huge changes that took place with and after the industrial revolution. Science has made tremendous progress, which has led to an impressive development of all sorts of technologies.

Today, there are similar concerns because of the expected population increase of three billion people between 2000 and 2050. Some claim that feeding such a population would require the equivalent area of three or four Earths.

This may be a nice wish, but the fact is that there is only one. The FAO (Food and Agriculture Organization of the United Nations) estimates that current agricultural production needs to increase by 70% by 2050 to meet the demand of the world population.

If one Earth is not enough, there is only one conclusion: there would be too many people. The only possibility then would be the massive death of the excessive numbers, be it because of famine, of disease or wars. This is not an exciting prospect, but there is no reason to think that this is the only future scenario.

Oil has been a key element in the transformation of agriculture during the 20th century. It has allowed the development of powerful machines. Oil revolutionized mobility and transport. In this period of cheap energy and highly efficient new production tools, agricultural production soared to levels never imagined before.

Because of oil, a new society centered on mass consumption appeared. Cheap oil, or at least perceived as such, allowed the development of fast delivery of goods from all over the world. Cars became the vehicle of choice for shoppers. Drive-through fast food outlets and large supermarkets, with parking lots, became the model for distribution and consumption.

This model is now seriously challenged because of the consequences of its excesses. The cost of the impact on the environment has never been factored in the cost price of the goods we consume. We over-consumed and wasted our resources. The consumption society has contributed to an increase of the level of contaminants in the air that we breathe, in the water that we drink and in the food that we eat. It has created mountains of non-biodegradable garbage, and it has depleted essential resources to almost the point of no return.

In agriculture and food, it is now necessary to envision how to produce food when oil will not be as cheap and available as it used to be. The oil era helped increase production, with its set of positive effects and its set of negative effects. The world population is facing major challenges. In order to overcome them, the rich countries must undergo changes that go beyond what most of them are currently willing to give up. The reserves are shrinking and oil will inevitably become too expensive to buy and to produce.

The carbon emissions, direct and indirect, that oil produces need to be reduced if we want to have a chance of maintaining an environment in which the human species can survive. Oil will follow the same path as coal during the 1980s. Another energy source will replace it and we already have all the technologies and the resources to make this happen. So far, the main resistance is the price of the alternatives, but this will change.

Humanity has also demonstrated an amazing ability to adapt and innovate in order to overcome problems that often seemed impossible to solve at first. Food production will have to be more efficient than ever. Despite all the progress made in agriculture, our farmers still have one major weakness: their very limited ability to control the climate or to avoid natural disasters. They have been good at selecting plant varieties and breeding the best farm animals they needed to produce efficiently, but they are still as vulnerable and helpless as they were in the early age of farming when it comes to dealing with drought or excessive precipitation, or to facing an infestation of pests.

The purpose of this book is to present the many areas of food and agriculture that need to be addressed and the problems that need to be solved to feed a growing population. Challenges are always a source of opportunities.

There is no doubt that the future of food will see much innovation and new technologies, new production techniques, new products, new distribution strategies, new transportation systems, new packaging ideas and preservation techniques. In the following pages, I have gathered the topics that will influence our decisions and the solutions that will be available to feed more people. Some solutions are about science and technology. Some of them are highly controversial and the debate is sometimes very passionate and emotional.

Our future depends on our choices. Human nature can deliver the best as it can deliver the worst. Politics and finance sometimes bring their share of controversy.

A number of companies appear in the book. I chose to name them because they offer interesting or innovative solutions. Some may succeed, some may not, but people who try to make the world a better place need to be praised. Humans have thrived because they created tools and developed the ability to think and create new ideas. Our future success depends very much on our resourcefulness and our ability to use our minds for the best.

I wish you happy reading and I hope this book will motivate you to become an active part of the transformation of our food production and food supply.

Christophe Pelletier

Introduction

Agriculture has become an increasingly complex activity. Ensuring food security remains a challenge. The future of agriculture depends on many factors and on human ingenuity to innovate and produce more efficiently. In spite of all the technical progress, access to food and production of food follow basic principles. This introduction will review the essential truths about agriculture and food security.

Food production is an essential economic activity

If we do not eat, we die. It is possible to live without cars and computers. Life would just be a little less convenient. It is not possible to live without food.

Agriculture is crucial because not only does it provide the necessary food, it is also the world's largest economic activity. According to the FAO, agriculture employs about 1.3 billion people and it provides employment indirectly to an additional one billion people.

Farmers play a very important role in human societies and farming is not the romantic activity some city residents tend to believe it is. Farming is hard work performed by men and women who have to make a living from it. In order to have farmers and a productive agriculture in the future, it is essential that they make money.

There is only one Earth

Although humans have acted during the last century as if the Earth had infinite resources, this is not the case. The reality is simple: more people need more food, and there is only one planet on which to produce it. It is necessary to either be much more efficient or develop new production areas, using methods that will not compromise the future. Failure to achieve these objectives will result in a sharp increase of food prices, which will lead to social unrest and probably armed conflicts.

Economy is the management of resources to ensure the survival of our species

The word "economy" comes from the Greek words *oikos*, meaning house or habitat and *nomos*, meaning administration. A sound economy is one that keeps the house (the Earth) in good standing. By looking at the economy in this manner, the triple bottom line concept is a logical and natural one. The triple bottom line is a way of looking at economic performance and its environmental and social consequences, not just financial criteria. Money is only one of the components of the economy. Keeping our actual houses in good standing simply makes sense. To achieve this, we need to take the proper actions (policies), use the proper resources (natural resources, land and money) and define the roles of the people involved (labor). No normal person would stack up garbage on his or her own property. Yet, when it comes to the planet, our actions have been very different. The landfills have accumulated non-biodegradable garbage, groundwater has become contaminated with minerals and dangerous gases pollute the air. The reason for this illogical behavior is simple: in most cases, the effect of environmental damage will come later and in a different place, while garbage in our house is here and now.

Everything that is not sustainable has no future

Anything that is unsustainable is doomed, and therefore it will disappear. There cannot be any argument against sustainability. Unfortunately, the debates about defining the parameters and allocating the accountability for sustainability delay effective action. A clear example of this has been the Climate Change Conference in Copenhagen in December 2009. During this summit, no final agreement was reached and countries placed the blame on each other.

Everything that is rigid is neither flexible, nor adaptable

Adaptability has been a key element in the evolution of life, and as the famous quote wrongly attributed to Charles Darwin said, *"It is not the strongest of the species that survives, nor the most intelligent that survives. It is the one that is the most adaptable to change".* [1]

This statement is relevant when it comes to the way we think of the future and of how our systems and structures function. The first reaction of most people is to resist change. Yet, when change is necessary to ensure our survival, resisting it can compromise our chances of success and make us waste precious time.

Agriculture is about managing living organisms and their environment

Since the day our ancestors started cultivating plants in the Fertile Crescent (the region going from Eastern Iraq to South Turkey, Lebanon and Northern Israel), farmers have done their best to improve plants and animals.

---

[1] This statement would have been a paraphrase of Darwin by Leon C. Megginson, a management sociologist of Louisiana State University, although it has also been attributed to Clarence Darrow.

However, controlling the environment, especially the climatic conditions, still remains a challenge. Farming also includes managing the microorganisms that live in the soil and on food products. Agriculture is not just crops in production, but it is a whole ecosystem at work. Agriculture is about balancing all the interactions between the crops in production and all the other plants and animals that live near and in the field, even though they do not have a direct economic function. Yet, they fulfill functions that one must neither ignore, nor neglect. From a sustainability point of view, an essential part of farming consists of ensuring that all the cycles of water, of organic matter and of soil preservation function properly.

Without water, there is no agriculture and there is no life

Water is an essential element of life. Everything that reduces access to water or makes it unfit for consumption is a threat to survival. Everything that will help save water and keep it clean will be invaluable to humanity. There is no doubt that water will become a strategic commodity, of much greater importance than oil is today. Remember that a person can live without food for a couple of months, but cannot survive without water for much more than two or three days.

Food is power

This may disturb some idealists. Unfortunately, food has been used as a bargaining tool in the past and it will be used as such in the future, too. For example, food aid can be selective and governments can decide either to help or to put other nations at a disadvantage. Similarly, veterinary restrictions or import levies can be a great weapon to protect the domestic agriculture from foreign competitors. Such a power is not just for government and international politics.

Companies use it to their own advantages, too. They can be active by lobbying governments to help pass legislation that will serve their interests. Through lobbying, they can create a situation of quasi-monopoly to force their partners in the food production chains to accept conditions that they would not otherwise. The power that comes with the ownership, or at least the control, of food will be a source of growing tension in the future.

One billion poor people suffer from hunger while the rich eat too much

According to the FAO, there are about one billion people worldwide suffering from hunger today, which represents about one out of seven people. While there are many reasons to explain this number, such as climate, local infrastructure and bad policies, the main culprit is poverty. When people have money, they can access food, regardless of where they live. This is how markets work.

This situation is not limited to poor countries. Even in the rich Western countries, a percentage of the population suffers from hunger. For instance in the USA, a report from the USDA Economic Research Service stated that 14.6% of American households had difficulties putting food on their tables in 2008.

According to the FAO, there are also one billion overweight and obese people worldwide. They suffer from ailments that result directly from their excessive consumption like heart disease, stroke, obesity and diabetes. When such diseases take epidemic proportions in a society, it means that something is fundamentally wrong with their diet and lifestyle choices. In these countries, governments will have no choice but to take action to change the situation.

Affordable food is not the same as cheap food

In order to feed the world population, food must be affordable. The price is only one parameter, though. Proper nutrition is just as important. Agriculture and food industry must provide balanced diets and reasonable portions for a price that everybody should be able to buy. Of course, the cheaper food is, the more affordable it is, but producing cheap food at all costs might end up costing much more than it seems. The concept of cheap food brings two main risks. First, when food is cheap, people tend to over-consume, which leads to potential health problems. Secondly, when consumers do not realize the true value of food, they tend to throw it away or waste it. Considering the amount of inputs to produce food, such as energy and water, the concept of cheap food leads to a waste of precious resources.

The world population is increasingly concentrated in cities

All statistics show the same trend: the world's population will be more and more concentrated in urban centers.

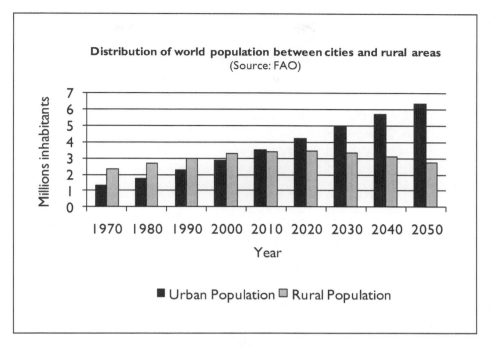

The FAO estimates that today 47% of the population lives in urban areas and they expect this proportion to reach 70% in 2050. Today, there are about 3.6 billion people living in rural areas, and this number will drop to 2.7 billion people in 40 years from now. Therefore, rural populations will decrease by 25% to go back to the level of 1980, while urban population will almost double from 3.2 billion to 6.3 billion! This will have a major impact on the way that food will be produced and delivered to the people.

Humans are not rational because they have emotions

People rarely eat according to sound rational nutrition. For the people who can afford food, the remembrance of experiences, such as the ones that remind them of what they ate when they were children or the desire for an immediate comfort feeling play an important role in their choices. For the people who cannot afford a decent ration, the choice is based on financial aspects. They eat what they can, not what they should.

Fear and greed are two incredibly powerful emotions that impair judgment and cause some serious mistakes. The fear of a food shortage will result in people hoarding food at the local grocery store and even fighting with each other, even if there is no actual food shortage. All it takes is a rumor. Greed is what drives speculators to enter food markets and drive prices up. Fear and greed are the source of many market cycles in agriculture. When the price for a product is high, more farmers want to profit from the good market and they all rush into producing more of it. The result is usually an overproduction that causes market prices to drop, and then most farmers do not make money. As they are afraid of losing more money, many of them decide then to stop producing, only to see the few who remained in the business make good money, because the drop in production caused prices to rise again.

These essential truths create a good foundation to examine the future relationships between human populations and food availability, the natural conditions to produce food and the creativity of humans to find solutions to their problems.

PART I

The Underlying Dynamics of Food Supply and Demand

Changing Demographics and Shifting Economic Power

The growth of the world population is not spread evenly between countries. The demographics will have an effect on both production and consumption. The age pyramid of the different countries will influence the future economic and demographic evolution. An interesting indicator is the median age, which divides the population in two equal groups. Half of the population is younger than the median age and half is older.

All industrialized countries in North America, Australia, New Zealand and Europe have a high median age, close to 40. At 44, Japan has the highest median age in the world. This is the result of a longer life expectancy and a decreasing birth rate. The industrialized countries are not only getting older but their population is hardly growing. In Russia and Eastern European countries, there is a decrease of population because of low fertility and emigration.

The population in Latin American and Asian countries (except for Japan) is still growing at a strong pace. Their birth rates have been slowing down, while their life expectancy has increased. Both regions have relatively young populations with median ages below 30 for most countries.

China shows a different situation than most of its Asian neighbors. The median age of 34 is rather high. This number is the result of the one-child policy that China introduced in 1979. China's population is growing slowly.

Africa and Arab countries have more than half of their populations under 25 years of age. This is the result of high birth rates in Arab countries and, for Africa, the consequence of the AIDS epidemic.

In Arab countries, 65% of the population is younger than 30. A problem that Arab countries face is a high level of unemployment, of 25% among young people. Half of these 25% are first time entrants in the job market. In many African countries, half of their populations are younger than 20. Uganda has the lowest median age in the world at 14. Africa and Arab countries are showing a fast population growth, except for South Africa because of AIDS.

The evolution of demographics is going to influence the future political international relationships. Food and agriculture will play a significant role in this transformation.

Asia, Africa and the Middle East face serious problems to feed their own people. Their populations are growing rapidly and these countries face a high risk of social unrest if they cannot develop their economies and provide their young populations with employment and food. By 2050, seven billion people out of the total nine billion will live in these three regions.

Today, Asia represents about half of the world population and the continent is still showing strong growth. This part of the world is growing economically, especially in industrial sectors and the services sector. These businesses will need more people coming from rural areas to work in the factories and offices. In Asia, the agricultural population now represents between 30% and 70% of the total active population, depending on the country. The migration of farmers to the industry and services will fuel a further urbanization boom. This will change the agricultural structure, as there will be more consumers than before who do not grow food anymore. These regions have specific climatic and soil conditions that will require great care to ensure the sustainability of agriculture. Many countries in Asia are not self-sufficient today and they will need to have access to food from other regions.

South America is a net exporter of agricultural products and, in particular, countries like Brazil, Argentina, Uruguay and Chile play an important role in the global trade of agricultural commodities and food products.

Although the population in Latin America is growing strongly, both South and North America will still have large areas of agricultural land and both continents should remain net exporters in the future. This favorable situation will give these regions economic and political power in world trade negotiations.

Changing demographics will affect the dynamics of the world economy. The wealthy industrialized countries still will play a leading role for some time, simply because this is where the wealth for consumption of goods is, although consumption patterns will change in the future due to the pressure to improve environmental performance. The strong development that is happening in emerging countries is the direct consequence of the consumption society and of financial markets. Most manufacturing activity has moved away from industrialized countries to the now emerging countries for the simple reason that the cost of labor was low, which reduced the production costs and the price to consumers, which stimulated consumption. On the other side of the business deals, countries like China and India, by welcoming foreign corporations found a great way to develop their own economies and create employment, thus averting risks of social unrest.

After the death of Mao Tze Tung, China has changed its course cleverly. The government realized that the country needed to open to the outside world more and to develop its economy to ensure social stability. We all know what has happened in the last 30 years and now China is playing a dominant role in the world economy. During this period, the Chinese leadership has been working towards food security because they know it is essential to social stability. As the Chinese economy is growing, so is the middle class.

The development of the Chinese economy has a typical pattern of farmers finding better paying jobs in factories and the cities grew around the new economic activity, followed later by the service industry. The Chinese leadership showed a great dose of pragmatism because opening the country to capitalistic foreign multinationals and creating a free economy within a one-communist-party political system was against the thinking of the dominant ideology.

5

The Great Recession of 2008-2010 has caused a shift in economic power. About 70% of the American economy was based on retail sales before the economic crisis. Credit defaults and reduced access to loans is going to limit growth possibilities. The US economy runs on stimulus money. The national debt and the budget deficit are at an all-time high. China on the opposite disposes of large cash reserves and can finance many projects without issuing debt. Their middle class will grow and consumption will increase. The objective of the Chinese government to grow a middle class from 300 million people today to at least 800 million by 2025 is on its way to completion. The Chinese middle class is gaining more spending power. For the first time, more cars were sold in China than in the USA in 2009. China will soon produce for its domestic market. Factories will depend less on exports. China is taking economic leadership over from the USA. International trade will shift to China and Asia. This is even truer for agriculture and food. With half the world's population on the continent, Asia is going to become the main food consumption market and it will not be able to be self-sufficient. The populations in all emerging countries are changing their diets as they become wealthier and they all tend to consume more meat and other animal protein. The result will be a much stronger demand for agricultural commodities, which will greatly benefit the countries that have the land, the water and the resources to produce more.

Food supply strategies will increasingly show similarities to oil supply strategies. Politics are going to become increasingly important. There will be aggressive moves from countries that are not self-sufficient, but there will be a point when this will not be enough and regional conflicts will happen. Some exporting countries will also take a more aggressive stance on prices and on supplies, but they also will have to be aware that too much arrogance might end up in tension. Much more than today, food will join energy, trade agreements, diplomacy and military threats in the arsenal of international negotiations.

The strategies for food supply will lead to new economic zones. The Mediterranean region is the interface between Europe, Asia and Africa. Between all the countries with a coast on the Mediterranean Sea, the region produces a wide variety of food and possesses an extensive knowledge of agricultural practices. The Mediterranean also offers a variety of seafood, both from fisheries and aquaculture. Climatic conditions play a role in limiting agriculture in most parts of the region. Demographics around the Mediterranean are unbalanced. There are aging populations with slow growth in the European part and there is a demographic explosion in Northern Africa. The European side of the sea is self-sufficient. On the African side of the Mediterranean, food security is difficult to achieve, especially when the population keeps on growing. Having a strong food supply in the North while more people will become food insecure in the South is making a migration scenario likely. Because of the colonial past, many of these countries have ties, and immigration from the South to Europe has taken place regularly since the old colonies have gained their independence.

Migrations will create many opportunities for trade, as the connections between the countries will grow stronger under influence from the new immigrants. Of course, the immigration flow in the region is more than simply an economic issue, but it brings strong cultural and religious tensions, too. A managed integration supporting the development of wealth is an absolute necessity to avoid conflicts. The existing political and religious tensions, combined with an imbalance in food security, give the region potential for major instability. European countries of the region and their counterparts in Asia and Northern Africa will need to meet and develop coordinated policies for the Mediterranean region. This way, they can determine strategies to manage climatic, economic, political and food security challenges. There is great potential for a win-win situation if managed properly. The idea of creating an Economic Zone around the Mediterranean has been brought forward by the French President Nicolas Sarkozy. It is not a new idea, as in ancient times trade between these countries was one of the pillars of the economy of the region.

Because of their geographic location and logistics, the ties between the former Soviet republics and the Middle East will become stronger. The Black Sea countries can provide the region with grain. This region also needs to create more political and economic stability. In March 2010, the First Deputy Prime Minister of Russia, Igor Shuvalov, declared that Russia, Kazakhstan and Belarus are considering the possibility of having one common currency.

Migrations in the North-South contact area between Asia and Central and Eastern Europe are likely. The region spanning from the Black Sea region, the Caspian Sea region, the former Asian Soviet Republics, Russia, China, Iran, Pakistan, and to some extent the Arabic Peninsula and India is sensitive because of oil, which generates a large part of the revenue of Russia, Iran and Arab countries.

It is also sensitive to food supply, as some of these countries cannot grow much because of desert conditions, while others have rich agricultural land. In the long-term, food imports are going to weigh increasingly economically and politically. Many of the region's countries have comfortable revenue from oil, although depending on the quality of their oil fields, the price of oil that they need to receive in order to balance their budgets varies greatly. Qatar needs less than US$25 a barrel to balance its economy, while Saudi Arabia needs around US$50 and Iran needs US$90. These numbers will affect how much they can spend on new projects. This is a politically sensitive region. Several countries in the region possess nuclear weapons. Religious radicalism is also part of the dynamics. These conditions call for very skillful diplomacy to ensure a harmonious cooperation. Food will play a role in multilateral negotiations.

In Asia, due to population growth, trade activity within the region will intensify. While much of the past economic growth has come from manufacturing of products and outsourcing of services for the West, the local market will gradually increase its share in the local trade. China is the engine of growth and it seems logical that a new economic zone will appear around it, including the ASEAN nations, China, South Korea and likely Japan.

India is a particular case in Asia. It is somewhat isolated. The Himalayas to the north make road connections with China difficult. To the west, the conflict with Pakistan obviously does not create favorable conditions for open trade. On the east side, India has substantial trade activity, but the neighboring countries still are suffering from economic weakness, and therefore have limited potential. India still suffers from food insecurity and it needs further economic development. India will have to engage in trade agreements with the large economies of the region. When it comes to food and agriculture, the main weakness in the region is that China and Japan, two economic giants, are and will likely remain net importers of food. India, the third economic Asian giant might follow them if it cannot boost the efficiency of its agriculture.

The situation in the Americas will evolve. With NAFTA in the north and Mercosur in the south, it is just a matter of time before an economic zone appears in Central America, probably under influence of either one, or both, of these two entities, first with bilateral trade agreements, and later through multi-party agreements. Mercosur will expand to all Latin American countries eventually. Latin America has also the advantage of a common language, except for Brazil, and shares a cultural heritage. Because the South of the USA is also in a linguistic transition, where half of the people in Florida and California speak Spanish as a first language, the entire American continent will have closer economic relations than it has been in the past. It is likely that populations from Central America will migrate north to the USA and they might become the American farmers of the future.

The Quest for Food Security

The FAO defines food security as "*the situation in which all people, at all times, have physical and economic access to sufficient, safe and nutritious food to meet their dietary needs and food preferences for an active and healthy life*".

Food is one of the most basic needs of all living organisms and the human species is no different from any other. During evolution, human populations have gradually shifted from hunting and gathering by acquiring the ability to select and raise a combination of plants and animals that can provide them with food all year round. By being able to have a source of food located nearby, their dependence on "good luck" decreased and their chances of survival increased. Yet, even in the 21st century, humans have not quite emancipated themselves from going into the wild to find food. Fisheries and nomadic populations are examples of dependence on wildlife. Knowing that food is there when needed is the most valuable aspect of agriculture. It removes uncertainty, creates food security and creates the conditions for economic prosperity, which is necessary for societies to grow and develop. The development of agriculture has been a major element in the settlement of populations into communities. Agriculture has shaped societies far beyond what many people may realize. Creating food security has allowed the creation of villages and cities. Villages and cities have always appeared near sources of drinking water and food. The growth of this mosaic of settlements has resulted in the establishment of kingdoms and nations that have spent and still spend large amounts of time and money to establish their sovereignty and fight to control resources.

This was true 10,000 years ago and the global politics of today simply follow the same logic. The word politics come from the Greek word *polis,* meaning city. The entities that have derived from the development of agriculture are now defining the politics and the policies of food security to meet the needs of a growing population.

Although agriculture increases food security, production still depends on environmental conditions, such as weather, diseases, pests and weeds.

Except for greenhouses where computers program the number of hours of light, the temperature, the humidity and the distribution of water, agricultural activities are still subject to the climate. Too much rain may destroy the crops or may erode good quality soil, or a long-lasting drought will dramatically reduce the yields, or force farmers to sell their cattle earlier than planned, as there is not enough feed for the animals.

Climate change has the potential to affect food security significantly because it might affect the yields of crops, and thus affect the availability and the price of food. It also could change the ecosystem in such a way that diseases and pests could occur more often and more strongly than in the past.

Diseases and pests have always been causes of lower agricultural production. For instance, a type of stem rust fungus, named Ug99 by the scientists after its appearance in Uganda in 1999, has the potential to wipe out 80% of the world's wheat production if it spreads. The UN considers this fungus a major threat to the world's food security.

Insects are well-known pests with devastating effects on crops. For instance, the locust outbreak of 2004 in West and North Africa caused major damage. Mauritania lost half of its harvests to the insects.

Weeds are less spectacular, yet just as effective in reducing food production and therefore undermining food security. According to the FAO's numbers, weeds limit crop yields to such an extent that the world loses the equivalent of 380 million tons of wheat a year, or about half of the 2009 expected world wheat production! With the simplistic assumption that this wheat would feed people only a basic diet of bread, it could feed about one billion people, which is the estimate of the FAO for the number of hungry people in the world.

Dealing with hunger is not an easy task. Currently, the FAO estimates at about one billion the number of people suffering from hunger. With an additional two billion people expected on the planet in the coming 40 years, food security needs to be on the agenda of all nations. According to the FAO, agricultural production must grow by 70% to meet these needs, although no one seems to have developed a plan to achieve such a goal. Forty years go by very quickly.

Wherever it happens in the world, hunger is not the cause, but only a symptom that something in the society is not functioning properly. Hunger is often the result of poor political or economic choices by the leaders of the countries where it happens. The lack of infrastructure certainly contributes to make the situation worse in many cases, but the cause of hunger in all cases is poverty. Poverty is usually the result of unemployment or wages that are too low. Education and good health are necessary to get jobs that pay enough. Unfortunately, in many countries, both education and health care are lacking dramatically. There are many great programs all over the world to fight hunger, and many companies participate as part of their commitment to communities. The FAO has set the goal of eradicating hunger by 2025. It will succeed only when the world will be effective in the fight against poverty. The issue goes far beyond the sole scope of agriculture and food. It requires action at all levels of society. The purpose must be economic development everywhere in the world, not just agricultural development.

In 2010, Brazil has included food security as part of the citizens' basic human rights in the constitution. The Brazilian President Luiz Inácio Lula da Silva wants to pass the Fome Zero (Zero Hunger) program that the Brazilian government started in 2003 to reduce poverty, hunger and child labor, into law as well. This program seems to have mixed results, according to the sources, but it has delivered some positive results, just not as many as some had expected.

The G8 (economic group consisting of the USA, Canada, the UK, France, Germany, Italy, Japan and Russia) decided in July 2009 to commit US$12 billion for more agricultural development in developing countries in the following three years. By doing so, they clearly signal a decision to shift from the former food aid approach to a farming aid policy by stimulating long-term investments in agriculture. It is also nice to see that world leaders look at the issue in a more sensible manner than in the past, shifting from "*Give a man a fish, he will have food for a day*" to "*Teach him to fish and he will have food every day*", to paraphrase the Chinese proverb[2].

Reducing food waste is an absolute necessity to improve food security. Food waste is one of those topics that rarely make the headlines, yet the numbers that come out of surveys are simply stunning: 40% of food production does not reach the plate! Further analysis of the wastage showed two distinct situations. In developed countries, most of the waste happens in the later stages of the supply chain, often far from production areas. In developing countries, the waste takes place mostly in the early stages of the supply chain, rather near production areas. This is quite sad, as the food had been produced. It was ready to go to market, but because of lack of proper storage and infrastructure, it rots and molds. This also represents a major waste of all the energy, the often-scarce water, and the fertilizers used to produce this food. This is an environmental waste. The financial waste is not negligible either. This food should have generated revenue all through the production and supply chain. Instead, it generates no money at all.

---

[2] Quote sometimes attributed to Confucius and sometimes to Lao Tzu.

Unlike developed countries, food is relatively expensive compared with income in developing countries and consumers make sure to not waste it. If improving infrastructure in developing nations can help preserve food, the way to deal with waste in the developed world will take place at food outlets and households. According to the FAO, the cost of fixing the infrastructure is US$83 billion. The world agriculture GDP is estimated at US$3.6 trillion. Although finding data about the actual value of the post-harvest losses is difficult. By making the bold assumption that half the GDP originates in the developing countries, the 40% post-harvest losses represent globally a loss of GDP of 20% of the total food production. If 80% of the potential agriculture GDP were worth US$3.6 trillion, the post-harvest losses would represent 20% of 3.6/80%. This equals US$900 billion. Even if this estimate were off by a factor 10, which is quite unlikely, the value of post-harvest losses would add up to US$90 billion. This means that fixing the infrastructure problem would have a payback time of less than a year!

In 2004, the University of Arizona published a report about the situation in the USA. Their estimate of food waste was that almost half of the food produced in the USA is never eaten. Although some losses are inevitable in the supply chain, their report estimated that 14% of the food bought by American households is thrown away, 15% of which is sent to garbage without even being opened. Not only could the lost food have been eaten, but also the environmental impact of food waste is substantial. According to the University of Arizona research, cutting half of the food waste would reduce the environmental impact by 25%, because of reduced landfill use, soil depletion and application of fertilizers, pesticides and herbicides. Recent USDA studies indicate that 25% of food never reaches a plate.

In the UK, research by the government's waste reduction agency, WRAP, found that one third of all food bought in Britain is thrown away, of which half is edible.

In a 2007 article from The Guardian, Liz Goodwin, the WRAP's chief executive said about the environmental impact of food waste *"If we stopped the amount [of food waste] that we could stop, it would be the same as taking one fifth of cars off the road."* About a third of the food waste in the UK comes from households. Food manufacturers account for about 20%, food service and restaurants for about 15%, and retailers just under 10%.

In Australia, food waste makes up half of the country's landfills, according to estimates.

According to a new study by the United Nations Environment Programme released in early 2009, at the global level, estimates of food going wasted are that over half of the food produced globally is lost, wasted or discarded because of inefficiency in the human-managed food chain. According to UNEP Executive Director Achim Steiner, *"There is evidence within the report that the world could feed the entire projected population growth alone by becoming more efficient while also ensuring the survival of wild animals, birds and fish on this planet."* A statement this strong is worth verifying. If today's food production is 100, with a waste of 40%, the world actually consumes only 60. FAO claims that food production needs to increase by 70% to meet the needs of the population in 2050. This means that the available food must be 60 x 1.70 = 102, compared with 100 as gross production now. Achim Steiner's statement is consistent and correct.

With 40% food losses, we currently feed decently six billion people, of which one billion are overweight, while one billion people are malnourished. Theoretically, we can cover the nutritional needs of 11.6 billion people. By reducing food losses from 40% to 20% would help to free food to cover the nutritional needs of 2.3 billion people. This means that we could feed 9.3 billion people. This is not by 2050, but anytime from now, if we actually work at it.

Strategies to Build Food Security

Food security concerns will force governments to make strategic choices between agricultural policies, trade agreements, import policies, market regulations mechanisms and outsourcing. Considering the importance of food security for the economic and political stability of these countries, such decisions will be taken beyond the individual borders and they will take regional collective actions.

The first step in creating future strategies is to calculate the population and its required needs for proper nutrition. The base of the diet worldwide is made of grains. The three main species, wheat, rice and corn, accounted for about 87% of all grain production and for 43% of all food calories in 2003, according to FAO numbers. The production of animal protein is a greater challenge. When their wealth increases, people tend to replace plants with meat and other animal products such as eggs and dairy in their diets. Farm animals consume large amounts of feed, which competes with human consumption.

Once the objectives are determined, the policymakers will have to make the plan to achieve food security. Depending on their specific situations, different countries will develop different strategies.

The main exporters of agricultural and food products will keep on thriving as long as they produce sustainably and they make sure their own people have food security. Food commodities will be in high demand in the years to come. Countries that are not self-sufficient will consider different possibilities. The most logical one, although not always realistic, is to reach the level of self-sufficiency by developing their own agriculture further. This is not always an easy solution, and it usually requires strong financial resources.

Unfortunately, many countries still do not have access to enough funding to develop their agriculture. Poverty is a hindrance for progress and their situation remains dire. Some countries, such as China and some Arab countries, foresee a chronic food deficit. A different strategy for them is to purchase or lease land abroad to outsource additional agricultural production.

Of course, the other strategy to achieve food security is to trade with partners with which the country can be interdependent. In order to have a stable and predictable relationship, the country needs to be a producer of what the partner needs. As the WTO (World Trade Organization) negotiations linger without reaching any agreement, more and more countries choose to engage in Free Trade Agreements (FTA) to secure exports and imports. For example, Egypt has now secured 3 million tons of wheat from Russia every year. Another example is the creation of a meat trade zone between Russia, Ukraine and Belarus.

The post World War II European Union policies are examples of successful actions on food security. The EU, which started as the "Common Market" with only six countries in the 1950s, developed agricultural policies to stimulate the production of food in the member states, and it used high levels of subsidies to achieve the objectives. Some may say that the plan worked a little too well, as the EU has for years been known to produce surpluses without having markets for some of its agricultural products. This is how the EU created a "butter mountain" that required the implementation of milk quotas in 1984, and a different payment system to the farmers to solve the problem. This surplus situation was used to great extent by the former Soviet Union as part of its food supply strategy. The Soviet Union used to buy large quantities of old food at very low prices, as the EU needed to empty the cold stores, just to make room for more subsidized surpluses.

The involvement of governments in self-sufficiency programs is paramount for success. The Green Revolution that started in Mexico in 1945, with the cooperation of the Mexican government, the Rockefeller Foundation and the Ford Foundation, delivered amazing results.

It transformed Mexico from a net wheat importer into a self-sufficient country in 10 years and into a net exporter in less than 20 years. This success motivated a similar project in India. The Indian government and the Ford Foundation coordinated the actions. By improving plant breeding, developing irrigation and fertilization, India was able to face successfully a potential famine and the country became a net exporter of rice. Between the 1960s and the 1990s, the yields of rice increased from 2 tons/ha to 6 tons/ha and the cost of production was reduced by two-thirds. The Green Revolution also shows how useful non-governmental organizations (NGOs) are in agricultural development. Today, the Bill & Melinda Gates Foundation can play a similar role for Africa as the Rockefeller foundation played in Mexico and India.

Because of their actions at the local level and their cooperation with governments, NGOs have already made many improvements possible, such as in sub-Sahara countries. In Niger or Burkina Faso, food production has started to increase.

Agricultural development is a work in progress. It requires a continuous effort because the work is never finished. For instance, the food security situation of India remains very fragile. Today, more than 200 million Indians are malnourished and the production level has stagnated while the population has kept on increasing. India has four times as many inhabitants than the USA. Its territory is about 40% of the size of the USA's not including Alaska, where agriculture is very limited. India faces a situation comparable to what the USA would face if its population were 3 billion people. These numbers demonstrate how huge the magnitude of the task of the Indian government is. In 2007, India initiated its National Food Security Mission (NFSM).

This project aims at increasing the production of rice, wheat and legumes through area expansion and productivity enhancement in a sustainable manner in the identified districts of the country. The goal for the production increase by the end of 2012 is 10 million tons for rice, 8 million tons for wheat and 2 million tons for legumes.

The project will work towards restoring soil fertility and productivity at the individual farm level. Its goals also include creating employment opportunities and enhancing farm profits to restore confidence amongst the farmers. To achieve these goals, the Indian government will implement the project through active engagement of all the stakeholders at various levels. It will promote improved seeds, Integrated Nutrient Management (INM) including micronutrients, soil amendments, Integrated Pest Management (IPM) and resource conservation technologies along with capacity building of farmers. The government will monitor the flow of funds to ensure that interventions reach the target beneficiaries on time. The various interventions proposed will be integrated with the district plan. The targets for each identified district will be fixed. The implementing agencies will monitor and evaluate progress to assess the impact of the interventions for a result-oriented approach.[3] After three years, the results of the NFSM are mixed, as climatic conditions strongly influence agricultural production.

Northwest of India, another BRIC (Brazil, Russia, India, and China) country is working on a food self-sufficiency program. The Soviet Union may be gone, but Russia is still struggling with food security. They want to develop their agriculture and especially their meat and poultry production. For 2010, the Russian government has set up a US$2-billion program to develop the meat processing industry.

The country has already made serious progress. For instance, pork production increased by 26% in 2009 compared with the year before and the growth will continue in 2010. Russian poultry production showed a solid increase, too. Production increased by 14.9% in 2009 compared with a year earlier. Early in 2010, the Russian President Dmitry Medvedev announced the Food Security Doctrine to make Russia self-sufficient with the most necessary foods before 2015. The goal for Russia is to produce at least 95% of its grain needs, 80% of the sugar, 80% of the vegetable oil, 85% of the meat, 90% of the milk, 95% of the potatoes and 80% of the fish.

---

[3] Government of India, Ministry of Agriculture, Department of Agriculture & Cooperation, National Food Security Mission, Operational Guidelines, August 2007

A limiting factor is the ability to compete with cheap imports that are badly needed because of the limited financial resources of Russian consumers. By importing the cheaper meat and meat cuts from countries where it is cheaper and more efficient to produce, Russia can bring affordable food in the country without needing to sell the expensive parts to rich countries that are already oversupplied. Such a situation could make it difficult for the Russian meat industry to be profitable. The frequent change of policies about import duties and restrictions of all sorts is disruptive for market stability. The only short-term effect of import restrictions seems to be a higher price for the Russian consumer.

In other regions, a number of organizations resembling OPEC are being set up to control or at least influence the markets of the commodities they produce. Their objective is to stabilize prices, increase food security, develop agricultural production in their area and increase their bargaining power in world markets. The strong price increases of agricultural commodities in 2008 and the strategic role of food security have been the triggers to set up these organizations.

One example is the plan to set up a rice cartel in the ASEAN (Association of Southeast Asian Nations) region by Thailand, Vietnam, Laos, Cambodia and Myanmar in order to control the rice market. ASEAN countries, China, Japan and the Republic of Korea show strong interest in transforming the East Asia Emergency Rice Reserve Pilot Project into a permanent mechanism under the ASEAN+3 Emergency Rice Reserve (AERR). In South East Asia, the ASEAN member countries initiated the AERR in 1979. The purpose then was to establish rice inventories in the region to face and cope with a shortage of rice. This has been work in progress and the Emergency Rice Reserve has shifted from a storage initiative to a market regulating organization.

Another example is the idea of creating a Black Sea Wheat Pool, between Russia, Ukraine and Kazakhstan. Their objective is the same. They want to have more control and more bargaining power in world markets.

They are gradually taking market share away from the USA, which is still the world's largest wheat exporter. This group of nations is now in the top five of world exporters. From an agricultural point of view, these three countries certainly show great potential, although the rich dark Chernozem soil has suffered serious degradation in the past. To succeed, these countries need to set consistent policies and develop a plan of action to turn the region into a major player. If the crops can exploit the potential of the soil, the Black Sea region will become a supplier of choice. Considering the regular conflicts between Russia and Ukraine on natural gas, one can wonder if such a partnership will hold, though.

In 2010, eight nations from the Pacific region (Papua New Guinea, the Marshall Islands, Kiribati, Solomon Islands, Tuvalu, the Federated States of Micronesia, Nauru and Palau) have set up a tuna cartel. The ocean area that they cover is as large as one and a half time the size of the USA. Their objective is twofold: they want to increase their share of the profits from tuna fisheries and they want to be able to monitor proper sustainable fishery practices.

Because the previous avenues do not provide enough food security, some countries are looking for land tenures abroad. The discussion about these foreign investments is controversial.

The debate is loaded with emotions, ideology and politics. There are many interests at stake. What are the different parties involved looking for in these land deals?

The host countries are interested in developing their agriculture, their infrastructure and their economy. They want long-lasting social, economic and political stability by offering their people food security, proper housing, health, education and prosperity. To achieve these objectives, they welcome all investments that support these objectives. They have the land, they have the work force, but they lack the capital. Foreign investors have a variety of goals depending on who they are and what they are. China, Arab countries and other Asian nations involved in these transactions are looking for an additional reliable and sufficient source of food.

The drawback of the economic growth in China is the environmental cost. Pollution is affecting the climate and it has made water unusable for drinking and for agriculture in some regions. Water is essential for food production and it is even more so for productions like meat, produce and rice, which is what China needs. China is the world's largest producer of many agricultural products, such as rice, wheat, eggs, pork, potatoes and many types of vegetables This not enough, though. Because of water scarcity, degraded soils and a high density of population, China is facing a critical situation to ensure food security. The Chinese have no choice but look beyond their own agricultural potential and imports. This is why they have now engaged in purchasing and leasing land abroad, mostly in Africa. Venturing in Africa is not new for the Chinese. They have been active in projects on that continent for decades. The Chinese are also buying farmland in Brazil. For instance, the China National Agricultural Development Group Corporation has plans to grow corn and soybeans. It has been allowed an annual budget of US$ 2 billion to realize the objectives and secure grain supplies to China.

The population in Arab countries is growing fast, but they face a specific situation: a large proportion of their land is a desert. This is a serious limitation for food security, and although they have developed industrial agriculture activities, they simply cannot produce enough. Arab countries are coming to the realization that trying to intensify agriculture further would deplete their reserves of drinking water rapidly and irrigation has caused the salinity of soil to increase. For these reasons, Saudi Arabia decided in 2008 to reduce its wheat production by 12.5% per year to save its water reserves. During the 30 years prior to this decision, the Saudis had a production increase and self-sufficiency policy. The unsustainable effect on water reserves forced the country to look for land leases abroad. They have concluded that they will not be able to produce all they need on their territories and they do not want to depend solely on imports at world market prices, as those will increase in the future.

Paying now for the land and controlling the cost of production is a more predictable approach to control food prices that these countries will have to pay in a couple of decades from now.

These agreements are anything but new. Colonial powers and corporations did something similar in the past. What makes this trend more dramatic is its pace and magnitude. China and Arab countries are leading the movement, as they need more food. Africa offers a lot of agricultural land that has not been developed into commercial production. This looks like a great opportunity for more agricultural production, at least from the point of view of Asian and Arab countries. Rice, wheat, corn, sugarcane and palm oil are the crops the investors want to develop.

Many African countries have shown interest in such deals, and Sudan, Mali, Ethiopia, Congo and Mozambique are among the most active. Similar deals are happening in Asia, too. Indonesia, Pakistan, Myanmar and The Philippines are among the countries most in demand.

These deals are causing much suspicion since a similar deal made by the South Korean company Daewoo in Madagascar sparked social unrest and ended up in the fall of the government of the African country in 2009. The United Nations is developing a code of conduct to regulate those investments, but this code would be only voluntary and not applicable before late 2010. It will not have much effect, as investors have a lot of time to complete deals before the code of conduct comes into effect. Moreover, the voluntary nature of this code makes it virtually ineffective.

The money invested will have to create jobs for the population of the host countries. It is in the interest of foreigners who buy land to create economic activity by training and by employing the locals for the projects they create. It is as important for the success of the investors to feed the Africans as much as it is to feed their own people. The prosperity of both sides will depend on this simple fact. For the host countries, it means potentially dramatic changes in the structure of rural areas and of their infrastructure.

They will need to manage this with the utmost care to ensure a proper transition of their societies. The economic boom in emerging countries would never have taken place if the foreign corporations had not employed the locals.

The question that needs to be answered is "Will this work?" It is difficult to answer today, but two opposite scenarios are possible. One is win-win and the other is lose-lose.

In the win-win scenario, both sides of the land deals receive what they are looking for. The host countries will develop and become prosperous. The foreign countries will get the food they need, which will help them socially and economically. It might not be as much as they would wish for, but the benefits will outweigh the little disappointments. Not only will both parties benefit, but the whole world will, too. There will be less international tension.

The less seductive lose-lose scenario will happen as soon as one of the parties does not receive what they hoped for, or when they feel short-changed. If the foreigners do not get the food supply they expected or do not make money, they will leave, look for options somewhere else or maybe they will sue. The host nation will have missed an opportunity. If the host country loses, the tension will turn ugly. There will be violence. Africa would have its own version of the Grapes of Wrath. Burning fields or violence against foreign farmers' staff is possible. In this scenario, the Africans will not have prosperity, their countries will stagnate, and the foreigners will not have food. This will cause problems much further than Africa only and the world will face serious tensions. What happens in Africa will affect us all, for better or worse.

However, such deals are not just between countries. There are more and more private investors buying or leasing land. Corporations have a different objective. Their purpose, as well as their responsibility, is not towards a particular nation. They want to be in the agriculture business, because they expect the sector to become lucrative in the future. People need to eat and when supplies become tight, the profits should be attractive.

The companies want to show a nice return on their shareholders' investments. Their attitude will depend on how fast and how much they want to achieve. Private investors have similar objectives as corporations, although they might have different timelines in mind. Investors see agricultural commodities as being very attractive in the future. The supply and demand data certainly supports their point of view, and they want to get a strong return on their capital. Financial institutions like investment banks are investing in countries including Ukraine, Brazil and China.

Jim Rogers, a famous investor, is a strong believer of agriculture. In an interview, he declared *"If I'm right, agriculture is going to be one of the greatest industries in the next 20 years, 30 years."*[4] He is the adviser of a fund that is buying farmland in Brazil and existing farms in Canada, and starting to farm them. The fund is clearing the land, fertilizing it, irrigating it and hiring farmers.

More investments are needed in order to develop a proper infrastructure between production areas and markets. Further technical support will be necessary to improve the yields. Such land deals and investments are not limited to Africa or Asia. A similar trend exists in Europe and in the Americas. Even with great potential, many farms in Ukraine are for sale and there are few buyers. This region needs to develop its economy to attract more people, and especially farmers. Foreign farmers, in particular from France, show interest in Ukraine. Libya has recently contracted some land in that country for its food needs. In 2009, Sprott Resource Corp. launched One Earth Farms Corp. with a goal of becoming Canada's largest corporate farm. In its first year of operations, One Earth Farms secured approximately 13,000 acres (5,200 hectares) of cropland in the Canadian Prairies through partnership with the First Nations to grow crops as an investment in agricultural commodities.

---

[4] Interview on CNBC.com, Jim Rogers Buys Land, Starts Farming, 3 March 2009

Who Controls Food Production?

Agriculture has evolved from producing locally for a local market with a straightforward production chain, to becoming more complex and structured over time. With the trend towards more integration, traceability and globalized markets, the roles and the bargaining positions of the various players have changed. This evolution has caused uncertainty in food ownership. Between the retailer, the wholesaler, the farmer, the owner of the land on which the crops are grown, the futures contracts trader and the feed supplier to name a few, it is not always clear who the owner is or, better said, who is actually in control of the food supply. Without farmers, there is not much food in the stores. Without seeds, farmers cannot grow much food. Without food, there are no futures contracts to negotiate. It is important to define the ownership, because it influences where the food goes, too. The decisions will not be made in the same way if the food belongs to the country and the people who produce it, or if it belongs to a corporation that prefers to sell it abroad. Conflicts are possible.

Corporations look primarily at markets and they try to maximize their profit. It is their mandate. Governments have a different perspective, as politicians want to have happy citizens, so that their position of power can continue. All they want is to avoid social unrest. Potentially, it can lead to new regulations and even to the possibility of nationalization if companies and governments do not agree. As long as there is no severe supply imbalance, the current situation will stay as it is. The players who have the most power will try to strengthen their position and influence other deciders to their advantage.

Yet, this kind of consensual vagueness about who the owner of food is will eventually cause some major shake-up.

The day that the world will have a serious global shortage, riots will erupt. Many questions will arise about how much and what kind of power politicians and corporations should actually have on food supply.

In 2008, the world saw the power of financial markets on the price of food. Inflation rose when the prices of all commodities, oil and agricultural commodities in particular, skyrocketed. In many countries, food related riots took place. Even in the rich Western countries, consumers were hoarding large quantities of food items in supermarkets, out of fear of an imminent shortage. The media publicized the cause as the increased demand because of the growth of the population in emerging countries. The inflation had other causes than just supply and demand for the commodities.

On financial markets, the demand for future contracts for these commodities was rising strongly, but the demand was only on paper. Future contracts had been introduced as a tool for the producers of commodities to fix a price in advance for their production. As such, it is a good system that offers more security, and especially more market predictability to producers. A futures contract is a standardized contract to buy or sell a specified commodity of a determined quality at a certain date in the future and at a market-determined price. This system eliminates the risk of future market price drops for the farmers. Many players who were trading these future contracts in 2008 were investment banks, financial institutions and private investors, mainly hedge funds. These people are not physically involved in the trade of the commodities, and most of these traders have never been on a farm. Using borrowed money, they traded more contracts than the quantity of the underlying physical commodity actually existed. This created the impression that demand was high. It was but only on paper. The speculators wanted to create a momentum in the market so that the prices of the contracts would increase significantly, to make as much profit on the paper transaction as possible when they would sell. This would not be bad if the futures prices were not becoming the official price in the real economy.

Unfortunately, it is not the case and many people have suffered the consequences. Inflation increased and social unrest took place while there were no major actual physical shortages. The best demonstration for this is 2009: although the population had continued to increase further, there has been no global food shortage. Actually, food prices decreased at the retail level, as well as at the farm level.

These futures contracts have now become investment products that are not connected anymore to the real market numbers. They are priced by the market on paper with high leverage levels, but because they are published as the market prices, they can directly influence the prices of goods to consumers.

In the future, a drop in the value of the US dollar will encourage financial investors to hedge against inflation by rushing into futures markets. This is exactly what has been driving the price increase of commodities during 2011. For investors and especially speculators, commodities have now become currencies. They do not represent actual products, and the investors do not link them to the consequences that will hit the real economy. They will create inflation by giving the impression that demand is much higher. The inflation that would result from a weak US dollar would make the US Federal Reserve increase interest rates. This combined with a slow economic recovery would lead to stagflation. In such a scenario, the USA will be severely affected, since commodities are traded in US dollars. A strong US dollar is necessary for the stability of commodities markets. The food price increases of 2008 and 2011 have showed how vulnerable a large part of the population is for their food supply. It is likely that such a situation will repeat itself, and this time for real physical reasons, not just because of the trading of derivatives. There will be inflation, there will be riots, and there will come a point when the risk of social unrest will force governments to intervene.

Governments are aware of the risks that speculation on the futures markets for commodities has on the economy and on possible social unrest.

If there are signs of excessive speculation, they will intervene and regulate the futures markets much more tightly. This affects the economic situation directly.

Government action will take various forms, depending on the magnitude of the crisis and the location of the social unrest. A shutdown of the futures markets as it happened in India in 2008 is likely to occur. The futures market for basic agricultural commodities was so disrupted that the Indian government decided to halt futures contracts for potatoes and chickpeas during the summer of 2008. Government intervention will result in a profound change of the rules according to which these markets function, probably allowing only companies and individuals directly involved in food and agriculture to trade. The surge of investments in agriculture is already worrying many. What would happen if African "rebels", as they are always called in such situations, decide to regain ownership of the land leased to China or to Arab countries, because they are hungry and they do not accept anymore seeing large volumes of food grown on their land being shipped abroad?

If the price of food increases too fast, governments might decide to intervene by fixing the price of the most basic foods, or even to limit the amount of food people could buy. The French government used to fix the maximum price of bread. During World War II, there were food ration coupons. The Chinese government has a policy of only one child per family. Rationing food is not any more intrusive or extreme.

In such extreme situations, who will own the food? Power struggles will have to determine that. What will be the value of intellectual property if what is at stake is survival? Will political leaders bully corporations, or will corporations move away from countries? These will always be lose-lose scenarios, with hard confrontations.

While in the USA, such disputes generally lead to court, other countries have different ways of dealing with differences of opinions. In China, even the almighty Google could not get the People's Republic to change its rules. It had the choice between complying and leaving.

In Russia, the head of state reminded large corporations like Shell and BP who the owner of the country, and especially of the oil, was in 2008. When market conditions changed months later, they became good friends again, though.

In more extreme cases, direct government intervention and nationalization of companies will take place. Venezuela did already this during 2009 by nationalizing a pasta plant, a rice mill and a supermarket chain owned by foreign companies and by seizing temporarily a local sardine cannery, under the reason that Hugo Chavez wants to protect food security of his people. "*It is the duty of the State to guarantee the population's food security, as the sardine is a strategic product for the Venezuelan consumer*" according to the Venezuelan President. One can argue the Venezuelan leadership is extreme. Yet, some people take desperate measures when they face desperate situations. What would happen if a global food shortage threatened the stability of countries or of entire regions?

Morals and responsibilities will be more important than ever. It is essential to maintain a balance of power between all parties involved in the food production and supply chain.

In the supply chain that starts with the DNA of crops and farm animals and ends on the consumer's plate, not all links have been created equal. The strongest links are the ones at each end of the chain.

Genetics, through selection and breeding, but also more recently with genetic engineering, plays a critical role in food production. The genetic material, be it vegetal or animal, will affect directly the production performance of the farm, through the genetic potential of the traits it contains. Yields, growth, water efficiency, disease resistance (or sensitivity) or feed conversion ratio (FCR, quantity of feed needed to produce one kg of meat) all derive from the genome of the plant or of the animal.

These parameters have a direct effect on the cost price and the profitability of the farm.

A major share of the economic value depends on who owns this part of the chain, and how the bargaining power between the genetic companies and the farmers is distributed.

In the sector of seeds and genetics, there is a growing responsibility resting on the shoulders of the executives of breeding and genetic engineering companies. A bit more than a century ago, there was much more genetic diversity in agricultural crops and farm animals. The diversity has shrunk significantly and the world faces the potential risk of not having the right genes available to face a natural situation that would eradicate plants or animals, because of their potential inability to resist and to adapt to the new environmental conditions, such as drought or diseases.

It can take several years before the results of a breeding and selection program can appear clearly, depending on the type of production. Selection companies that foresee the future needs of food markets properly win the competition, as they select on the right characteristics. Genetic selection is capital intensive and high risk. This is why farmers can choose only between a limited number of suppliers. This gives them a strong competitive advantage with farmers. The market of genetics is a small market with players that have a strong bargaining power. This also gives them a strong influence on the food supply chain.

The genetic pool used to be a collective asset. Farmers could keep some of the seeds they produced to plant the next generation. There was no patent on genes. With the rise of genetic engineering, genes have now become intellectual property that farmers can use only by signing contracts including many legal obligations. They cannot reuse the seeds. They have to buy the next generation from the seed supplier again. The genetic heritage of thousands of years is becoming privatized. One can wonder who has ownership, and what the consequences will be.

At the other end of the chain, the power lies in the hands of who has access to the consumer market and to the best customers.

Understanding the consumers and being connected to the right channels to serve the best market segment is of critical importance for the profitability of the negotiating parties. All through history, traders, brokers and marketers, depending on the names they receive, have always been in a strong position. Many of them have earned much more than small independent farmers have. If Fair Trade has become a symbol, it is because trade has always been unfair to farmers. One can wonder if it will ever change. Jim Rogers tends to think so, as he claims that in the future, *"farmers will be the ones driving Lamborghinis, instead of the stockbrokers today"*[5]. The agricultural boom may indeed come in the future, but more than the people actually working the land, the investors and food brokers will benefit the most of the creation of value in the food production chain.

Weakness is why farmers have organized themselves in co-operatives a long time ago, in order to have more control on the marketing activities of the production chain. Processing companies also wanted to have more bargaining power against the retail companies. They consolidated and, through mergers, have created major industrial blocks. To maintain their dominant position, they integrated and subcontracted farmers to produce the commodities for them. This, too, results in many cases in farmers losing their independence and trading away some of their potential profits to the integrated groups.

In the second half of the 20th century, the retail industry has become a major participant in food value chains. Everyone who has negotiated sales with large retailers knows how powerful they are, not only in terms of commercial negotiations, but also about changing the food industry to serve the consumers' wishes. Since the power becomes increasingly concentrated at both ends of the chain, large retailers and the suppliers of genetic material will compete eventually for the control of food.

---

[5] During the same interview on CNBC.com, Jim Rogers Buys Land, Starts Farming, 3 March 2009

The outcome of this confrontation will decide who, between agribusiness and consumers, has the final word on food.

Since the end of World War II, the position of the consumer and the structure of retail have undergone major changes. The rich industrialized countries represent the largest part of the world's consumption, and their societies have thrived on cheap oil, cheap food and cheap consumer goods. In the years following World War II, Western society changed to become what it is today. First, the part of the population living in rural areas and busy with agricultural activities was substantially higher than today. From levels around 50% before the war, industrialization has led to low one-digit percentages nowadays. Another significant difference was the disposable income of consumers. Then, the largest part of household expenditure was for basic essentials such as food, housing, clothes and shoes. Having a car was a luxury and television was just a novelty broadcasting an amazing one channel. These were the early days of the consumption society. Consumer goods were starting to become present and, in many cases, they were a reflection of what was already going on more actively in the USA. America was the beacon of the world and American lifestyle was becoming a trend. Nonetheless, consumption was not as active as today, simply because credit was not as easy to get, either. Supermarkets and malls were starting to emerge, but until then consumers were buying what they needed from specialized stores, such as the baker or the butcher. The offer was still about basic ingredients, as women were not involved in the professional life as much as today, and homemakers were cooking the meals for their families. This was about to change dramatically.

As TV was new, so were TV dinners and other convenient foods. From a limited assortment of basic consumer goods with little differentiation, and therefore a limited number of options, all sorts of food products offered in many sizes, packaging and flavors emerged. Supermarket shelves are full of all the goodies and modern consumers can now experience the pleasure of hunting and gathering in a surrounding that will not disappoint them.

Today, in rich countries, it is impossible to come back home from the grocery store and say that, unfortunately, there will be no food for dinner tonight. The society wants you to consume. The system has been very effective. In the "old days", the consumers had little influence on production systems. This has changed, thanks to efficiency. The industry's ability to overproduce everything has made the price of food drop, if expressed in constant money. With more disposable income, the abundance of cheap food has created a more demanding and more critical consumer.

As mass production came along with mass media, consumers are now flooded with information all day long, every day of the year. Since their area of expertise is limited, especially when it comes to agriculture and food, because so few of them have actually ever been on a farm, their only source of information is what they see on TV and what they can read on the internet. Mass consumption has been the ideal support for the development of large retailers. The specialized small stores have lost a lot of their market share, and actually, they are now re-emerging inside the supermarkets. At first, supermarkets were selling brand names and their role was rather limited to selling those products. As time went by, they also decided to fight the A-brand products to improve their margins, by developing their own private labels. This has meant a significant change in the way retailers had to look at quality and liability, because from that moment, the brand was theirs, and they had to make sure the customers would be satisfied.

In the food and agriculture sectors, a number of food scares have taken place during the last few decades, and have deeply influenced how consumers and retailers look at food, with significant consequences for the production side of the business.

In the 1970s in France, the hormone scandal in veal caused the sales of veal to plummet. Consumption never really recovered as consumers found alternatives. There was another white meat available: turkey. Although it was mostly an item for Christmas, a new industry developed, offering consumers similar products such as roasts or scaloppini.

The hormone scandal helped develop turkey farming beyond what the sector probably had ever thought possible, and as most products were parts and special cuts, it changed the parameters sought after in selection and breeding.

In the mid 1990s in the United Kingdom, BSE, also known as mad cow disease, caused a shock. Consumption of beef plummeted in most European countries. They closed their borders to British beef for years, and the retailers started to ask more questions about production methods. The trend started in the UK, but quickly expanded in all other European countries. Then, retailers started to hire their own agricultural specialists, because they wanted to be able to offer guarantees to their customers that the food they bought from their stores would be safe. The BSE scare forced governments to set up Food Safety Agencies. Since the disease had been transmitted by meat and bone meal produced from infected sheep, the animal feed industry came under intense scrutiny. This resulted in a ban on meat and bone meal into animal feeds in the EU. The dioxin affair that came up in Belgium in 1999 fuelled these concerns further. Fat used to make animal feed was contaminated with high levels of dioxin and PCB, which are carcinogenic substances. Although the problem started with chicken feed, it affected all animal productions including aquaculture. Beyond BSE, many more practices came under review, and the rise of reports on bacteria resistance and antibiotics being "recycled" into humans through the drinking water increased the pressure to change production systems.

Animal welfare became another subject of controversy and housing and husbandry methods will change, too. European regulation of animal husbandry methods has undergone major changes over the last 15 years.

The tethering of sows has been banned since 2002 and keeping layer hens in cages will not be allowed anymore in 2012. A similar ban on layer cages will also take place in the Canadian province of Manitoba in 2018. Castration of piglets is under review in the EU, while this procedure has been required to take place under anesthesia in Norway since 2002.

There will be a strong focus on reducing densities. This will improve animal welfare and reduce the environmental impact of animal husbandry. The EU is also considering legislation to ban the sale of meat produced from EU livestock that has suffered from poor welfare.

In April 2010, the European Food Safety Authority (ESFA) opened an online public consultation process for genetic selection in chickens and animal welfare. The EU wants to assess the effect of genetics on welfare and resistance to stress in chickens. This follows other consultations on health risk assessment of foods, on the impact of GMOs (Genetically Modified Organisms) on non-target organisms, and on pesticides.

The concepts of food safety, transparency, traceability, and all the issues about production systems, densities, pollution by manure, and environmental impact of agriculture have gained ground in Europe for about two decades. The same trend is now starting to take place in the USA, where new food safety legislation is being developed. Compared with European consumers, their North American counterparts have been rather docile and passive about food and agriculture until recently. The number of E. coli outbreaks in ground beef in the USA, or the listeria case that caused 27 deaths in Canada in 2008 are just illustrations that more work on food safety is not a luxury. North America and eventually the whole world will have to deal with more regulations and more restrictions on food quality, food safety and agricultural practices.

There will be drastic health procedures to reduce pathogens entering the food chain and to prevent risks of contamination during processing, packaging and storage. With the use of antibiotics, and in some countries the use of hormones, as a standard procedure, it should not be a surprise that some people question the sustainability of such systems. The fact that the movie "*Food, Inc.*" was nominated for best documentary is a clear sign of such a change. Those who fight against this trend do not have a chance of winning the battle.

Instead, they need to negotiate good efficient procedures to guarantee the quality the consumers demand, in a cost effective manner.

Retailers will increasingly take the lead in food quality and agricultural practices, as these fit into corporate social responsibility. In Europe, they have been proactive in that direction for many years. The world's largest retailer, Wal-Mart, is increasingly pushing the sustainability agenda. When retail leaders decide that these are the critical issues, it is only a matter of time before the other retail chains and their suppliers follow their lead and adopt similar measures.

The Current Turning Point

Over the last century, oil has played, and still plays a central role in the world's economy. Everything in current society has been influenced by the use of fossil fuels. Because oil is such an effective and cheap energy, it has been highly successful at transforming the way of life. Without oil, there would not have been the same possibilities for mobility, for mechanization and automation. Manufacturing, agriculture or fisheries would not have become so efficient. There would not be such a bonanza of cheap goods to consume. There would not be the malls and supermarkets of today. There would not be the concept of suburbia, with people commuting alone in their cars back and forth to work every single day. Without oil, there would not have been such a fast and aggressive globalization of the economy. Without oil, there would be less comfort, at least in rich countries, because unfortunately, this model of society benefited only a minority of the world's population.

In agriculture, oil has been the engine of major efficiency improvements, due to mechanization and farming machinery. Automation of many tasks on farms, together with use of fertilizers and herbicides has increased yields and productivity. Because of cheap oil, mechanization has replaced human labor. This has led to lower production costs through intensification and industrialization. Cheap oil also allowed agricultural commodities to be shipped all across the world to support other food related activities such as animal feed, animal husbandry, and food processing.

Consumers in wealthy countries are so spoiled that even off-season, they can eat whatever they like, because someone will bring it to market from a location in the other hemisphere.

Yes, oil has brought rich countries a lot of convenience, an incredible level of comfort and plenty of food, but the cost of environmental damage has not been included in the cost price. It was easy to overlook, since it takes a lot of time for Nature to show the signs that her flexibility has been pushed to the utmost limits. Emerging countries that are benefiting from the economic development brought by relocation of manufacturing and outsourcing of services would like to have the same way of life. This will not be possible because energy, natural resources, consumption, food and agriculture are all reaching a turning point.

This economic model did not factor in the long-term effects, and these are serious. The intensification of agriculture has led to the deterioration of soils because of too intensive monoculture (cultivation of a single crop on a farm). Pollution by chemicals and manure caused water pollution that contaminates the drinking water sources and the rivers. Emissions of greenhouse gases threaten the climatic conditions and the survival of humanity, unless humans act efficiently to reverse the trend.

Climate and food are almost impossible to separate, as agricultural production depends greatly on climatic conditions. Since the beginning of farming, farmers have always looked anxiously to the sky, hoping rain would finally come or it finally would stop falling to avoid any catastrophe and to ensure a good harvest. In all cultures, there is evidence of rituals and prayers to ask the help of divinities to have plentiful harvests, and therefore food for the community. The inability to control climate conditions is a major weakness in agriculture. Of course, there are techniques that can help dealing with temporary adverse situations, but a long-lasting drought or an excess of rain can ruin food production.

Climate change is nothing new, as the Earth has undergone several ice ages and warm periods before. The continents have been exposed to different climatic conditions, as they shifted and changed positions on the globe, but this is the first time the change can directly be linked to the activity of one of the living species on the planet.

Human activities have a serious impact on climate. The emission of greenhouse gases has the potential to affect productions, farming systems and affect yields. Because of the use of fossil fuels and deforestation, agriculture is a substantial contributor to carbon dioxide emissions and climate change as well. Further, agriculture is the main contributor to the emission of methane coming from rice cultivation and cattle, and the main contributor to the emission of nitrous oxide coming from nitrogen fertilizer use. Regardless of what people believe causes the problem and of which numbers they choose to look at, it is clear that the climatic conditions to grow food are changing. It is necessary to have a proper strategy to cope with the problem and to be able to meet the demand of an additional two billion people.

According to the US Environmental Protection Agency, five factors of climate change can affect agricultural productivity[6]:

- Average temperature increase
- Change in rainfall amount and patterns
- Rising atmospheric concentrations of carbon dioxide (CO_2)
- Pollution levels such as tropospheric ozone (the troposphere is the lowest part of the atmosphere; it contains about 75% of the atmosphere's mass and 99% of its water vapor and aerosols)
- Change in climatic variability and extreme events

An increase in temperature can have both positive and negative effects. It can limit growth in regions where heat is already a problem, it can increase evaporation from the soil, or it can create droughts, but it also can increase production in areas that were usually cooler and where plant growth was slow.

Higher temperatures could increase the area of new arable land, especially in areas where the ground was previously frozen, such as in Siberia or Northern Canada.

---

[6] US Environmental Protection Agency, Agriculture and Food Supply, Climate Change - Health and Environmental Effects, 15 October 2009

Higher temperatures would make ice caps melt, which could result in a higher sea level and cover agricultural areas. Countries like Bangladesh, India and Vietnam could be seriously affected. Higher temperatures also will affect glaciers and, according to the United Nations, Himalayan glaciers could potentially disappear, with catastrophic consequences. They estimate that 2.4 billion people depend on water coming from the rivers originating in the Himalayas, such as the Ganges, the Indus, the Brahmaputra, the Yangtze Kiang, the Yellow, the Mekong and the Salween. The progressive disappearance of glaciers in the Rocky Mountains in North America can lead to serious droughts in the Canadian prairies and the Great Plains in the USA. This would cause a drop in crop production, bring adverse conditions to cattle farmers and significantly reduce the predictability of crop production. The USA and Canada are among the largest exporters of grains and if the environmental conditions in their production areas were to affect yields negatively, there would be a noticeable effect on commodities markets.

Changes in rainfall can affect the level of moisture in the soil and the level of soil erosion. Too much rain can also create conditions for diseases to develop or for crops to rot on the fields. According to the IPCC (Intergovernmental Panel on Climate Change), an organization established by the United Nations and the World Meteorological Organization, precipitations will increase in high latitudes and decrease in most subtropical land regions by as much as 20%, and they predict local extreme precipitations events to increase because of climate change. More rainfall would result in more humidity. Combined with higher temperatures, it could result in higher risks of fungal diseases and other pests.

Higher levels of atmospheric CO_2 could act as a fertilizer and have a positive effect on plant growth. Wheat, rice and soybean could benefit from higher yields for this reason, although a change in temperature and precipitation might limit the positive effect on crops, depending on the conditions. The same would apply for weeds.

Climate change is expected to alter the level of ozone in the low atmosphere, as this level depends on both emissions and temperatures. Higher levels of ground level ozone limit the growth of crops.

Change in the frequency of dramatic and extreme events such as droughts, heat waves, floods and hurricanes, are expected although it is difficult to forecast their location and magnitude. In late 2009, unusual tornadoes and floods hit Brazil causing Brazilian officials to realize that their country is probably more vulnerable to the effects of climate change than they thought. Considering how critical export of agricultural products is for Brazil, and how necessary their commodities are to other regions of the world, this situation is likely to affect their policies. *"The northeast will lose one-third of its economy if we do nothing"*[7], the Brazilian Environment Minister told in an interview to Reuters. In 2008, Brazil agreed to reduce the Amazon deforestation by half, in order to fight climate change, but more needs to be done. The irony for Brazil when it comes to climate change is that the only crop to benefit from higher temperature is sugarcane, which they largely use for the production of biofuels.

In the course of 2010 and 2011, dramatic climatic events occurred in many regions. Russia suffered from a drought that signaled the start of active speculation on agricultural commodities. The food inflation that followed was the reason for a worldwide concern about how the world would cope to feed the expected nine billion inhabitants by 2050. In 2011, China suffered from drought, too, and so did France. The cost of such climatic events is quite high. The French government considered to support the farmers with a financial relief package of one billion Euros.

During the first half of 2011, the USA suffered more than 500 dead because of tornadoes. The floods of the Mississippi River caused much damage as well.

---

[7] Reuters, Climate change threatens Brazil's rich agriculture, 1 October 2009

Climate is not the only key element of agriculture undergoing major changes, so is soil. The causes of soil erosion are water, wind and tillage. As stated by the European Environment Bureau, soil is the basis of 90% of all human food, livestock, fiber and fuel. Further, they also state, "*The permanent loss of soil due to sealing is continuing at high rates, increasing flood risks and reducing groundwater resources. The rapid loss of organic matter poses a threat to long-term soil fertility and contributes to the problem of climate change. Contamination with chemicals via air or direct input through pesticides, fertilizers, manure and waste leads to a loss of biodiversity and a growing accumulation of persistent substances, with potentially irreversible negative impacts on human health and economic activities*"[8].

The ISRIC (International Soil Reference and Information Center) carried out the GLASOD (Global Assessment of Human-Induced Soil Degradation) study[9] in the late 1990s. This study is so far the best research available on soil degradation. It estimates that 15% of ice-free land is deteriorated to some extent. It attributes 56% of the degradation to water erosion and 28% to wind erosion. The degradation is not caused by erosion only, but it includes all human activities. The fact that a number of countries that play an important role in agricultural production have very degraded soils is of concern for the future.

In the USA, the entire Mississippi River basin from North to South and California show the most degradation. All of Central America is damaged, too. Arid regions have the same problem. The Middle East and the majority of Arabian Peninsula, Morocco, Tunisia, Libya and the countries south of the Sahara have high levels of soil degradation. All of Europe has degraded soils, but the worst cases are in Eastern Europe, from Poland at the north to the Black Sea region in the south.

---

[8] European Environment Bureau, EU soil policy, "From neglect to protection" The need for EU level legal protection

[9] UNEP/GRID Arendal, Philippe Recacewicz, Degraded soils, 2002

In Asia, the problem spreads over most of India, Pakistan, large parts of China, Indonesia, The Philippines, Thailand and Vietnam. In Africa, Madagascar and South Africa are the most affected by the problem. South America is relatively better, although parts of the Brazilian States of Paraná, Mato Grosso, Minas Gerais and the Nordeste region have very degraded soils.

Many of the regions vulnerable to desertification are regions where the population is growing. This shows how critical dealing properly with climate change and soil deterioration is for food security. Clearly, the Middle East is very vulnerable for food shortages. The strategy to purchase or lease land to develop agriculture in Africa by foreigners will have to be carried out carefully, as many African regions are vulnerable, too. India is facing serious risks. Brazil needs to manage its agriculture cautiously. Australia, one of the largest exporters of wheat is also vulnerable to desertification.

The European Commission Institute for Environment and Sustainability reported that erosion is still a serious problem in northwest and central Europe, and is on the increase. In parts of the Mediterranean region, erosion has reached a stage of irreversibility and, in some places, erosion has ceased because there is no more soil left. It attributes the main causes of soil erosion to inappropriate agricultural practices, deforestation, overgrazing, forest fires and construction activities.

Nature had developed its own way of protecting soil thanks to vegetation covers, such as forests and grassland. These are effective in keeping the soil in place. Agriculture needs arable land. Transforming grassland and forests into agricultural land has been an ongoing process. Urban development also contributes to the exposure of land and its degradation.

Proper tillage methods and the use of organic matter are helpful to reduce the risks of excessive soil erosion. Organic matter strengthens the structure of the soil and binds soil particles together, thus making them less susceptible to be taken away by water or wind. The use of mulch is also effective.

Much of the past damage has been the result of excessive and too deep tillage as well as compaction by heavy machinery used to work the fields. At the same time, farms became more specialized, and they did not have access to manure as mixed farms used to. The "modern" farmers replaced the organic matter fertilization by mineral fertilizers making the soil much more sensitive to rain and wind erosion.

Because of the distances food travels, huge quantities of organic matter are moved around the planet. Bananas from Ecuador eaten in North America or soybeans from Argentina used in animal feed in Europe are examples of organic matter being moved without being brought back to its original location. There are many similar examples because food production is a global activity. Eventually, organic matter produced on the countryside ends up as organic matter in the cities. To ensure the sustainability of food production globally, it is necessary to develop a strategy to restore the cycle. The management of agricultural organic matter will take place in cities, too and not just in the rainforest.

Organic matter from and back to food production is not just about plant waste. It also includes what is left of food after being processed by humans and farm animals. Maintaining a proper level of organic matter is of critical importance to maintain the fertility and the integrity of the soil. In the times when mixed farms were the norm, and the economy was mostly local, the cycle of organic matter was preserved in a natural manner. The wheat was used for milling and for feeding some of the farm animals. The food produced for the farmer's family originated from the farm, too. The farm animals would eat the food waste, and the straw would be used as a litter for the farm animals. The manure was left to rest and mature until the fertilizing season. The manure mixed with the straw was a good fertilizer rich in organic matter and rich in minerals.

The organic matter, mostly rich in carbon, would help retain the minerals in the soil and prevent leaching after rainfall. The circle was complete, as the animal feed and the litter originated both locally from the same land on which the manure was to be spread.

With the arrival of modern commercial farming, based on capital, cheap oil, specialization and intensification, the cycle has been broken. Many farms that previously used their own manure replaced it by mineral fertilizers because they have no other choice, as they do not keep animals anymore. Organic matter content in the soil gradually decreased, which, combined with inappropriate agricultural practices, caused some of the soil degradation.

The disruption of the organic matter cycle is not just about crops. Another major factor in the imbalance of organic matter is intensive animal husbandry. One of the drivers of intensive animal husbandry has been the ability of the animal feed industry to produce highly concentrated feeds that increase the production per animal.

With the growth of the animal feed industry, large quantities of raw materials have been transported over long distances to feed the animals produced close to the consumer markets in the rich industrialized countries. In Europe, a number of regions have developed intensive animal production, such as The Netherlands, Denmark, Northern Germany, Brittany in France, the Po Valley in Italy and Cataluña in Spain. If it had not been for the import of all the raw materials for feed, these regions would not have been able to feed and produce the number of cows, pigs and poultry they did. European livestock has been grown and has produced manure with feedstuffs coming not only from Europe, but also in large quantities from North America, South America and Asia, where these crops were grown according to the modern intensive commercial agriculture model.

Some countries have been running a deficit of organic matter, as they have exported it to feed European livestock. Since these farms do not keep animals, they can only replace the minerals exported with the feed raw materials by mineral fertilizers.

The countries with intensive animal husbandry produce high quantities of animal products, among which are large quantities of manure. Since most of intensive animal husbandry farms have little land, their regions have ended up with huge manure surpluses, causing a surplus of minerals in the soil.

This is how excessive amounts of nitrates, phosphates and heavy metals have entered the local environment with serious consequences. For instance, in the Netherlands, the fertility of the soils came under threat because of high levels of phosphates. In Brittany, the quality of the drinking water has been seriously deteriorated because of high levels of nitrates, making tap water unsuitable for pregnant women and infants.

Because these minerals end up in streams and rivers, the natural conditions of these rivers have changed, sometimes to such an extent that algae thrive on these nutrient-rich waters and colonize the rivers and seashores at the expense of other species that had been present until then.

Considering that phosphate mines are running empty, a proper management of this mineral is necessary. The future source of phosphates will be manure and from sewage. Ideally, the manure should be shipped back and returned to the land where the crops used for animal feed originated. However, it is quite expensive considering the distance and the high water content of manure. This is not a practical solution.

Not all manures are equally useful. For instance, cattle manure has a good agricultural value when mixed with straw and it would easily find a nearby destination. Chicken manure, too, has a good agricultural value, and since chickens produce manure with a high dry matter content, it is easy to pellet and transport over longer distances. Pig manure contains more than 90% of water and its agricultural value is rather poor, which makes it less interesting for crop farmers.

Manure surpluses happen every time on intensive animal farms with too little land. Unless these farms can write contracts with agricultural crops producers who have the land to receive the entire manure surplus, this situation is without an acceptable solution.

During the 1980s and 1990s, The Netherlands tried all sorts of manure-agriculture contract regulations.

The industry has been creative and innovative to find ways of processing, dehydrating and reducing the volume of manure, but every time they came to the same conclusion: the solution costs too much and it is not economically viable. In the end, the country came to the only conclusion possible, which was to reduce the number of animals held on intensive farms.

The combination of growth of the population with the improved wealth in emerging countries makes the challenge of feeding the world even greater. The example of China illustrates this. The Chinese consumer is changing and as families have more money, the diet is changing, too. In the large urban centers, the level of wealth has risen to levels similar to that of Western countries. This comes with an increasing number of cases of obesity among the younger population. Meat, fruit and vegetables are more in demand and rice consumption is decreasing, although the demand for rice will still increase at the national level.

The FAO estimates that meat consumption in China will reach 85 kg per capita on average by 2030. This number was only 50 kg in 2000. A population of 1.5 billion people increasing its meat consumption to this extent will weigh heavily on the demand and the use of agricultural commodities and water resources. The change of diet might be the biggest challenge that future agricultural production may face, not only in China but also worldwide. From a volume and price point of view, one can wonder if such consumption numbers are sustainable. China cannot keep up with domestic demand. It will have to import large quantities of soybeans and soybean meal, and it will become a small net importer of corn in the coming years. The increased demand for animal feed will push prices of agricultural commodities up.

This trend will take place all over the world. With economic growth, the need for animal products increases. This means that animal husbandry requires more feedstuffs coming directly from agriculture such as grains or legumes.

According to USDA statistics, there are about 60 billion chickens, 800 million pigs and close to one billion cattle produced per year in the world for human consumption. In 2006, aquaculture represented a tonnage of 51.7 million metric tons, about the same as fisheries volumes. These numbers keep growing. Animal feed is not the only market to compete with direct human consumption.

The competition is getting fiercer for agricultural commodities with the development of biofuels. According to the IEA (International Energy Agency), the land cultivated for the production of biofuels represents "only" 2% of the total global agricultural land. However, if the land was average arable land, it could represent 2% of the food potential. Expressed in consumption numbers, it represents the equivalent of food for 140 million people worldwide. According to the same IEA, the most ambitious scenario indicates a level of supply of biofuels to increase to 700 million tons of oil equivalent in 2050, representing 26% of the total transport fuel demand, compared with 20 million tons of oil equivalent in 2005.

Yet, they recognize that most of the growth of biofuels production would have to come from the second generation of biofuels to be produced from ligno-cellulosic biomass, such as straw, wood residues or grass. Such a 35-fold increase in 45 years cannot come from arable land, since it would then represent an impossible equivalent of 70% of the current arable land. Another report from the USDA describes how the share of corn used for ethanol production has increased strongly over the past years. In 2001, only 7.5% of the corn was used for ethanol. Because of the incentive programs of the Energy Independence and Security Act of 2007, this share has jumped to 23.2% in 2009.[10] In 2011, 40% of corn produced in the USA was aimed at the production of ethanol.

Since the USA produces almost half of the world's corn, their ethanol production represents large areas of land and reduces significantly corn availability for animal feed.

---

[10] USDA, Economic Research Service, Ethanol and a changing agricultural landscape. November 2009

Agricultural production must increase in the coming decades. To meet the needs, farmers will need better and more productive plants and animals.

Genetics have played a key role in all improvements in agricultural production. Selection of plants and animals has been an ongoing process in agriculture through the centuries. Since the purpose of agriculture is to provide food security, it is logical that farmers always try to select their best plants and animals to meet all their needs, be it production levels, the ability to resist adverse conditions, diseases and pests, or to offer more predictability and guarantee a revenue. With the rise of industrial commercial agriculture focusing on standardization and high production, selection and breeding have left aside many genes that did not have a direct economic advantage. Plants and animals are now very productive, but agriculture is left with a major unknown: how much diversity has been lost in the process and what could this mean if the conditions of production were to change?

For instance, in India, before the time of colonialism, the number of rice varieties was estimated at 400,000. This number dropped to 30,000 by the middle of the 19th century and it has decreased by several thousands more during the Green Revolution that started in the 1960s.

Genetic improvement is not limited to productivity. There are concerns about whether the modern plants are more sensitive to traditional diseases than before. A number of crop failures are a reminder that this risk of sensitivity to disease exists. For instance, potato blight caused a famine in Ireland in the 19th century. The grassy stunt virus caused a severe loss of rice in Asia in the 1970s. Similarly, the loss of about 15% of the corn production in the USA in 1970 because of the corn leaf blight, caused by a fungus, has been attributed to selection.

Another problem with breeding and selection is that pathogens evolve, too. According to the USDA, over 400 species of pests now resist one or more pesticides.

In animal husbandry, the loss of genetic variety is just as much of a concern. Selection and especially the use of artificial insemination have sped up this process. While in the past, farmers would inseminate their cows with a local bull or their sows with a local boar, artificial insemination created the possibility to collect large quantities of sperm, keep them in liquid nitrogen and send them over long distances.

This has contributed to increase production levels quickly. For instance, the average milk production per cow is about twice as much today as it was 40 years ago. However, high producing cows also are more prone to health problems and have to be replaced more often.

The FAO estimates industrial specialized livestock production grows twice as fast as mixed farming systems (crops and animal production combined), and six times as fast as traditional grazing systems. They are concerned about the loss of genetic diversity and they have created the Domestic Animal Diversity Information System to help countries map their livestock genetic resources and take action to preserve genetic diversity.

They estimate that a third of farm animal breeds face extinction. One of the causes is the import by developing countries of higher producing breeds, from developed countries, that tend to replace the local breeds. Genetics will have to take into account feed conversion efficiency and carcass quality even more than today. Since it takes more energy to deposit fat than to grow lean muscle, there will be a further shift in the choices of breeds towards leaner ones.

A highly productive animal has relatively lower maintenance needs. It consumes relatively less water and feed. For these reasons, the commercial breeds will gain more popularity with farmers at the expense of the often less productive traditional local breeds. This requires the proper care, though, because such a strategy brings the risk of further loss of genetic diversity. To balance this, conservation programs will be put in place for environmental conservation and management purposes.

It is crucial to maintain as many genes as possible because selection and breeding are dynamic processes that need to adapt to and anticipate future changes, not only in the natural environment, but to consumers' choices, too. For instance, as life became more comfortable and people could live in heated houses and workplaces, the need for energy for maintenance changed. In the past, people needed fat in their diets to get the calories they needed for their manual labor as they worked in relatively cooler conditions. Now, less demanding physical activity and more comfortable housing have reduced this need for fat consumption.

Consumers started to demand leaner meat. This meant a change in the selection of pigs, and since money talks, farmers receive more money when they deliver leaner pigs. This brought breeding companies to select on different criteria than before. As the need for convenience increased and consumers were looking for boneless white meat, parts and especially deboned breast meat drove the growth of chicken consumption. Breeding companies had to select on new criteria to meet the new demand.

In Europe, when milk quotas were implemented in 1984, selection shifted from mostly quantity to the quality of the milk, such as protein percentage and selection changed focus, too.

Due to new consumer trends, and marketing, some old breeds have found a new future. For instance, in Spain, the Iberian pig fed on acorns in semi-wild conditions has made a comeback. This breed might not have the profile of the modern intensive pork producer, but consumers looked for an authentic typical ham to share with friends as tapas: the expensive, but delicious *"Pata Negra"*. Similarly, in Japan, old cattle breeds have found a new popularity as beef specialties.

If the land has been put under serious stress by human activities, so have the oceans. Since the 1970s, catches have increased dramatically, because of the emergence of bottom trawlers (powerful vessels with huge fishing nets sweeping the ocean's floor catching all types of fish) with state-of-the-art technology and efficiency.

By the end of the 1980s and early 1990s, it became clear that this type of vessels caused major damage to fish populations and to ocean ecosystems.

Not only do these vessels catch too many fish, they also catch species that are not commercially valuable or they catch fish that are too small. The pressure in the nets caused by the weight of fish they catch is so high that a large proportion of fish is crushed and therefore unfit for the markets. Actual numbers of fish discards are not easy to find, but there are estimates that close to 25% of the fish caught is discarded.

A notorious example of overfishing is the collapse of the Newfoundland cod population in the early 1990s. The first colonists in the 15th century described the fish population as almost infinite. The highly efficient super trawlers of the second half of the 20th century caught in 15 years as much cod as what had been caught between 1647 and 1750. In 1992, six populations of cod collapsed. The population of the Northern cod, which used to be the largest cod fishery in the world, saw the volume of the cod juveniles drop by 99%! Overfishing is one reason, but poor administration and lack of foresight also contributed to the disaster. Although there is a moratorium on cod fishery, the cod still has not returned, and it looks doubtful that the natural conditions are there anymore for this to happen.

Newfoundland's economy has been hit severely by the loss of this economic activity. However, when protected on time, fish stocks have the possibility to recover and get back to normal levels in a rather short period as the recovery of anchovies in Peru illustrates.

One of the reasons behind overfishing in general is the overinvestment made in the fisheries sector. Not only are the vessels huge, but the number of boats is also far above the real needs. A 2008 UN report from the World Bank and the FAO mentions that even cutting the worldwide fleet by half would not decrease the number of catches.

Other estimates from the Monterey Bay Aquarium indicate that the global fishing fleet operates at 2.5 times the sustainable level, and 75% of world fish stocks are fully exploited, overexploited or have collapsed. Deep-sea fisheries receive many subsidies, especially on fuel costs, which contribute to keep overcapacity and over-efficiency to deplete wild fish stocks. Research from scientists Daniel Pauly and Ussif Rashid Sumaila concludes that without these subsidies, deep-sea fisheries would simply lose money[11].

This means two things. First, fish is too cheap because the revenue to fishermen does not cover their actual costs. Secondly, fishermen use oil for a system that is economically and environmentally not viable. Dismantling the subsidy system would certainly help by having the fish market reset to the actual prices consumers should pay for fish. Of course, it would affect affordability of fish and the survival of many fishing companies, but the current situation is unsustainable.

More governments are taking action to reverse the trend and prevent the collapse of fish populations. It will not be easy, but there are a number of ways to address it, such as fishing quotas, which have proven to deliver encouraging results. In the most dramatic cases, a strict fishing ban would be the last resort.

---

[11] American Association for the Advancement of Science, The Last Wild Hunt: Deep-Sea Fisheries Scrape Bottom of the Sea, February 2007

PART II

The SIMPLE Way Forward

A New Way of Thinking

Compared with the previous economic revolutions, such as the Industrial Revolution of the 19th century and the Green Revolution that started after World War II, the future will have to include one dimension that has been neglected in the past few decades. While most of the progress made during these revolutions was of an economic, scientific and technological nature, the next one will also include preserving and repairing the environment.

In the course of the 20th century, the dominant model for agricultural progress has shifted. From an agriculture that used to rely mostly on human labor and with limited capital, food production moved towards an intensive system. Farmers gained more land as quickly as possible and they created capital-intensive farms with a high level of mechanization that replaced human labor with bank loans and subsidies from governments. This approach did not apply only in agriculture. It has been the dominant economic model in Western countries, which encouraged many developing nations to adopt it.

In the course of 2010, world population will pass seven billion people. There were only 2.5 billion people in 1950. Their impact on the environment by then had been relatively benign. In the past few decades, science and technology have brought many improvements. Medicine has made tremendous progress, human life expectancy has increased and food production has reached a level of productivity like never before. It has come at a cost, and choices are necessary for humanity to survive. With two more billion people to join the world population by 2050, and with an intensive agriculture that has already met a number of limitations because of its success in increasing output to levels unknown before, the time has come to reassess how to allocate land, capital and labor.

59

Considering the difficulties farmers have to face in order to meet today's food demand, meeting tomorrow's demand will be an even bigger challenge. Yet, farmers have many tools and many possibilities to improve the performance of agriculture.

The universal model thinking will not work in a diverse environment. During the 20th century, humans have gradually chosen to ignore their biological nature and they approached economy in an almost mathematical way. During the last 50 years, it certainly has resulted in cost reduction, mass production and attractive pricing to consumers because of economies of scale, standardization and intensification. It is true until the time the potential for progress shrinks to close to zero. Moving a factory to replace workers paid at $8.00 an hour by workers paid at $0.50 an hour delivers great financial results, even if the productivity of the cheaper workers is lower. Over time, they will become as productive. Yet, when the labor costs reduction is less than half a dollar an hour and the employees are productive enough, there is not much margin for progress left. Therefore, the effect of globalization will fade, especially since transportation costs to bring the goods from distant low labor costs countries to the rich consuming countries will increase.

Agriculture has reached the point where the one-fit-all model cannot work anymore. The way forward consists of thinking of a combination of models, much like Nature has shaped her creatures to adapt to different environments. Similarly, there is a need to integrate old empirical methods, even if science has not explained yet why they work. New farming models will appear. Some farms will be large and others will be small, and yet both will be efficient. The gap between organic farming and industrial farming will gradually disappear. They will learn from each other and integrate the benefits of both approaches. Commercial farming will make sense in certain conditions and in certain areas, while subsistence farming will be the solution of choice in other places, but all in a modern way. Sustainability and modernity are not mutually exclusive but they actually support one another. All the discussions that try to oppose systems are actually counterproductive and biased.

Environmental, climatic, economic, social and cultural conditions differ strongly between regions. All the actions that bring progress in their particular conditions will be accepted. Critical and pragmatic thinking is necessary to adapt constantly in the best way possible for the short term as well as for the long term.

Innovation is going to flourish as never before. Humans have more knowledge and more technological resourcefulness than ever before. By looking back in time and seeing how many things have changed, even in the course of one's life, it is easy to realize how much potential there must be for food production to improve.

All the main forces that have shaped the world and societies during the last century have now reached a critical point, and this situation is about to create a different future for all of us.

As natural resources are being depleted, they are simply going to become more and more expensive. It is the law of supply and demand, and it will affect the world economy profoundly.

Cheap oil will soon be gone, which is probably the most dramatic change the world will face. Beyond the issue of global warming, expensive oil means two simple things. First, everything produced with large amounts of oil is going to become substantially more expensive. This is the negative part, at least when looked at from a consumer's perspective. Secondly, and this is much more optimistic, many alternatives that could not compete economically on the short term with oil are going to become attractive. As these alternatives become economically viable, they will become cheaper to manage and to produce. After all, it is not a new process. Coal underwent the same situation. Today, the world already has all the technology it needs to replace oil. There would be some short-term economic disadvantages to do so, but humanity certainly would survive. All it will take is to accept to change the way of life, especially in the West.

For a couple of generations, the industrial world has been filling the needs of the consumption society and for instant gratification. For many people, this is the only model they know. It is only natural and human that the necessity of a profound change meets resistance and disbelief, especially by those who have enjoyed the system the most. The consume-and-throw-away mentality that leads to having all of the natural resources ending in a different form on landfills, dissolved in drinking water or emitted in the air has no future. It is necessary to look at materials with a new attitude, and to aim at a zero-waste world. Another economic system must take over. Production numbers and volumes will not be the only parameters.

Changing lifestyles dramatically, and within a rather short period, actually corresponds to grieving the loss of abundance, which is not easy as comfort is addictive. To understand and to manage this process, it is interesting to look at it with the famous Kübler-Ross model in mind that describes the five stages of grief as Denial, Anger, Bargaining, Depression and Acceptance.

This model describes rather well the process countries are going through in all the debates and the negotiations about environment and climate change, including agriculture and food production methods.

So far, the world has not quite passed the third level. Many people and organizations are still going back and forth between the first three stages. Some are still in denial or angry, mostly in the materialistic and rich countries. Others already see the necessity to negotiate deals to ensure the future. For instance, a poll held in October 2009 revealed that more than half of the Americans stated they did not believe in climate change at all. Many industry lobbies still try their best to resist change and deny having a responsibility in the problems. Countries blame each other for creating the situation and demand from others to make more efforts.

Yet, there is a gradual move towards acceptance, as more and more companies regularly release statements in the press about their sustainability programs. Although it is sometimes difficult to identify what is actual action from what is PR, this trend is positive because it shows that now everyone is aware of the issue. Some retailers have already taken the lead towards more sustainable business. Because of their position in the supply chain, they are in an ideal position to lead and change the way humans consume and produce. The ones who will take the right actions will emerge as the winners, and the ones who are stalling or passive are simply placing themselves out of the game.

The SIMPLE Way Forward

The future of agriculture and food, just like the future of all economic activities is SIMPLE. This acronym stands for Sustainability, Innovation, Market orientation, Pragmatism, Leadership and Efficiency.

Sustainability

All that is needed to succeed is to rediscover common sense and understand that Nature works through cycles. Until the consumption society, sustainability was the normal state of affairs. There was no excessive waste. Maintenance and recycling were common. Sustainability is not just about the environment and people. It also includes financial sustainability. In order to succeed, sustainable activities must be financially viable, too.

Innovation

Humans have been successful because of their ability to think and create new tools and methods. The first tool set the path and people will continue innovating because innovation improves the quality of life and contributes to make wealthier societies.

Market orientation

Being market-oriented is the best way to reduce waste and benefit both the economy and the environment. Markets bring supply and demand together to ensure that needs are met. The need for food will only increase and markets will play a central role in future food supply. Market-oriented is different from marketing-oriented, which consists of creating a demand for something that is not a basic need.

Pragmatism

When facing tough challenges, rigidity rarely helps. Pragmatism is the expression of flexibility and readiness to adapt. In agriculture, all possible systems will deserve consideration, even the ones considered old-fashioned. Combining today's technology with an open mind can be the way to improve the efficiency and the relevance of these old techniques. Future agriculture will be a variety of systems adapted to the local environmental, economic and socio-cultural conditions.

Leadership

Success will depend greatly on the quality of the leaders, be it in politics, in business, in science, religion, education and all areas of society that have the power to make people take action. Strong leaders are needed to focus on the long-term collective advantage more than on personal short-term rewards, because of elections every few years, quarterly results of companies or share price on the stock markets. The performance indicator will shift from merely financial to success in fighting poverty and malnutrition.

Efficiency

As population numbers increase and because resources are limited, or in some cases have already been seriously depleted, the only way to provide for the needs of humanity will be to be efficient. It is not only true for production, but also for waste. Efficiency reduces the level of inputs. Nothing can be lost; everything has to be transformed.

Sustainability and Modernity: a Joint Effort

Sustainability is about allowing Nature to do its work at its own pace, staying in balance and allowing natural cycles to complete their courses.

There are two groups of unsustainable activities. The first one consists of activities that continuously deplete a source of basic essential needs. The second one consists of activities that continuously increase the level of harmful components in the air, the water and the food.

Sustainability is the way human societies have lived for thousands of years, simply because the scarcity of goods made conserving and recycling a necessity for survival. Only over the last 50 to 60 years has humanity seemed to forget, because of the consumption frenzy and the abundance of goods thought to be about infinite. This explains why until recently, sustainability seemed to be almost a revolutionary concept. Thanks to the increasing awareness about climate change and the endangered environment, sustainability has now become a widespread concept through all industries. The food value chains have embraced it like everyone else.

Since one cannot live without eating for much longer than two months, cannot live without drinking for much longer than two days and cannot live without breathing for much longer than two minutes, these cycles can be reduced to just a few critical areas for life.

- The cycle of air is necessary to remove the contaminants, so that air remains breathable.

- The cycle of water is necessary to remove the contaminants that can make it undrinkable.

- The cycle of soils is necessary to preserve the fertility of the soils, and thus allow a continuous agricultural and livestock production to feed people.

The population increase will put more pressure on the environment. As demand for food will continue to increase, sensible management of water resources, of the soils and of ecosystems will be a key factor for the success of agriculture.

The importance and the obvious need for sustainability appear already in the definition of the word. What is not sustainable disappears eventually. There is no need for any further philosophical or political discussion. Survival can come only from sustainability. All processes in Nature that deal with life are about recycling of organic matter in one form or another, and about balance. If the environment is favorable for a particular species, this species thrive and its population grows quite fast, to the point where it exceeds its abilities to provide for itself in its original ecosystem. Then, it starts to use more resources than Nature can replace, resulting in a strong reduction of the population because the weakest cannot find food and perish, or because the high population density makes the spreading of diseases much faster than it would otherwise.

At the beginning of the consumption society, mass production seemed attractive because nobody factored in the cost of cleaning up and of repairing the damage. It became obvious over time that depleting natural resources at such a pace would bring problems. Yet, humanity is still trying to postpone the moment when the cost becomes too high and a change of attitude is necessary. It is quite difficult to change habits.

The problem only gets bigger as now people from emerging countries also wish to have the same standard of living as in Western countries. Materialism, selfishness, overindulgence and the search for instant gratification are the wrong attitudes. To be sustainable, the world needs to be frugal and thrifty. Humanity must live within its means.

Yet, the situation is changing. As a good banker would, Mother Nature is now sending some clear signals that living above our means is not possible anymore. If attitudes do not change, the price will be high, and higher the longer the delay. Demand will keep increasing and this will cause inflation. Governments will pass more regulation on environment and sustainability, which will increase costs. Inflation will reduce consumption and the business environment will be difficult. In the short term, the goods providers will face a problem. Corporate earnings will disappoint the markets.

Mother Nature, like any good banker, knows no mercy. She does not do politics and she does not discriminate. The financial crisis happened because financial resources were mismanaged. During the recession, many people lost their homes because they could not pay their mortgages and they moved somewhere else. The situation about the environment is different. Since the Earth is humanity's only home, foreclosure is not an option. A similar crisis is waiting to happen with natural resources and agriculture. There is one major difference, though. Unlike what happened with the financial system, there will be no bailout.

Sustainability and modernity are compatible, but from all economic activities, agriculture seems to have a specific status. While everyone seems to agree that most of the polluting industries with unsustainable processes or products must work on a cleaner future through new technology, agriculture could only have a future by downsizing. Where are the voices to demand to get rid of large factories, and go back to small local workshops, or to get rid of cars and ride bicycles again?

Food is a special topic, though. It is loaded with emotional and psychological symbolism. The most vocal proponents of sustainability seem to reduce the possibilities of sustainability to only organic and small-scale farming. This is simplistic and untrue. This thinking may fit in the wealthy North American city baby boomer nostalgia of things that never were. They can afford to pay for organic foods in specialty stores or on farmers' markets. In Western countries, the organic market is growing fast, although it still represents a small percentage of total consumption. Consumers are longing for what they perceive as being more natural and environmental, although they make their choice based mostly on emotional criteria more than rational ones. The trend for authentic and for local food is also gaining momentum, and there is no doubt that these market segments will gain a growing audience. Unfortunately, the health and environment-friendly food market is not affordable for everyone. From a global perspective, the current Western model of organic production and farmers' markets are not in a position to become the dominant model for food consumption, because it is not affordable for most of the world population. However, it will help some farmers to stay in business and contribute to the local economy. Yet, the organic approach will prevail eventually and serve the majority, but it will grow thanks to innovative techniques on large-scale, efficient and rational agriculture, not on small individual farms scattered over the country.

It is possible to envision a world with small extensive farms as the only model. This is a very different type of world than what the current trends indicate, though. Such a model requires the majority of the population to be working in agriculture. Food would be more expensive to produce and there would be less disposable income to spend on other goods. This would have consequences in the rest of the economy as well. There are better alternatives.

The research and the development of better practices using modern and efficient techniques need to receive more publicity and encouragement.

Humanity has reached its highest level of scientific and technical knowledge ever. Combining old empirical techniques with new technologies will bring the best of both worlds. Farmers can be very precise and efficient in the use of water and of fertilizer to feed the plants with exactly the right amount of what they need when they need it. By combining the old and the new, they can protect and improve the fertility of the soils, reduce the use of pesticides and herbicides in crop production, and reduce the use of antibiotics in animal husbandry. All the techniques that the small-scale organic farmers currently use can be implemented on a larger scale. Feeding an increasing world population mostly concentrated in cities will require large-scale efficient and sustainable agriculture. The main challenge is to figure out the right economic model. Large-scale sustainable agriculture will require a different distribution and use of land, capital and labor from the current organic farming, but there is no reason why it should remain small-scale.

What is lacking today to make the move to the future is a clear plan. There is a tendency to stick to the present, and to some extent to the past. The world needs people who will combine the principles of sustainability with modern technologies. The development of sustainable practices will come from leaders who will determine the successful models. These models will take into account the local situations and consider without prejudice the best possibilities.

The environment and the economy function within a closed system of finite resources. Nothing is created out of nothing and nothing disappears completely. Everything is transformed, either from something else or into something else. Sustainability depends on the ability of producers to manage these apparent shortages and surpluses. The solution is not extracting more. It is about finding a use for the by-products.

By looking at the Earth as the only home, and humanity as a good tenant who does not want to accumulate garbage where it lives, people need to change their attitudes towards waste.

71

The goal must be to create zero waste. The sense of organization of human societies is one of the reasons why people do not see the problems they create. For instance thanks to garbage removal, once the garbage has been collected and it is on its way to the landfill, it looks like the garbage has gone. It does not seem to exist anymore. It is not true, but it looks that way and it feels that way. The only exception is when the garbage collectors go on strike. Then it becomes clear how much garbage is actually produced.

For agriculture and food, the system works in the same way. The ecosystems play a regulating role through the cycles of soil, of water and of air. This is true until the day these systems are overwhelmed and do not have the ability to process more of the garbage, be it gases, minerals dissolving in the drinking water or lost fertility of the soils. The system runs at its maximum. Anything that exceeds its capacity is not processed and it ends up accumulating in the environment, with all the risks that this brings for human health and, eventually, for survival.

The concept of zero waste is quite simple. Nothing can leave the factory, the farm, the workshop, the store or the house unless it has a useful destination. If it does not have any, it is necessary to consider this simple choice: there is a use for the waste produced or then there is no alternative to keeping and accumulating it. This is a powerful way to look at sustainability, because it forces people to think about their actions and their consequences.

Another factor in dealing with waste is money. A large part of waste is produced simply because what people throw away is cheap and they have enough money to replace it. It feels convenient.

The options to work towards zero waste fall into three categories.

- Reducing the amount of garbage generated by buying different products
- Reusing some of the goods, thus extending their life
- Recycling the garbage so that it has a new value for the producer or for someone else

Some European countries have been running green waste recycling programs for a few decades. All organic waste from fruit, vegetables and plants is brought to a separate garbage bin. The organic matter is recycled into compost. Recently, a British company called Vertal Ltd. has started a plant specializing in large-scale processing into compost after transformation inside large aerobic digesters of food waste from the London area. The final product is ready for use and can be spread on the land to return organic matter in the soil.

Food companies can also play a significant role in reducing waste by taking action at the source. A leading American deli producer initiated actions that illustrate how waste reduction programs make sense both financially and economically. In 2008, they reduced the quantity of packaging materials by 5.2 million pounds (about 2,390 tons). The reduction includes cartons, paper sleeves, thinner glass jars, plastic trays or shrink-wrap. Not only does this program have a direct effect on the packaging of their products, but it indirectly also saves a lot of resources, such as a significant reduction of paper fiber, less trailers on the road using fuel and less petroleum for plastics of all sorts.

Although food production appears mechanical due to industrialization and standardization, the difference compared to manufacturing of other consumer goods is that agriculture deals with living material. The "average" or the "model" is true only within a certain statistical domain, and there is always a margin of error.

Regardless of how sophisticated techniques and technologies have become, a field is not an isolated system. Farming today still depends for a large part on external factors such as climate, pests and diseases. All that farmers can do is to take all the possible and available preventive measures to reduce this dependence, but their power is limited compared with the damage Nature can cause. The agriculture of the future, starting now, cannot ignore this truth.

Farming will take into account all the interactions that exist between the environment and the production unit, being the crops and the livestock. These interactions are both direct and indirect.

The group of indirect interactions covers the complex relations that exist between the farm and the environment, especially the ecological function of the farm for all the other forms of life, visible and microscopic, vegetal and animal. A field is a complex ecosystem in which many living creatures establish their territories and fulfill their roles in the ecological balance and the survival of other species. This type of interaction is always difficult to assess, because of Nature's resilience. It takes time for signs of imbalance to appear. If the populations of some species are depleted, others thrive and for quite some time, everything seems normal. Yet, when the balance between species has shifted beyond a certain point, natural calamities occur, such as an insect plague. Since ecology is a balance of many balances, the disaster often has several degrees of separation with the cause of the imbalance. This is why such calamities, and especially their magnitude, generally come as a surprise. Ecosystems are comparable with a set of gears, in which every wheel is a sub-system. One wheels starts to turn, making another wheel turn and so on. The initial action sets the whole system in motion. To manage the whole system properly, it is important to understand the relationship between all the sub-systems, too.

The other type of interactions, the direct ones, covers two areas. One is the kind of inputs the farming unit receives, or in some cases undergoes from Nature. The other is what the farming unit releases in the environment. This type of interaction is much easier to manage because the farmer walking through his fields or among his animals can notice any deviation rather easily.

To an experienced and capable farmer, the five senses are quite helpful, although they are not always sufficient. With today's technology, it is easy to spot imbalances and take samples for further investigation. There has been degradation of soils and pollution of groundwater and air. In some areas, this has already exceeded what is acceptable from a sustainability point of view, and action is needed. Farmers have already implemented new techniques. Governments have set new and stricter rules to stop the degradation, and to reverse it gradually over time.

Just as the degradation was a slow process, restoring better farming conditions will be also a long and slow process that could clash with short-term economic interests.

It is important to realize that even with developed technologies, farmers and food producers can only manage Nature, but they cannot beat natural laws. Living organisms are constantly adapting to their environment and any change that takes place induces changes in the vegetal and animal populations. Antibiotic-resistant bacteria, herbicide-resistant weeds and insecticide-resistant insects are the best illustrations of such an adaptation of Nature to agriculture and the food sector. If the agricultural community cannot manage such risks properly, the world might find itself back in the pre-penicillin and pre-herbicide era, but with much tougher adversaries.

An essential part of agriculture is soil. It has many functions, such as storage and release of moisture and minerals, so that they are available for plants. The soil, because it contains so many life forms such as bacteria, worms and insects, is an ecosystem of its own, and it fulfills a role of recycling organic matter into fertilizer. The function of the soil could almost be compared with the function of the liver in the human body. It filters, stores, releases the essential nutrients, and excretes toxic substances. When the liver is sick, the body shows visible signs that something is not functioning properly, for instance by turning yellow. A vegetal population will also give signs of the health of a soil. The appearance of the crops, their growth, the presence of weeds and their type, can indicate the health status of the field.

All the techniques protecting the soil from degradation are preserving future agriculture. For instance, techniques like limited tillage, or even zero tillage, burying crop residues for matter organic enhancement, or harvesting techniques that leave a higher stub of plants on the fields to protect the soil from wind erosion all prove beneficial.

The economy of the future will not be as much about consuming anymore, but it will be about managing the Earth. In this model, the agriculture of the future is going to be much more complex. It will include the ecosystem as an integral part of the operations. Although it will increase the number of parameters to monitor and the complexity of running the operations, the development of technology and software will greatly assist farmers in their tasks. Farming will not be about production only anymore, but about managing what sustains the farm. It will be about having a comprehensive approach of the total supply chain as well. It will take place locally at the farm level, but the agribusiness will have to do its share at the global level.

In the future, many innovations will come to market and governments will get more involved to change how to produce food. There will be actions to reduce excess gases in the air and excess minerals, especially coming from manure, in the groundwater and rivers. Stricter rules on food safety will also address residues, from chemicals such as pesticides and from antibiotics.

Depletion of resources will be addressed, too. There will be more regulations, new techniques and new technology to protect soils and preserve them from erosion, to manage water in a more efficient manner and reduce unnecessary waste. More concerns will grow on the loss of genetic diversity and of biodiversity. Deforestation and depletion of wild fish stocks will face more action and stringent action plans will come to stop the damage and to rebuild the resources.

Innovation: Adapting to a Fast-changing World

The purpose of innovation is to create new solutions to improve the quality of life and help societies to cope better with the environment. Two main drivers lead the pace at which the world is changing: the increase of population and technology. Technology helps meet the demand by increasing efficiency, but every technology has its limitations. The meeting point between the increasing needs of the world population and the physical limitations to meet those triggers innovation.

Several major areas of interest for humans have been constantly stimulating the process of innovation.

- Reducing the amount of difficult physical labor
- Developing more efficient tools and techniques
- Developing better communication systems to access knowledge and information
- Surviving
- Improving health and extending life expectancy
- Enhancing mobility and speed
- Improving the quality of life
- Saving time
- Saving money
- Providing more possibilities for leisure and entertainment
- Enabling some people to increase wealth

All these drivers of innovation will continue to play a central role in the quest for new solutions and to adapt to the future.

Further development of better and more efficient machines and robots will keep contributing to eliminate difficult physical labor and boring repetitive activities. Using computerization, software development and artificial intelligence, these machines will become increasingly sophisticated and efficient. They will allow people to have better working conditions and jobs that are more interesting.

Combining all sources of data with an ever-increasing processing capacity and further miniaturization will support farmers in their decision-making. Satellite technology will develop further and offer more possibilities for monitoring and measuring. New applications of these technologies will greatly increase efficiency and reduce waste of inputs. Precision farming will become increasingly important in tomorrow's production systems. Improving the technical performance in the agribusiness will deliver higher production and financial savings that will contribute to keep production costs and consumer prices under control.

Genetics and nutrition research will be the base for the development of plants and animals that are more productive, that will transform nutrients and water more efficiently into food products. New types of fertilizers, herbicides and pesticides will come to market. The continuous improvement of food safety will lead to the development of new techniques and products to reduce pathogens in food products.

New technologies will bring new challenges. Yet, innovation does not have to be high-tech or capital intensive. Farmers have always been very creative in bringing simple effective solutions and they will keep doing so in the future.

Opposite forces are engaged in shaping the world of the future. Accepting change is always a slow and often a difficult process. There are those who see the possibilities and those who see the drawbacks.

Supposedly, the first train was going to make cows stop giving milk. Probably, the first caveman who drew a picture of an animal on the wall was considered by some as a great magician, and by others as pure evil. The first agriculturalist who decided to plant a seed in the ground instead of going hunting with the rest of the tribe probably had to endure sarcasm, especially when the hunters brought back food and the seed still had not come out, yet. Such a struggle is useful because it shakes immobility, opens new doors and prevents people from rushing into the unknown without thinking first. In this process, the main problem is the pace of change. It takes time for people to leave their comfort zone and adapt. Over the last century, this pace has just increased steadily, thanks to more and more efficient technology.

By the end of the 19th century, which is only the lifespan of the oldest living person, there was no car industry, no antibiotics, no commercial airlines, no TV, no internet or cell phones, no supermarkets, just to mention a few things taken for granted nowadays. The change has been dramatic, and it has affected the way people live today. More than 60% of the products that exist today did not exist 10 years ago. By extrapolating this number to the decades to come, some more spectacular changes will take place.

Innovation is in constant motion. Yet, even with such a pace of change, traditions still play an important role. Even with many modern gadgets, most cultures keep their specific characteristics. Their respective values do not evolve as much as the "things" do. These just become part of the culture. This is an important point when it comes to innovation. A product or a service must meet a need. If it does not, it will either fail or at best be a fad. While many changes will come over time, consumers will still be looking for some level of tradition in foods. They may ask for authenticity, regional specialties and recipes, or choose to buy directly from farmers. It is not a rational process, but it is more about the perception of "true" and "natural" production systems. After all, nostalgia is a constant of human emotions, too.

Two useful questions stimulate the search for better, new and creative solutions. The first one is *"Why not?"* which Robert Kennedy used in one of his speeches: *"There are those who look at things the way they are, and ask why... I dream of things that never were, and ask why not"*[12]. The second is *"What if?"* What would happen if there were an oil shortage tomorrow? What would happen if oil cost $300 in six months from now?

So far, alternatives to oil all faced the major problem of their relative costs. The demand for energy increases and the supply side does not have much potential for increase. There has not been any significant discovery of new fields. Exploration and extraction become more and more expensive. This was true with oil at $30-50 a barrel, but with a price of $100 as the norm in sight, the economics of energy, and especially the momentum of energy sources, look quite different. It has happened before, when coal replaced wood, and when oil replaced coal. Everything that could be produced cheaply before, because energy was cheap, will face a cost increase. It is necessary to review the economics of food to avoid a severe price increase that many people will not be able to afford. The transition will be gradual, and the oil producing countries will resist change. Indeed, if oil becomes obsolete, the economies of the Arab world, Iran, Russia and of other countries like Nigeria, Venezuela, or Canada will be affected negatively. The potential economic setback will cause social unrest for many of these countries if they do not develop new economic activities.

As usage of renewable energies increases, their cost of production will drop, and the relative price differential between oil and the alternatives will make the latter ones the winners. The economy and the environment will both benefit. The development of wind power, solar energy, geothermal energy, biofuel or hydropower opens the doors to a new future. An interesting documentary called *"Here Comes the Sun"*[13] made by the Dutch TV station VPRO in 2008 shows the possibilities.

---

[12] This quote is a paraphrase of a line in George Bernard Shaw's play "Back to Methuselah"

[13] The English version of this show can be viewed on YouTube

Such a change will affect agriculture in the future. As oil becomes gradually obsolete, agricultural systems and equipment will have to adapt, too. In the total supply chain, all industries will be affected by the change and they will have to find new solutions. These sectors are machinery, nitrogen fertilizer, plastics and packaging, refrigeration industry and transportation. From a cost point of view, what happens with oil will probably not be relevant because energy, regardless of its nature, will become more expensive. Governments have always helped agriculture with subsidies on energy in one form or another and they will continue to do so.

The main challenge will be to develop equipment that can do the work without losing productivity in order to be able to have a similar output from the land.

A number of alternative energy systems for farm animal housing are being tested, such as solar panels or LED lighting. The only aspect that needs further investigation is the cost of production. Technical performance is unchanged.

In 2009, The Israeli Ministry of Agriculture organized a contest to develop more environmental layer hen houses. The winning project reduces fossil fuel consumption, as it is equipped with solar panels, wind turbines and it can generate its own energy with the hen manure.

One of the solutions for agriculture comes from space. Satellites are gaining more presence in agriculture. Farmers have been using GPS systems for some time during the harvests. It optimizes the harvest by regulating the direction and the speed of the tractors and of the harvesters. The system measures the crop density and steers the machines. This optimization of trajectory of the tractor and of the power used to harvest reduces fuel consumption, which saves money and reduces the burden on the atmosphere.

Satellites are the modern way of land assessment, too. Not only is it accurate, but it proves to be much more cost-efficient than former techniques such as soil analysis.

By measuring the electro-magnetic radiation reflected from the ground, a whole region can be scanned at once, and farmers can review their whole farmland area. On such maps, shortages and surpluses of minerals appear in different colors. Farmers can see with high precision the properties of the soil, the quantity of crop being produced, and the levels of various minerals and moisture in those crops. This technology will help make the management of the farmland much more precise. Farmers can see the differences between fields and the discrepancies within one field. By knowing where plants are lacking fertilizers and where they might have received too much, the farmers can optimize the fertilization plan. They can prevent waste and the leaching of minerals. It serves the technical and economic performance of the farm, and it preserves the environment. Satellite information will also be useful in the monitoring of pests and diseases by locating and identifying the areas of activity.

By linking and loading the information from the satellite to farm management software, market information and meteorological data, farmers will be able to make better decisions faster and thus maximize their revenue. It creates the amazing possibility of having farming operations carried out virtually without the input of the farmer. The data on plant growth will be read directly from space and projections of yield and date of harvesting will be available on the screen. The farmer's role will become more one of control and supervision. The computer will coordinate, present the data and send instructions.

Similar developments will come in the seafood sector. Systems will be able to locate and monitor schools of fish from a longer distance than today's systems. Fishermen will then know where to go, and how much to catch. The vessels could be steered from space the same way as the tractors on the crop fields. Monitoring from space will also help government organizations record, control and enforce fisheries activities. They can help ensure the sustainability programs are followed properly, preventing risks of overfishing.

Satellites will also help aquaculture farms to monitor their level of production, and deal with environmental problems, such as the development of algae blooms or the possible risks of interaction with wild fish stocks.

More and more, machines and robots will replace people for difficult, boring and expensive labor-intensive activities. Jobs will evolve to supervision of processes. In food production plants, robots have been present for some time, such as the ones transferring cans of drinks from the conveyor belts to the final packaging. Robotics is engaging in new fields, and the tasks of robots are driven increasingly by food safety concerns. By reducing the amount of handling by people, and replacing them by robots, there is hope to reduce the number of contamination risks in food plants. Robots have become able to handle delicate products without causing physical damage. For instance, Pepperidge Farms, a US high-end brand cookie manufacturer, uses robots to collect, stack and place the cookies into individual paper nests that are then stacked inside retail packages. In 2009, a new robot manufactured by Applied Robotics Solutions has received approval and certification by the USDA. It handles meat and other fresh and frozen food products.

Not only will the machines become "intelligent" with technology, other areas will offer possibilities for robotics in agriculture and in food plants. The list of projects and applications is long and here are just a few examples to illustrate the broad range and the creativity at work in the mind of researchers.

A project supported by the USDA is investigating the possibilities of having robots helping in orchards, designed to improve fruit quality and lower production costs.

According to Sanjiv Singh, research professor of robotics, who leads the Comprehensive Automation for Specialty Crops (CASC) Program *"Growers will receive early warning of diseases and insect infestations, as well as continuous updates on crop status. With this information, growers can make timely decisions that will save them money and improve the quality of their crop."*[14]

One device under development is the weed control robot. It is still in the early stages, but on a small scale, the results are encouraging. The prototype called Lukas, developed by Halmstad University in Sweden can help organic growers replace the labor-intensive manual weeding. Their first estimate was that the robot could reduce the cost of weeding by half. This project also demonstrates that organic farming can be mechanized and use high-tech instruments.

Wageningen University and Research Centre, in the Netherlands, has been investigating ways of using robots in labor-intensive activities, such as greenhouse crop production. They have been working on robots to pick cucumbers and other robotics projects aimed at leaf picking for tomatoes, harvesting roses, and various mechanization projects for cut flowers like Gerbera and Chrysanthemum.

A few years ago, the National Agricultural Research Center of the National Agriculture and Bio-oriented Research Organization in Japan, developed a robot to plant rice. The robot uses a GPS system for direction and can work without supervision. Japan has more and more difficulties to find young people who are interested in doing this kind of work, and they are already working on developing the "robot farm", where robots would carry out the farmer's work. If there is one country in the world where there could be farms without farmers just run from a control panel room, Japan will be the one.

---

[14] In: Robotics News, Carnegie Mellon Developing Automated Systems To Enable Precision Farming of Apples, Oranges, 20 November 2008

In aquaculture, MIT (Massachusetts Institute of Technology) is working on developing gigantic cages that can travel the sea in search of better environmental locations with higher water quality and where fish waste would not be as problematic as is currently the case in coastal areas. The plan is to have these cages being able to power themselves with solar energy.

Innovation will also contribute to a new generation of solutions for herbicides and pesticides. In addition to potential residue issues, one of the problems with chemical herbicides is weed resistance. So far, 180 weed species worldwide have developed resistance to chemical herbicides. It has become a major concern because the resistant weeds invade fields and affect negatively crop yields. Alternative solutions need to be developed. One of these solutions is bioherbicides. These products are made from active agents that originate from a living organism. They are produced with bacteria and fungi that can attack a broad spectrum of weeds and destroy them. Researchers believe that biological herbicides may be less vulnerable to genetic variations in plant populations, which makes these products appealing. Another factor stimulating the search for bioherbicides is the problem of invasive weeds. Many such weeds are associated with waterways, and therefore require products with a lower ecological impact. Biological herbicides, however, need to be effective at a competitive cost to be an economically viable alternative.

The development of biopesticides is not a new field, as the first product in this category was approved in 1990 for large-scale field-testing of genetically engineered insecticides to kill pests that attacked tomatoes, potatoes, eggplants, and ornamental trees. In the USA, the EPA (Environmental Protection Agency) has approved more than 200 biopesticides now sold in more than 800 products. Some are quite effective in their highly targeted uses, and none of them causes residual damage to the environment.

According to the EPA, biopesticides generally affect only the target pest and closely related organisms, in contrast to broad spectrum, conventional pesticides that may affect a wide variety of organisms from birds to insects and mammals.

Biopesticides are effective in small quantities and they decompose quickly, resulting in lower exposures and fewer pollution problems than with conventional pesticides. Users need to be familiar with managing pests to use biopesticides effectively. They must be used as a component of Integrated Pest Management (IPM) programs. This combined approach decreases the use of conventional pesticides, while crop yields remain high. These products still represent a small share of the pesticide market, as they do not compete economically with chemical pesticides for large-scale agriculture, yet. Their main use is in niche markets, mostly gardens and small-scale organic farming. The producers are optimistic and they expect a growth of as much as 10% to 20% per year in the near future. Their market presence may be limited now, but biological solutions to fight pests will gain more interest in the future for two main reasons. The first reason will be an increased regulatory pressure to preserve the environment and to safeguard food safety, and it might affect the market of chemical pesticides significantly in the future. The second reason is the further development of genetic engineering, which will bring the large companies to this business, as they will look for alternatives to chemical products, just like the oil companies are investing in all sorts of renewable energies. Biotech companies are already engineering plants to be resistant to diseases and to pests. They are familiar with this field, and they could combine their work with the development of biopesticides for geographical areas where genetically engineered crops are not allowed, but where there is much interest for environmental-friendly alternatives to chemicals, such as the European Union.

The interaction between production aspects and food safety and environment is also fuelling the debate about genetics. Genetic engineering and traditional breeding will become increasingly intertwined in the future. They will join their respective areas of expertise into combined genetic improvement programs.

Eventually, these two disciplines will be merged into one science of DNA. There will be an increased number of joint ventures and mergers between genetic selection companies and biotech companies.

Genetics are a key element of the food production chain because of the qualities that they can provide to living organisms to perform in their production environment. By focusing on true improvements and on the sustainability of production systems, combined breeding and genetic engineering programs will bring constructive solutions. All it requires from the stakeholders is vigilance. To solve such problems, the people in charge of the programs will have a heavy moral responsibility towards society because the choices they will make will affect the longer term and humanity's ability to survive.

To overcome the loss of genetic diversity, a vault built into a mountain in Norway on Spitsbergen Island, near the North Pole, is housing an increasing collection of seeds. Already one-third of the world's seeds varieties are stored in this new version of Noah's Ark. The objective is to keep 1.5 million specimens. The purpose is for humanity to preserve genetic diversity, be able to adapt to very different climatic conditions and survive.

In agriculture, breeding uses the selection and the mating of the best individuals in order to produce generations that deliver higher performance on selected criteria. This can be done only with the genetic pool naturally available as it comes with the individuals. When genes are not there, they cannot be used. Genetic engineering can help fill this gap and speed up the process.

Genetic engineering is a controversial area. Applying this technology requires thorough thinking because the products interact with other life forms. The consequences of pollination with non-GMO plants need to be considered very carefully. Plants producing toxins to protect themselves from pests could kill useful insects, such as bees that play a critical role in the reproduction of many plants. Such side effects are very difficult to assess, because genetic engineering is a very young technology. Nobody can say with absolute certainty how long the effects on the ecosystem could take to manifest.

If nothing seems to have happened after 10 years, does this mean that the technology is safe?

The debate between the proponents of the precautionary principle and the entrepreneurs who see more upsides than risks in the technology will continue. The precautionary principle states that if there is no scientific consensus that the technology is not harmful to the public or the environment, it should not be used. The fact that in the EU the precautionary principle is a statutory requirement explains the position of the Europeans about GMO policies.

Genetic engineering will evolve in the future. It will move from a support activity to, for instance, herbicides, to address the challenges of the agriculture of tomorrow, such as drought resistance and soil salinity. The real problems to solve include a broad range of topics. They include technical performance and yields of plants and farm animals. Genetic engineering will increase the efficiency in the conversion of nutrients and water. It will develop plants and animals that have a stronger resistance to diseases, in order to avoid severe production losses. Its application will help eliminate debilitating traits that make the plants and animals vulnerable. Genetic engineering will provide alternatives to antibiotics, to herbicides and pesticides. Another area of research will be to improve the quality of final agricultural products. Genetic engineering can contribute to producing healthier foods by influencing the protein content, the amino-acid profile or the fatty acids profile contained in grains, legumes and oilseeds. For example, work on developing the introduction of a gene in soybean that would allow the plant to produce oil with a higher content of omega-3 fatty acids is currently being carried out. Such modifications could create the ability for plants to produce certain molecules such as medicines that are technically difficult and expensive to produce synthetically. For example, genetically modified tobacco has produced active molecules that can cure inflammatory diseases and possibly diabetes.

The topic of GMOs is sensitive. They are used widely in North and South America, but other regions are reluctant to use them. This is the case of the EU, where there has been a moratorium on GMOs since 1998.

It does not mean that the EU will never allow genetically engineered crops in Europe. It just will take place on the Europeans' terms. An exception to the overall ban is the authorization given by the EU to use a genetically modified potato in 2010. Europeans do not really need GMOs because their agriculture is very productive and efficient. Technical performance of Western European farmers is high, in particular because of the high quality of their genetics. Western Europe does not have food shortages or any major insect plague or weed infestation that would really require GMOs. The price of food in Western Europe is quite affordable without GMOs and people want natural food. The rejection of GMOs came originally from the UK retail sector after the mad cow disease disaster. It was not the time to take any chances. Strong cultural differences between Europe and the USA explain their positions on the use of genetically modified crops. The Europeans do not want to see their food production falling into the hands of a few corporations, either. When GMOs solve specific European issues, they probably will be accepted. In the USA, consumers did not have the same critical attitude as in Europe and the agribusiness started using GMOs without opposition. There seems to be a different trend growing and American consumers are starting to challenge their food production system more and more. When the debate becomes open in the public opinion, which is only a matter of time, one can wonder what the position of retailers will be. In the power balance within food value chains, the strong links are the providers of genetics and the retailers. A possible situation in which the large and powerful retailers would say no to GMOs would give the debate a new dimension, as the balance of power would shift.

Until recently, China had taken a cautious position on GMOs. At the beginning of 2010, the Chinese Ministry of Agriculture announced that it will develop the domestic seed industry. One of the objectives is to help consolidate a fragmented industry and have seed companies with more capital structure to work on plant improvement. Currently, there are about 7,000 seed companies in China. This program also includes the development of genetically engineered plants.

They will develop genetic improvement programs that correspond to their needs at home and abroad, like in Africa. The sector of genetics will see more competition and the Western seed companies will soon face a powerful competitor on world markets.

A better understanding and predictability of long-term effects is paramount in agriculture and food production. Actions in genetics need to guarantee the long-term balance of the ecosystems, in which weeds, although of no economic interest, are a part, because once an ecosystem has been altered, it has been changed forever. Genetic improvement programs must ensure to preserve, in whichever form, genetic diversity and survival of vegetal and animal species, because once extinct, they are lost forever. Long-term fertility of soils is another highly critical part of the protection of food supply, because once sterile, the land is lost almost forever.

Genetic engineering is not the only controversial topic in agriculture and food production. Nanotechnology is a new field in agriculture and food production. It is the technology of building structures from atoms, molecules or molecular clusters to make materials and devices with new properties. It offers a wide variety of applications in a number of important areas such as food safety, traceability, the use of chemicals and waste.

With nanotechnology, agriculture and food production will be able to use very efficient devices and sensors that can aid in decision-making. For instance, in Controlled Environment Agriculture (CEA), which is an intensive hydroponics greenhouse system used in the USA, in the European Union and in Japan, nanotechnology is a great fit for the already sophisticated computerized management system that optimizes growing conditions.

There is also a lot of potential for precision farming, in which nanoparticles can be used to store and release pesticides and herbicides in a targeted and controlled manner. Nano-clay capsules can store fertilizers and release them slowly, requiring only one application during the cycle of the crop.

The use of these capsules saves time and fuel to the farmer, and reduces the use of chemicals, too. Further, nanosensors can be used to measure crop growth, help diagnose diseases even before the farmer can visually notice them, or help him carry out microbiological tests and get results within an hour. They help farmers monitor soil moisture, temperature, pH, nitrogen availability, and in the future, they could open the path toward a remote farm surveillance system.

In the area of pest control, using nanocapsules is useful in Integrated Pest Management (IPM). Problems can be identified earlier and plants can be treated much more effectively. This technology is already used in human medicine and nanotechnology could treat farm animals, too.

Nanotechnology is already used for water treatment, and there seem to be many possibilities in that particular field to help solve existing environmental problems. For instance, the American firm Altairnano from Reno, Nevada produces lanthanum nanoparticles that can absorb phosphates in water. This product offers good possibilities to reduce algae growth in ponds and rivers.

Similar applications of nanotechnology can be used to decontaminate soils and groundwater by using iron particles that help break down dioxins and PCBs into less toxic carbon compounds. They also can help remove arsenic from drinking water, which is a problem occurring in many regions.

There are nanotechnology applications for the food production industry, too. Some nanodevices can be used to tag food items. They can be of great use to ensure traceability and to help optimize the supply chain. Some of the world's leading retailers are investigating such devices made out of silicon. It appears to be too costly at this early stage. There is no doubt this will change in the future.

Food packaging is an area with potential, and there are new packaging materials in development. Nanotechnology helps reducing the risks of food contamination.

Some systems reduce the ability of oxygen and gases to travel through the plastic wrap, which extends the shelf life of the product. Other food packaging systems are aimed at controlling the level of humidity, of oxygen, reducing bacteria counts and eliminating any problems of odor and flavor. Antibacterial packaging using silver nanoparticles is in development and the applications range from plastic cling wrap to plastic bags, containers, even teapots and kitchenware. Packaging containing nanosensors are made of carbon nanotubes or of titanium dioxide that can be activated by UV rays to help detect microorganisms, toxic proteins or food spoilage. The firm AgroMicron, from Hong Kong, has developed a spray that contains a luminescent protein engineered to bind to the surface of microbes such as Salmonella and E. coli. When it is bound, it emits a visible glow that allows the detection of contaminated food or beverages much more easily.

Developing molecular food manufacturing, which consists of building food from component atoms and molecules, is already a possibility. Although this is far into the future, such a technology could allow a more efficient and more sustainable food production in which fewer raw materials are consumed. The food produced in such a way would have a higher nutritional quality.

If nanotechnology seems to offer possibilities for food production, some people express concerns and it could be the next controversy in the food business. Nanotechnology in food is relatively new and very little is known about the long-term effects of using these components. Because it is so young, food safety regulations are not properly written to deal with nanocomponents, and the status of the nanoproducts is unclear. One of the concerns is that such particles could bring health risks because of their size and of their chemical composition that make them potentially very active in the human body. These new possibilities are promising, but it is important to remain vigilant and to address the risks as well.

The fight against pathogens is critical in food production. Since the beginning of the use of antibiotics, there has been a gradual rise in antibiotic resistance.

It is a natural process, but it has become a problem because antibiotics could become ineffective, with serious consequences for human health. Beside its use in human medicine, the use of antibiotics as growth promoters and therapeutics in animal husbandry has contributed to the problem of bacterial resistance to antibiotics used in human health.

Antibiotics have been used in animal husbandry since the early 1950s to prevent and treat diseases and improve feed efficiency. Because of the risks of resistance to antibiotics, Denmark initiated a ban of antibiotics as growth promoters, with no major difference in technical performance. Other countries such New Zealand and the European Union did the same. This took place in the EU in 2006 and it followed an earlier ban from 1998 on feeding livestock antibiotics for growth promotion purposes that are valuable in human medicine. At the beginning of 2010, the parliament in Bangladesh has passed a bill prohibiting use of antibiotics, growth hormone, steroid and harmful pesticides in animal and fish feeds. The same trend is happening in more and more countries. The use of antibiotics will be limited to therapeutic use only and controls on residues will become stricter than they are now. A ban similar to the one now in place in the European Union will happen in North America some day as well.

The agricultural sector is already looking for alternatives to antibiotics that will preserve animal health and pose no threat to human health. Possible alternatives to antibiotics cover diverse areas such as novel vaccines, probiotics and phage therapy, to not only reduce or eliminate the need for antibiotics, but also to eliminate specific food-borne pathogens from livestock at the source, thereby reducing the risk to human health from contaminated food.

An area of research is on antibacterial products that function through different mechanisms than those of current antibiotics, or that can be used next to antibiotics.

This group includes antimicrobial peptides (AMP), incompatible plasmids, agents inhibiting bacterial growth, drugs inhibiting bacterial toxin production, compounds blocking resistance mechanisms, thus restoring antibiotic sensitivity, compounds interfering with the transfer of resistance between bacteria, decoy molecules redirecting a bacterium's resistance enzymes and alternative approaches such as use of ozone or essential oils.

An example of research of AMP is the use of potato protein in pig diets. The potato protein showed in-vitro antimicrobial activity against Staphylococcus aureus and E. coli, among others. The potato protein improved growth performance and feed efficiency thanks to improved nutrient digestibility. It also reduced the number of pathogenic intestinal bacteria. Other studies have demonstrated that potato protein can selectively inhibit harmful bacteria without negative effect on the beneficial intestinal bacterial flora, while antibiotics inhibit the growth of both beneficial and pathogenic germs. In human health, a team of German researchers have identified an antimicrobial peptide from hydra, a primitive sea organism, and found that it exhibited significant and widespread activity against bacteria including MRSA[15] and VRE[16].

Chitosan, a polymer derived from chitin, the main component of crustacean shells, is a possible alternative to antibiotics. This molecule has antibacterial properties, is biodegradable, and does not cause bacteria resistance. A team from the Basque Research Technological Center has carried out encouraging trials on the effect of chitosan as a growth promoter.

At the Istituto di Ricerche Scioccheze in Milan, Italy, two scientists are working on the production through genetic engineering of a new strain of antibiotics from green algae. The antibiotics are degradable in the digestive tract of farm animals, which eliminate the risk of bacteria resistance.

---

[15] Methicillin-Resistant Staphylococcus Aureus

[16] Vancomycin-Resistant Enterococci

These antibiotics can be used as growth promoters for meat production. Trials on pigs have showed that the FCR (feed conversion ratio) was 20% lower with these growth promoters. The researchers have also observed a substantial reduction of the FCR with chickens.

Probiotics could provide an alternative to antibiotics. Probiotics are microorganisms that bring health benefits when they are administered in sufficient quantities. The health benefits of probiotics have been known for many years. In a similar area, prebiotics, which are non-digestible food materials that beneficially affect the host by selectively stimulating the growth and/or the activity of established bacterial species, could also offer new possibilities.

Bacteriophage therapy is an old, almost forgotten, medicine that could find a second chance. Before the era of antibiotics, bacteriophages played an important role in the control of bacterial infections, particularly purulent infections. Bacteriophages are naturally occurring predators of bacteria. They can be effective antibacterial agents due to their specificity against a particular bacterial species and their lack of impact on other flora. They are highly efficient, safe to humans and non-target bacteria. They are very good at finding bacteria in hard to reach places such as biofilms and they could offer a potentially sustainable biological control of bacteria. During the last 50 years, research and treatment using phage preparations has continued in many Eastern European countries, but they have been abandoned in the Western World, although phage has continued to be of value in microbiological research, particularly in molecular biology, epidemiology and diagnostics. With the threat of antibiotic resistance, bacteriophage therapy is getting more attention again. Phages have been used successfully for several decades in human medicine in Eastern Europe, and they have appeared to be effective in a number of situations where antibiotics are inadequate due to bacterial resistance or poor blood supply. For example, phages have been used successfully in Eastern Europe to treat antibiotic-resistant bacterial infections in skin ulcers of diabetic patients.

In Canada, studies have focused primarily on phage products, such as lysine or synthetic molecules that mimic phage action. In the UK, research on bacteriophage therapy is being carried out on Campylobacter in poultry. Campylobacter is an elusive bacterium, which is difficult to isolate on poultry farms and in poultry meat. It is considered responsible for even more cases of food-borne disease than salmonellas are. In the USA, in a preliminary study led by Purdue University and the USDA ARS (Agricultural Research Service), researchers inoculated 3 to 4 week-old pigs with salmonella bacteria. They immediately administered the animals an anti-salmonella phage cocktail. Salmonella infection decreased by 99.0 to 99.9% in the tonsils and parts of the small and large intestines. The researchers also tested the efficacy of phage therapy in a production-like setting by inoculating four market-weight pigs with salmonella bacteria and placed them in a pen for 48 hours to allow contamination to occur. They then mixed two groups of healthy pigs, one receiving the anti-salmonella phage cocktail and the other a control with the infected pigs in the contaminated pen. Results showed significantly reduced salmonella concentrations in parts of both the small and large intestines in the pigs receiving the phage cocktail.

As the need for animal products increases, innovation is required to make animal production more efficient. Animal feed represents the main cost in animal production. Therefore, any performance improvement coming from the feed or from nutrition gives a competitive advantage. A feed mill is a rather simple process feed producers know well and master. Simply put, the recipe is prepared in the equivalent of a big kitchen blender. As a standardized industrial process, the focus for a given quality specification is to produce at the lowest cost possible. Feed has become a commodity and the challenge for feed producers is find ways to increase the added value to farmers. This can be looked at on two levels: the feed itself and its usage. Feed manufacturing itself can be incorporated in the production chain in different ways that will all have the same purpose of cutting costs. The feed company can be independent and market its own feed, or it can just produce as toll milling for a farmer or a processing company.

The actual added value lies somewhere else. It lies in innovation. Feed manufacturers are already active in this increasingly strategic area of the future for feed companies. Innovation will continue to cover many areas, from biology, nutrition, to feed technology with the purposes of further improving feed efficiency, and provide raw materials that are more efficient. In an age where availability of raw materials will become scarce because of the competition between animal nutrition, human nutrition and possibly demand for biofuels, everything that will help save and recycle resources will win. To achieve this objective, there will be new techniques to increase the digestibility of feed, to reduce the feed conversion ratio and to produce less manure. Feed companies will also work further on improving the texture and the other physical qualities of the feeds. More innovations in feed composition that will improve the feed efficiency by the animals are expected. For instance, the use of enzymes will increase further. Other developments, such as a promising sesame seed extract that can help replicate omega-3 fatty acids in fish feed, can help reduce the dependence on scarce and expensive fish oil, and offer substitution possibilities with more types of vegetal oil. In this case, fish would compete with other farm animals and humans for these oils, making them more expensive. There is also the development of algae as a feedstuff for farm animals. Increased competition for feed, and therefore its price, will stimulate the search for new ideas. The feed companies that will possess the latest scientific and technical knowledge, combined with a strong innovative capacity and the talent to locate and purchase the best mix of raw materials will in fact own some sort of an intellectual property. None of this is new, but the future changes will have more to do with the allocation of the activities in the feed value chain itself. The intellectual property is what they might need to sell in the future, instead of a feed their customers do not always perceive as a differentiated product. Feed and nutrition will become two distinct products and even distinct businesses. Feed mills will become franchises of nutrition and feed technology centers.

Market Orientation: More than a Strategy, a Necessity

Being market-driven is always the right approach, even when the market is friendly. The alternative, being production-driven will only bring gloom eventually.

A recent, and now famous example to illustrate this, is the construction industry in the USA until the subprime mortgage collapse of 2007-2008. Agricultural products tend to follow similar cycles and this story is just a reminder of the recurrent mistakes that occur. Builders forgot to be market-driven, which is the reason why they got into trouble. As their market was good, and easy, they became overconfident and instead of being business people, they actually became speculators. They assumed the market would not change, that the only way would be up, and they built more and more houses without having any contract at all, as they assumed there always would be buyers. By ignoring how markets function, the builders created their own demise.

Agricultural products know similar phases. In Europe, in the pig sector, this has been known as the "pig cycle". One good year for pig prices encourages farmers to put more animals in production, which results in an oversupply the year after. The prices drop and farmers prefer not to produce as many pigs anymore. It leads prices up again, and the cycle can continue. Overconfidence caused the salmon market to crash in 2000, after several good years.

All producers were confident, although by then all surveys showed that they all expected the market would become oversupplied and that many companies would end up in financial difficulties. Yet, in the same surveys, they all thought their own companies would survive. The result was a major market downturn with a strong consolidation of the industry, with no real winner.

When food prices increased worldwide in 2008, farmers increased the planted area and the crop production volumes. Since the market was good, suppliers of inputs such as fertilizers also increased their prices. The result has been that many farmers did not make that much money in 2009, as supply exceeded demand. The economic crisis took its toll on consumption, and the suppliers have cannibalized the farmers' margins. The planted area for the following year has decreased. The cycle continues.

The market-driven approach is also the most sustainable one. By assessing what the market needs, it is possible to adjust production levels to meet the demand. It will always result in a more balanced market, in more stable prices and in less waste, as nothing should go lost. No other approach has as much benefit for the environment and for the economy. Market-driven thinking is the key to prosperity and sustainability.

A production-driven approach can never optimize markets, as it always results in surpluses that need to be pushed in the market at a discount. Producing first and then having to find customers to buy the production is a sub-optimal way of doing business, as it consumes resources that are not transformed in added value. In such an approach, valuable resources usually end up generating economic and environmental losses. Producing what has already been sold is a lot easier and it is a much safer approach. Yet, this way of organizing business is still more the exception than the rule, especially in agriculture.

The example of India where farmers are planning to grow GMO-free soybean for the EU market where GMO crops are not allowed is a good illustration of how market-driven production can turn opportunities into business.

An opposite example of this approach is the frustration of African cotton farmers who cannot sell their production into the EU for the same reason mentioned above. They have been encouraged to produce something that their main market does not want and they cannot sell. The customer is always king. In this case, being production-driven affects the farmers' profitability negatively.

Being completely market-driven is not simple. Eliminating the production-driven thinking is a little theoretical, because when it comes to agriculture, there still is one element farmers never have under control. The weather can affect seriously the production plans. It can help produce more than expected if the weather conditions are good and it depletes the volumes if the conditions are adverse such as in the case of droughts or floods. Weather conditions make market-driven production a little more difficult, but the advantages outweigh the risks by far. Producers need to consider possible production setbacks and plan accordingly to supply the market.

As future agriculture will be focused on sustainable production, there will be new developments in the area of market forecasting, production forecasting, weather risk management and precision agriculture that will help produce in a market-driven manner.

Regardless which link in the value chain one represents, it is essential to consider always the big picture. In this picture, the consumers are a key element because they are the final link of the chain. As the final users, the consumers will always drive the activities and the profitability of the whole value chain. Although the interaction with the industry is left to the retail sector, the consumers' quality requirements will trickle down along all the other links of the chain. In the example of meat, what the consumer wants will have implications all the way back to genetics, and breeding companies know how critical it is for their survival to be able to anticipate these needs, as choices have to be made several years in advance. For breeders, the final products are the consumer products, not just the animals produced.

Animal feed goes far beyond animal nutrition. Feed is part of the consumer product specification and feed ingredients become eventually the consumer's choice.

Understanding the consumer is what makes successful value chains. Many companies fail because they do not listen or understand the consumer market.

Pretending to do so, with the help of new product development, sleek communication or fancy marketing concepts may help for a while, but it will not withstand the test of the consumer. Commodities always sell at market price and with no premium because they do not represent anything special to the consumer. Therefore, the only differentiation with the competitor's commodity is the price.

Agriculture and food products will flow towards the consumer market, and the information producers need must originate from the consumer as well. When building a value chain, it will always pay off to spend time understanding the consumers because they represent the strongest and most powerful link of the chain.

Health concerns of consumers will gain more influence in the future when they buy their food. More and more newspaper articles, TV programs and movies address concerns and criticism about the current production systems. Although the bad publicity is not always based on the most objective facts, it has been able to find a growing audience.

For now, consumers have a certain perception of how food is produced, and arguing whether the perception is correct or not it is rather irrelevant. Perception simply becomes the truth, and consumers act according to what they believe is true. Since most consumers have little or no knowledge of agriculture and food production, their only source of information is the media. Moreover, they have very strong, often idealistic and romantic opinions of how they think farming should be, regardless of whether it is viable or if it can provide them enough food.

Surveys of children raised in cities have shown that many of them do not make any connection between eggs and hens, or between milk and cows and calves. For many, it is not even a clear fact that in order to get meat, one has to kill an animal.

On the other side of the discussion, the agriculture and food industry is not connecting well with the public because its message tends to be too defensive and too technical.

Unfortunately for the industry, errors from the past (for example, the use of DDT) or cases from other industries, for example tobacco, contribute to cast a shadow on its approach of controversy and on its credibility. They must organize more Open House days.

The way consumers think will define the way they eat and how farmers produce. Many changes in consumption patterns, in production systems and in product offering are under way. Concern about environmental impact of food production and health concerns is growing. The depletion of wild fish stocks in the oceans, the interaction between aquaculture and wild fish stocks, manure and smell of intensive animal husbandry and impact of manure on soils and drinking water, deforestation of rainforest for ranching of beef or about growing GMOs raise many questions about the sustainability of current food production.

The area of the food production chain that will undergo the deepest change, although it may not be the most dramatic one, is food safety. This issue is present in all countries and governments have no alternative but to legislate on this matter. Consumers worry about food poisoning due to bacteria, such as E. coli, listeria, campylobacter and salmonella, but also about residues of pesticides or antibiotics, and the use of hormones in animal production. The crisis with melamine in pet foods with raw material originating from China has also created awareness over there about the food safety issue. China had another food safety scandal in 2008 with the sale of milk powder tainted with an industrial chemical that sickened 300,000 children. Tests carried out in Russia in 2009 have showed that more than 80% of meat products sold to consumers were below the veterinary standards for food safety. The region at the forefront of progress in the area of food safety is the EU, where preventive measures and inspections have already improved the level of food safety because the consumers are better organized and more critical than in North America or Asia. European consumers, helped by the media such as The Sun in the UK or Der Spiegel in Germany, have been able to gain a much stronger voice to influence industry practices.

Previous cases of salmonella or listeria infections, and of course the mad cow disease crisis, have left no room for the status quo. Eventually, North America will follow the European Union example, and adopt similar measures on farms, in processing plants and in the entire supply chain to improve food safety. All these changes in consumer attitude, legislation and population growth will affect production methods and the location of food production. Insufficient quality leads to rejections and closure of export markets. Shrimp farmers from Bangladesh have seen the European market disappear because of a high level of antibiotic residues. Vietnamese pangasius (also known as basa, a species of catfish) producers have been facing many problems with the USA because of antibiotic residues and because of anti-dumping claims.

In the USA, discussions of health care reform and the cost of obesity are becoming more intense. More and more people are questioning the fast food diet. Animal welfare is also a growing concern for an increasing number of consumers. The answer to many of these concerns has started to appear in the last few years with the growth of the organic market segment. Considering the growth and the performance of organic retailers, there is no doubt that organic foods have a growing audience.

Concerns about the environment are forcing retailers, food service and businesses involved in the production chain of food to make changes. Some of the actions they have taken can be seen as marketing or PR, but they also have become common business practice. Just a look at how many restaurants and supermarket chains have already implemented sustainable seafood programs indicates how serious the change in consumer attitude is.

Fast food chains are also actively working on reducing their environmental impact and setting standards on where they source their meat, based on environmental concerns, such as demanding the beef should come from ranches that do not contribute to the deforestation of the Brazilian rainforest.

Similar concerns are arising over the deforestation in Indonesia and Malaysia for the purpose of palm oil plantations. The concern for the environment is the reason why the French retailer Casino will stop using palm oil in its private brand food products by the end of 2010. The retailer will use only certified sustainable palm oil in cosmetics. Unilever and Nestle made a similar choice. They decided to stop purchasing palm oil from a large Indonesian producer under pressure of a Greenpeace campaign to preserve the rainforest and the habitat of orangutans.

In the sector of animal husbandry, much stricter regulations will apply in all countries, following the new regulations that have been put in place in the EU over the last decade. It is only a matter of time. The use of antibiotics as growth promoters and hormones will be eliminated gradually from production systems. Animal welfare regulations will become stricter. Only husbandry systems allowing enough recreation area for animals will be permitted. All of this is going to have an impact on how and where food is produced and at what cost. Systems will become less intensive, and progressively there will be more techniques to improve efficiency to compensate and keep production costs under control.

The Dutch province of Noord Brabant has recently passed a law that restricts the maximum size of livestock buildings to 1.5 hectares, with exception of 34 "agricultural development areas" in which the maximum size will be 2.4 hectares. This follows pressure from a public movement called "No to mega stables". In the Netherlands, the high density of human population with a high density of farm animals causes issues of manure smell. There are also fears of animal diseases and potential risks for public health in the case of outbreak flu-related epidemics.

The relative prices of various food products also need to go along with their relative health benefits. In North America, building a nutritionally balanced meal costs more than one made of cheap low quality fast food. It looks like only wealthy people can afford a healthy diet.

In the short-term, the economic crisis does not help making the population healthier, but things will change. Criticism about the American diet grows. The topic comes back regularly in the media and the actions of Michele Obama to fight child obesity start to have an impact in the industry, too. A number of food manufacturers have already announced some changes in the composition of their foods. Some will reduce the amount of salt in soups, deli products and prepared foods. Some will reduce the amount of sugar in their cereals. This trend will continue further in the future. The soft drink industry will also undergo a transformation towards healthier drinks. This will have consequences for the corn industry.

As the consumer changes attitudes, food production will change, too. The past 60 years have seen, at least in the Western world, the development of the consumption society. The emphasis has been on consuming always more, by having an apparently unlimited quantity of increasingly cheaper goods available. This evolution happened in the food sector just as well as it did in other consumer goods sectors. Marketing encouraged mass consumption, which supported mass production. Production costs were reduced due to intensification, technical and technological progress, cheap inputs and subsidies. Technical progress improved yields and productivity, while marketing aimed at creating more, and new, needs. Food has become standardized, industrialized, and processed in a wide variety of forms. The emphasis moved to convenience and comfort, which came along with the rise of mass retail distribution, cheap energy and suburbia. People lost the connection between themselves, the origin of food and Nature. Food became just things they bought at the supermarket, already packed in plastic or cardboard.

Now, society is aware that the high production of waste, be it packaging material, be it blemished products while still perfectly edible, be it the overproduction of manure and its minerals, or be it the use of antibiotics and pesticides, is not sustainable. Much progress has already been made to reduce waste and there is a growing trend towards organic and traceable production.

However, at this stage it is not clear yet whether it is a true change in consumer behavior or whether it has more to do with social status and marketing.

The understanding that it is not possible to keep on intensifying and wasting will bring a more fundamental change in how people consume in the future.

Food has a strong psychological connotation. Food is associated with experiences and, although there are differences between cultures, that emotional bond will stay.

The consumption society with all its excesses is coming to its end, and the current economic crisis, which also originated in the excess of having it all right now at any cost, could be the turning point. Intensification has already showed its limitations. The amount of waste is also reaching a limit. Energy is getting more expensive and this makes the production and the transport of food more expensive. The next evolution is probably going to be a balanced approach between consumption, which exists to some extent, and preservation. There will be different approaches to this balance between geographic regions, but sustainability is the only way forward.

With the current development of software and technology and all the concerns the consumers express about food, health and environment, there will be new tools to help process information and make nutritional choices. Today, nutritional information is shown on all food items labels, but few use it and many hardly know how to read them. It could soon change. As many people have computers at home, there will be software to allow them to determine and set up their own diets. Already, numerous websites have interactive programs calculating how many calories to eat per day, depending on the person's weight and lifestyle. Other websites help calculate the nutritional value of a meal by entering the quantities of the menu's components. Some iPhone applications offer this possibility, too. Other systems will take into account weight, age, level of physical activity, health risks and other biological parameters.

They will calculate what meals could and should contain. It will calculate how much to eat, depending on which menu combination to have for a particular meal or day. The computer will be connected to a kitchen weighing scale and the program will do the rest. The nutritional information could originate from a database or it could be directly transferable from the nutritional value label present on the food packaging. It will be no surprise to see the development of such software programs to be supported by governments and by health insurances as part of a broader health plan.

In animal nutrition, companies have been using optimization programs for many years. The programs compose the feed rations by entering the nutritional value of the possible ingredients and set limits to the level of inclusion of some ingredients based on nutritional and technical parameters. Last, but not least, these programs also include the price of the raw materials, so that it is possible to compose the best-balanced meal that meets the nutritional needs at the lowest cost possible. Such programs certainly could be quite useful for households to manage their food budget while eating healthy. The West has developed a society where people become obese by eating lots of food as quickly as they can, while they have less physical activity than previous generations, due to automation. Food is produced on intensive farms and feedlots where the animals grow and fatten as quickly as possible, as they eat lots of food, while not having much physical activity. Similarly, meat producers use hormones to boost growth and carcass quality, while body builders and sport professionals use steroids and growth hormone to boost their performance. These are intriguing similarities. This illustrates nicely the saying "We are what we eat".

Most restaurants will present their menus with thorough nutritional information on the side, in a similar way as food labels show, with indication of health benefits and restrictions. There also will be interactive programs that will enable customers to enter their personal information to have the meal tailor-made for them, with the relevant price adjustment when needed.

Of course, this includes the beverages as well, as they definitely can contribute to the overall nutritional value of the meal. In the new Health Care Law passed in the USA in March 2010, national restaurant chains with more than 20 outlets are required to provide their customers with nutritional information about the food they serve.

More and more foods in the future will be aimed at improving health. Genetic engineering will be the technology to help in this type of development. Plants will contain improved levels of molecules that have a positive influence on health, such as antioxidants or certain profiles of amino acids or fatty acids.

Another futuristic area for food is the "lab meat", where meat is produced from animal tissue growing outside the body of an animal. At first, this might sound like an odd concept, but there are some good arguments in favor of such a process. Theoretically, there would not be any risk of spreading animal diseases, or bringing pathogens to consumers. There are no by-products or waste as with traditional meat production and there is no manure pollution. Further, as the world population and the demand for meat increase, lab meat could be a way of reducing the pressure on the production of crops for animal feeds, thus reducing competition with human consumption. One such project is being carried out in the Netherlands, with the support of the Dutch government. A producer of sausages and deli products is participating. So far, there is no data available about the cost of producing meat in such conditions. The production cost of lab meat is its main challenge. If such meat goes into processing, grinding and soaking, the physical properties of the meat do not have to match exactly those of true meat, while it would offer a similar final product. A cost analysis will be necessary to see if it indeed has a future. So far, the texture of the meat is not what the researchers have been looking for.

Yet, they are optimistic about the possibilities and they expect such meat could be on the market before 2015. The physical appearance and texture of those final products might not be any different from the current ones.

Future Harvests

Pragmatism: No Food Left Behind

To succeed in meeting food demand and avoid social unrest, it is necessary to consider all available options and it is not possible to reject any out of prejudice or because of previous experiences. What may not have been an option ten years ago could be useful in the future. Over the past decades, and in light of the Green Revolution, commercial agriculture has chosen models that showed high performance, technically and financially, and has tended to exclude less efficient ones. These highly efficient systems have brought their own set of problems.

This approach of intensification, supported by capital and mechanization, did bring good results. Initially, the level of productivity was rather low and potential for progress was high. Now, with the current levels of production, intensification is no longer a synonym for efficiency. This subtle difference is relevant for the future, because intensification has already reached its optimum. Intensive agriculture may have reached a point where additional intensification will actually reduce performance.

The idea of an intensive production model farmers can implement and apply anywhere is also becoming obsolete. As the intensification model starts showing limitations, it is important to look at the production system as a component of a larger system that includes the environmental, economic, social and cultural conditions. A farm is not an independent and separate entity.

Future agriculture is not going to be about food production only. Farmers will have to manage the environment as well. This new dimension opens the door to opportunities, but it also sets a number of physical limitations. A new era is coming in which open-mindedness is an asset and excluding possibilities a liability.

111

During the 20th century, society has become increasingly technological and it seems that science has become the core of progress. Such an evolution is not bad, but the dominant trend has tended to reject, ignore or deny anything that science could not explain, or not yet. It explains why the agricultural sector has a tendency to replicate a certain model to solve apparently similar problems. Science, technology, heavy investment and large scale have increasingly become the only modern way to produce food. Any alternative has been regarded as archaic or non-viable.

The current idea that science must explain everything and that only what has been scientifically proven can be used is a major impediment to change. The recent history of human medicine is an example of such limited thinking. Alternatives, such as acupuncture or homeopathy have struggled to be recognized as treatment options because there was no scientific evidence of how they effectively worked, even though they have been used with positive results for many years, even centuries in the case of acupuncture. Another disadvantage of some of these treatments was that they did not belong to traditional Western medicine, and were considered inferior for that reason alone. Another non-official reason for alternative medicine to be contested was that the patients who would use them did not consume the synthetic medicines produced at great expense by the pharmaceutical industry. The role of science is to explain how things work, not to reject what has not been explained, yet.

Systems alone do not do all the work. The skills and capabilities of the farmers are essential in their success. Some farmers will do an outstanding job with high-tech tools and others will perform better with simpler tools that they master well.

The example[17] of a Dutch pig farmer who had an old traditional pig house illustrates this. The building did not meet any of the standards of "modern" pig housing.

---

[17] This is a farmer I visited during my early professional years

The house had an open layout, and it had no mechanical ventilation. In the late 1980s, such a farm was considered archaic over there. Moreover, he would not even consider changing his system, as he felt comfortable with it. He was not comfortable with the modern pig house. He obtained among the best technical and financial results in the country! Other farmers had opted for the state-of-the-art housing and feeding systems and they had lower results than this farmer did. The main reason for the difference in results was the farmers' ability to sense the climate in the pig house, and their ability to read the animals' behavior. There was no scientific evidence of why one farmer was better than the others were, but their respective levels of experience were an integral part of the performance.

Sometimes, it would be better not to wait for explanations about why some techniques work to use them. If they deliver results and they can be a solution in some situations, they should be used. Then the scientists should keep on investigating why and how they work. In the 21st century, humanity will need science to make further progress, but it will also need some old-fashioned techniques that contain a lot of wisdom passed on by previous generations.

This cold approach of science and technology contribute to some extent to the disconnect and the mistrust between the agribusiness industry and environmentalists.

Agribusiness, being a business, is about making money. Of course, this is acceptable as long as it does not jeopardize the future. This is where environmentalists play a role. They balance the power and challenge what the food industry does. This process is quite useful because it stimulates awareness of production methods. Such a debate is actually useful to prevent mistakes.

The problem is when the debate slides into the dogmatic and ideological area. Then, it is no longer about the general interest, but about partisan interests only. The debate shifts from the moral to the political.

There are aggressive opponents to the industry, unfortunately too often supported by the media, because sensation is good for ratings. Facing them, the industry tends to react too rigidly and too defensively, as they resist change, often because of short-term costs and profit concerns. Consumers can accept certain production methods if the industry explains why and if it can demonstrate beyond any doubt that the practices are sound. Justifying production methods by reducing the debate to making food cheap or by claiming there is "no scientific evidence to prove" there is anything potentially harmful does not answer the public's concerns. In the long term, this approach can actually be detrimental to business. The industry spends a lot of money for lobbying purposes, which saves money in the short term. Over the long term, if the industry's position is not serving the general interest, the inevitable will eventually happen. In such a case, the lobby money would be better invested in the systems of the future.

Sadly, both sides always claim to possess the absolute science to demonstrate their points of view. The main result is a confused public, since only a specialist of these matters could know who tells the truth. In a conference organized by Marks & Spencer on public perception of animal husbandry and animal welfare in the 1990s, the master of conference then brought up one relevant argument: the main source of scientific knowledge for the public over there was The Sun, not Scientific American! In the USA, the TV show of Oprah Winfrey, who has no agricultural background, has more resonance with consumers than the agribusiness with its army of well-educated scientists, technicians and PhD graduates.

Not everything is perfect in the agribusiness, as it is a work in progress. Any human activity has an impact on the environment. Even breathing is releasing CO_2 in the atmosphere. Sustainability is not about producing without any impact. It is about producing with effects that Nature can process in a timely manner. Consumers would understand that. All they deserve is to be informed properly, so that they can cast their vote when they shop by electing the good products and rejecting the bad ones. Eliminating bad practices is exactly what will bring benefit to consumers, and consequently to farmers, agribusiness and society.

As American consumers become more critical of the food they consume and as these concerns become present in the media almost daily, production systems will be under tighter scrutiny. Although the industry fights against many of the negative publicity, it will not win the PR war. The American consumer is changing. Therefore, the food they want will have to meet different criteria. The cases of the tobacco industry and the car industry are good examples of what can happen when health and environmental concerns influence consumer decisions. The agribusiness is experiencing a similar evolution and the current model of food production is about to change in America.

This cannot be done through confrontation only. It is necessary that the participants in the debate offer actual alternatives based on solid evidence, facts and thorough analysis. It is high time for the partisan debate to end, for both sides to recognize they do not know it all. They both can learn from each other. Industry leaders must realize that there will be changes, and some profound ones that will reshape the way they will do business. The environmentalists must realize that there will be changes, and that they will not have all they want. Eating is not an ideal. It is a necessity.

The relative economic power between corporations and the not-for-profit sector is evolving. The combined operating budget of all NGOs has now passed US$1 trillion, which puts this group among the largest economies in the world.

Therefore, the way of the future is cooperation between the industry and environmental groups. They will increasingly join their knowledge, their science, and their financial and business capacities to develop and support sustainable solutions. By joining forces, they will contribute to develop a better agriculture and find the most sensible ways to feed nine billion people while preserving ecosystems. Such an approach has already started.

The WWF (World Wildlife Fund) and Unilever have jointly created the MSC (Marine Stewardship Council), which certifies sustainable fisheries. The WWF is busy with a similar approach with aquaculture.

PepsiCo and the Carbon Trust initiated in 2009 a review of the carbon footprint of the company's Tropicana orange juice brand. They found out that 35% of the carbon emission came from the use of fertilizers and their applications. Together with one of the long-term orange farms, the company is now investigating the use of different fertilizers. Tropicana expects to achieve a reduction of as much as 15% of the Tropicana juice carbon footprint because of this decision.

In Brazil, the beef industry has agreed with Greenpeace on a moratorium on deforestation and they will not expand their ranches at the expense of the rainforest anymore. This Zero Deforestation Agreement was signed in October 2009. The first phase requires beef producers to register and map all the ranches supplying cattle to the processing plants. Six months after this agreement, the beef industry asked for more time as it could not complete the first phase on time. Regardless of the slow start, this type of co-operation is an improvement. It needs to be developed on a much larger scale!

The Global Harvest Initiative is a group of corporations and environmental organizations that look at the possibilities to double agricultural production by 2050 in a sustainable manner. They encourage agricultural development, innovation and private-public partnerships. They review trade and supply chain practices. The group includes NGOs and corporations such as Archer Daniels Midland Company, Conservation International, DuPont, International Conservation Caucus Foundation, John Deere, Monsanto, TransFarm Africa Corridors Network, and World Wildlife Fund.

Although it might sound contradictory, globalization could generate a new impulse for the development of a local economy, with energy as the main driver. The search for low wages led the trend towards globalization, causing corporations to relocate their manufacturing units to the emerging countries. Another pillar of globalization has been the ability to transport goods across the world at a low cost, as energy has been quite cheap.

The economic boom in the emerging countries, where employment has risen and where the standard of living has increased, on average, is a direct consequence of globalization.

Although the world is going through a difficult economic period, people must prepare for an increase of the price of oil. Higher energy costs and food prices will drive inflation higher, yet it should not reach alarming levels. Nonetheless, this cost inflation will push wages up in the emerging countries, while in the West where the main consumer markets still are, unemployment will stay high for a while and salaries will stagnate. The wage differential between those two groups of countries will shrink, while the cost of transporting goods will increase. In such a situation, some manufacturing will come back closer to the Western consumers' markets. At the same time, emerging countries will be able to develop a middle class that will drive domestic consumption, and thus sustain a certain level of economic momentum, even if their exports decrease in relative volume. A consequence would then be a global trend towards a more local economy.

Agriculture has followed the same pattern as other industries, and regions have specialized in the foods they could produce at the cheapest cost. The cost of production and of distribution to consumers depends largely on the price of inputs, such as energy, water, fertilizers and animal feed. Based on cheap fuel, the model was global trade and transport of foods over long distances. This is different from the local agricultural model that dominated until the 19th century.

The search for the lowest cost of production will not go away. The overwhelming majority of the world population has a limited budget and keeping food affordable is an absolute necessity. During the sharp food price increases of 2008, it became clear that it would not take much to create a panic and riots, because even a slight price increase is almost unbearable for most people, especially in developing countries.

Environmental concerns, the increasing cost of energy and transportation, and the emphasis on reducing waste will encourage food production to take place closer to consumption markets. Demographics will play a role, too, and the predicted increased concentration of the population in cities will reinforce this trend. The evolution is going to be especially noticeable for perishables, which are the food items the most sensitive to spoilage. There will be a reversal of the trend of the last few decades and fresh produce, fresh meat and fresh fish will be relocated gradually closer to urban areas to reduce waste caused by long transport and intermediary storage. For non-perishable products, such as grains, other commodities and frozen meat and seafood, the need for relocation will be of lesser importance, as long as these products will be brought to their final destination by boat. Water transport is the cheapest method and the one with the least impact on the environment.

The carbon footprint of food transport is often misinterpreted and miscalculated. Most of the arguments focus on the number of miles travelled, but not on the qualitative aspect of the transport. Depending on whether food is transported by road, by rail or on water, the results vary greatly. For instance, only 5% of exported products are transported by waterway in Brazil, compared to 61% in the USA Conversely, 67% of Brazil's exported products are transported on highways, compared to just 16% in the USA In the European Union, almost 90% of external freight trade is moved by water, and short sea shipping represents 40% of trade within the European Union in terms of ton-kilometers. The consequences for the environment, as well as for transportation costs differ greatly. A study carried out in 2002[18] in the USA shows the following comparison of freight costs and pollution between road, railways and waterways. The cost of freight in US cents per ton-mile was 0.97 by barge, 2.53 by train and 5.35 by truck. The emission (lbs. per ton of cargo) of carbon monoxide was 0.20 by boat, 0.64 by train and 1.90 by truck. For nitrous oxide, the emission was 0.53 by boat, 1.83 by train and 10.17 by truck.

---

[18] David V. Grier, US Army Corps of Engineers, 2002

There are also significant differences in carbon footprint between transporting fresh foods or frozen foods. A study carried out by Astrid Scholz, Ulf Sonesson and Peter Tyedmers on salmon showed that consuming frozen salmon transported by sea was the best environmental choice. Their conclusion was *"If seafood-loving Japanese consumers, who get most of their fish via air shipments, were to switch to 75 percent frozen salmon, it would have a greater ecological benefit than all of Europe and North America eating only locally farmed or caught salmon."*[19]

Another parameter in the environmental impact of the distribution of food is the filling rate of the transportation unit.

An efficient fleet of trucks organizing back transport for other goods can have a lower carbon footprint than a small truck used inefficiently to bring products to the city's farmers' market 300 miles away. In the choice between global or local, it is necessary to think in pragmatic terms because the reality is more complex than it may seem at first.

Pragmatism is also necessary in the debate about large-scale and small-scale farming. The Pareto principle, also more commonly known as the rule of 80-20, can help foresee the future of farming structure. This principle is based originally on the observation by the Italian economist Vilfredo Pareto that 80% of the land was owned by 20% of the population. Of course, extrapolating this to the 21st century agriculture is a theoretical exercise, but it seems realistic to assume that 80% of the food would be produced by 20% of the farms.

Two dominant trends will emerge: large commercial farms and small local producers. Mid-size farms will gradually disappear, as they will restructure to one of these two groups.

---

[19] From the New York Times article written by the authors, Catch of the freezer, 8 December 2009

The largest farms will keep increasing in size, but the number of farms in this segment will only increase slightly. Industrial agriculture will continue to be involved in mass production of commodities for global supplies, as it is today, but it will face increased pressure to be sustainable, which technically is possible. More efficient new systems and technologies will be the pillars of its growth and development. The requirements for capital will be high and the sector will be led by larger corporations, by an increasing level of capital by large private investors and, last but not least, by some governments. Agriculture will innovate further. It will use automation and mechanization to reduce the dependence on labor. Mergers & acquisitions will continue in the agricultural sector. A few large blocks will remain and dominate their sectors. Their mandate will be about more control of the natural conditions of production.

They will work on reducing to a minimum their impact on air, water and soil, by using less polluting transport methods, water preservation, effluent treatment and soil preservation. They will also have to engage in maintenance of their environment. The role of this type of agriculture will be to bring to market large quantities of affordable food to the masses. It will be included in food security strategies, which is where corporations and governments will interact regularly.

The number of small farms involved in specific productions, and directly linked to their local economy, will increase. Local food value chains will be set up in a market-driven approach. These farmers produce specialty products aimed at serving a specific segment either of the retail or of the food service market. This trend, which has been already initiated around concepts such as organic or authentic, will evolve into a more integrated local economy. The initial concepts will become less differentiated as food production in general, both industrial and traditional, will use more sustainable techniques. Contrary to the common belief, this local small-scale agriculture will be developed using efficient techniques, but will be based relatively more on labor and relatively less on capital than the current industrial model.

In this case, efficiency does not necessarily mean intensification. Although this type of agriculture is unlikely to be the solution to feed the world, there is no reason to underestimate its significance. Its market share will increase in the next decade.

Local food value chains will grow in two different environments. In developed countries, they will serve an increasing, but aging, population that is more demanding about origin and production methods. These consumers are ready to pay a premium for perceived better quality. The emphasis will be about quality, transparency, sustainability, traceability and as close to zero as possible a use of chemicals and pharmaceuticals.

In some areas, such partnerships will strengthen the local economy and the local communities. In emerging countries, the development of a local agriculture, and aquaculture, will be key drivers of economic development for under-industrialized and under-urbanized regions. Creating jobs in rural areas will also be a way of slowing down the migration of population to urban centers and limiting social problems, by creating satisfying economic conditions and by securing food supplies locally. Local value chains will be about meeting basic needs.

Currently, most people oppose modern agriculture and organic agriculture. They do not even seem to consider getting the best of both worlds. For the industrialists, organic is looked at as a regression to subsistence farming, while the proponents of organic farming look at any intensive large-scale operation as a threat to the environment. How could so many people be so wrong?

A study from the UK in 2009 concluded that organic foods are not nutritionally superior to regular foods. Of course, it did not take long for reactions to come. The pro-organics rejected the protocol used and therefore the conclusions. The proponents of industrial agriculture reacted satisfied. This is not surprising, because people choose their foods greatly based on psychological reasons. The debate around organic food is largely about choices.

The results of the survey were predictable, though. When it comes to nutritional value, many factors, such as location of the farm, climatic conditions during the growth period, stage of ripeness at harvest, can influence the quality of the products. Quality is much more complex than just the type of fertilizer or the use of pesticides.

The real debate between organic and industrial should not be so much about nutritional value as it should be about food safety. As consumers get more educated and have more choices, they will prefer something more natural and harmless, simply because it is more appealing and safer. Agriculture must be in a position to offer affordable and safe quality products. Organic foods are more expensive and this limits their market mostly to well-off consumers.

If organic agriculture is to become the standard to feed people, production costs and the relative price compared with industrial agriculture products must be lowered. Retailers are playing a central role. They dictate more and more how food should be produced. Retailers will get more involved in agriculture and they will impose more restrictions on suppliers about what kind of products they may use for crop treatment or more restrictions for better animal welfare. The market standards of the future will become "sustainable", "natural" and "traceable". It will not happen for emotional reasons, but for rational reasons. There will be pain to accept for producers to meet these requirements and the commercial negotiations will decide what the market price of natural foods will be.

The intensive production systems of the 20th century have caused many problems of soil degradation and of pollution, and there is no argument about this. These systems have also helped produce the quantities of food required to feed the increasing population. There is no argument against that, either. Organic farming grew as a reaction to bad practices. At least in its early stages, it has not shown the potential to feed the world, and the share of organic farming in total agricultural production is still marginal. This situation will change dramatically, once organic farming is not considered as an alternative form of agriculture anymore.

The problem with fertilizers is more the quantity used than their chemical nature. This is especially true for nitrogen. Mineral fertilizers are quite acceptable when used properly. They definitely enhance the growth of plants, but they are just a combination of minerals and they lack the organic matter. Manure is very useful because of its high content in organic matter. It is essential to use fertilizers efficiently by distributing the right fertilizer in the right quantities at the right time at the right place. The following two examples show how much potential there is to this approach.

A study carried out in Maryland from 1994 until 2002 by the USDA ARS compared light-tillage organic corn, soybean and wheat with the same crops grown with no-till plus pesticides and synthetic fertilizers. The addition of organic matter in manure and cover crops practiced in organic farming did more than offset the losses from tillage. In a follow-up three-year study, corn was grown with no-till practices on all plots to see which ones had the most productive soils. The organic plots had more carbon and nitrogen and yielded 18% more corn than the other plots did.

Research carried out over the period 2003-2006 by a team based at the Iowa State University, supported by the USDA National Research Initiative and the Leopold Center for Sustainable Agriculture compared the results of conventional agriculture with diversified, low-external input (LEI) farming systems. LEI systems use substantially lower levels of synthetic fertilizers and pesticides. The experiment included a two-year, corn-soybean rotation, a three-year corn-soybean-small grain-red clover rotation, and a four-year corn-soybean-small grain-alfalfa-alfalfa rotation. The results show the advantages of such a system. On the technical side, corn and soybean yields were as high or higher in the LEI systems as in the conventional system, and matched or exceeded average yields on commercial farms in Boone County, Iowa. Further, lower herbicide inputs did not lead to increased weed problems. On the financial performance side, without government subsidy payments, net returns were highest for the four-year LEI system, lowest for the three-year LEI system, and intermediate for the two-year conventional system.

With subsidies, differences among systems in net returns were smaller, as subsidies favored the conventional system, but the rank order of the systems was maintained.

Another difference between organic farming and industrial agriculture limiting the further development of organic production systems is the amount of labor involved, especially in high-wage countries. As more research demonstrates similar results can be achieved with organic techniques, and under pressure of stricter environmental regulations, organic farming will become as mechanized as commercial agriculture.

There will be a modern form of agriculture based on organic principles. It will also make use of synthetic substances with precision and efficiency, thus reducing the quantities used. Large farms will use this approach with the help of a new generation of equipment and machines to alleviate the problem of higher costs and higher food prices.

Traditional thinking is not enough. Thinking outside the field will be part of the solution. Although farmers have practiced agriculture in the open air since its beginning, would it be pragmatic to think this is the only possibility? The only way to bring new solutions for the future will be to use as many ideas as possible, in order to go beyond the current industrial model. The ideas and suggestions may be unconventional, but it does not mean they need to be revolutionary.

Some experts claim that, in order to meet food demand, two, three, or even four Earths are necessary. It will not happen, unless the universe sends some unexpected gift. Nonetheless, there are ways of increasing the area dedicated to food production. It is possible to expand in two directions: horizontally and vertically. The horizontal option is a limited one, because most of the land is already used, either for agriculture or for other economic activities or for urban development.

Nonetheless, land represents only 30% of the surface of the planet, and therefore there is the possibility to expand horizontally into the sea, too. The Dutch grew their country by developing polders using windmills, a sustainable renewable energy source. About half of the Netherlands is located below sea level and this country is one of the main exporters of agricultural products in the world. It is possible to grow food where there is no soil, by developing hydroponics, which is a highly efficient way of producing food with no soil and with little water, instead of developing more irrigation. Further, it has the advantage of producing food without dependence on weather conditions.

Another way of developing food production by expanding in the sea is aquaculture, which is the fastest growing food production in the world. Aquaculture provides for about half of seafood consumption, and the trend indicates that it will keep expanding in the future.

Aquaponics offers the possibility to combine aquaculture with crop production, using fish waste to fertilize plants and saving a lot of water by recycling it into the system. This system is already a form of vertical development as there is one layer for aquaculture, and at least one other for crops. Growing vertically will produce much more food on the same ground area, and this already addresses the problem of planet shortage. Vertical farming is not new, and there have been multi-floor animal husbandry housing systems for some time.

As the world needs more food, all possibilities to produce more need to be investigated. From a food production point of view, there will not be as clear a segregation between urban areas and agricultural areas as there has been during the 20th century. In the pragmatic world, there will be farming in the cities and there will be cities on the countryside. Urban farming is one of the agriculture sectors that will show strong growth in the coming decades. This trend will be a response to many issues. In many cases, the driver will be poverty. City residents will grow some food on small patches of land inside the cities. In other areas, it will be a political decision.

For instance, the mayor of the city of Detroit in the USA is developing a plan to remove all abandoned industrial compounds and re-introduce farmland within the city limits to create new economic activity.

Another sensitive discussion topic is animal production. The debate about whether people should or should not eat meat is passionate and very poor on pragmatism. For meat lovers, the answer is obvious, because meat tastes so good. For the opponents of meat, who live mostly in rich countries, the answer to the question is just as obvious, as meat is evil in all respects. As usual, the reality is a little more complex than simply black or white. Like many things in life, the truth lies somewhere in the middle. It is true that if there was no meat production, a large quantity of grains and other crops could be available to feed people instead of feeding animals.

Vegetarianism would free land and save large amounts of water, which would be positive. Nonetheless, meat has good nutritional qualities and fits in a balanced diet. There must be a good reason why when people have more money they start eating more meat. The French King Henry IV wanted every family to have a chicken in the pot every Sunday. It was his way of fighting poverty and improving his subjects' nutrition.

Traditionally, animal husbandry has played an important role in agriculture since the beginning of domestication of livestock species. Farm animals have been the source of high value protein through dairy products, eggs or meat. Keeping ruminants has been the only way farmers have found to transform the cellulose of grass into food. Grazing also contributes to bringing back organic matter on grasslands. When discussing animal husbandry, it is important to make a difference between extensive and intensive production systems. Extensive production systems usually are environmentally friendly, except when they are developed at the expense of forests. Intensive systems have become more controversial because they are run as independent production units, keeping a density of animals exceeding the normal number of animals per hectare that are naturally sustainable. The result is a surplus of manure, and especially of minerals.

In intensive systems, the link between land and animal density has been eliminated. Farms have specialized, either in crops or in animal husbandry. Intensive systems have been an efficient way of producing large quantities of animal protein on a limited production area, usually with imported feed and manure surplus.

Consumer attitude towards animal products differ between regions. In many of the developing countries, considering the low level of consumption and the poor diet that they had, the nutritional shift towards more meat brings them many health benefits. This is a comparable evolution with what took place several decades ago in the now developed countries.

Better nutrition because of a higher consumption of affordable high value protein has helped improve the health of the population. Along with the progress of medicine, this has largely contributed to a longer life expectancy.

Although the improvement in the diet has been beneficial, animal production has come under more scrutiny. What the future place of animal husbandry will take depends largely on which consensus consumers and industry will reach on production systems.

Activist vegetarianism is a relatively new phenomenon that seems to have appeared at the same time as Western societies started to consume excessively, which is true for meat, too. In the West, meat has become a commodity most people do not even identify or connect anymore with animals, farms, agriculture or Nature. In many cases, meat is covered with a batter, shaped as a stick with no other function than being a ketchup carrier. In the past, when meat was expensive, people used bread to dip in the soup or the sauce to fill in this function.

The strongest signal that attitudes towards diets are changing in Western countries is coming from some of the political leaders. In the USA, the Obamas expressed their desire for a little "farm" at the White House to grow their own vegetables.

In early 2010, the German Minister of Agriculture Ilse Aigner stated in a speech during the International Green Week in Berlin that consumers had to eat less meat. She was referring to the German Nutrition Society's recommendation of 300 to 600 grams (11 to 22 ounces) of meat per capita per week. For an adult, protein requirements indicate that 30 kg per capita per year are indeed sufficient to cover the nutritional needs.

People need a proper diet, but in wealthy countries, they simply exceed by far their nutritional requirements. In most Western countries, people eat close to 100 kg of meat per capita per year. There, people eat around 70 kg of meat too much annually.

A simple calculation shows what the effect of a diet change can mean for food availability. By counting the population of rich countries to 600 million people, a drop of individual meat consumption to 30 kg saves 42 billion kg of meat per year. This volume of meat can cover the normal nutritional needs (30 kg/capita) of 1.4 billion people. This represents all the meat needs of China, if each Chinese ate only the needed 30 kg per year. They have already passed this level, and many other developing countries are following the same trend. From a sustainability point of view, meat consumption should not exceed nutritional requirements. There is no need to eat meat every day, either. After all, a proper diet should include fish twice a week.

Leadership: Showing the Way of the Future

The quality of leadership will be of the highest importance, considering the challenge of feeding so many people in the future. All leaders, in politics, in corporations of course, but also all the quiet leaders in communities, in farming, in not-for-profit organizations, or in consumer organizations will affect greatly the progress that agriculture can achieve in the next decades.

Two old-fashioned, yet critical, qualities will be paramount: morals and responsibility. These two qualities have been missing in the way humans have looked at their future over the last 50 years, as short-term profit and hidden power agendas have shifted the focus away from the essentials.

Politicians are going to have to lead their countries through much more difficult food market conditions, as demand will rise. Prices will rise and supply will sometimes have difficulties meeting the demand. Their first priority will be to ensure food security because without it, they face the prospects of social unrest and the risk of being put out of power. Prosperity is not possible when food security is not there. Future political leaders must have the mandate to create the legislation that ensures food security for their people, and to create the conditions for agribusiness to supply only healthy and safe food.

The CEO's of corporations will also bear great responsibilities. They will have to show strong morals. By their actions and decisions, they will influence greatly where wealth is created and how it is distributed.

In the food sector, they also have the responsibility of going beyond their personal objectives, actively working towards a sustainable and sufficient food supply and ensuring that food safety is guaranteed. The purpose of the agribusiness is to provide food, not to take it away from consumers. Any position of monopoly or power can be exciting for them, but abusing their power would only deliver short-term results. In the food sector of the future, corporate responsibility will have to be a reality that goes beyond simple statements in the annual report. If corporations create chaos in the food markets, the social tensions that would result will create the conditions for strong resistance, not only from consumers, but also from governments all over the world. Future corporation leadership in the agribusiness, regardless of the place of the company in the total production chain must carry the mandate of offering affordable, healthy, and safe food, which is not the same as cheap food. Any food that can contribute to health problems, be it high blood pressure, cardiovascular risks, diabetes or obesity, should not be marketed without the clear mention of the risks they potentially bring to the consumer.

Their success criteria will go much beyond the financial performance of these companies. The triple bottom line will have to become the rule and it will be translated in the type of bonus packages the executives will receive. Such a change in performance objectives and accountability will not only change the roles of leadership and management, but it will also affect the financial structure of agribusinesses. Under pressure from investors, stock markets tend to induce a strong preference for short-term financial performance. Sustainability emphasizes long-term performance. Because of this fundamental difference, regulators will have to alter current market rules.

Leadership goes far beyond politics and corporations. For instance, a farmers' leader from Burkina Faso named Yacouba Sawadogo developed and taught techniques that helped increase agricultural production in the Sahel, which had been devastated by drought and desertification.

They used old techniques such as planting trees and shrubs to create better microclimatic conditions around plants. They dug pits and filled them with manure to increase the quantity of organic matter at the plant level. It helped reduce soil erosion and dehydration by the wind and by evaporation. This way, 300,000 hectares of land have been regained from the desert and have been able to provide half a million people with food security in a region where people had left because of the lack of food.

In Uganda, since 2004, the government has created the conditions for the development of rice production through a number of policies, the introduction of technology and by encouraging a number of private-public partnerships. The re-introduction of a 75% import duty has stimulated investment from millers and traders, as well as the introduction of more efficient rice varieties. Partnerships in agricultural research and extension services have supported the other actions. One effect of the policies has been an improvement of the income from rice for farmers. It became better than other crops they were producing previously. Production in 2008 was 2.5 times higher than it was in 2004. Good leadership delivers! In four years time, Uganda has moved from a country struggling with self-sufficiency to being an exporter, providing other African Nations, such as Congo, Kenya, Mali and Sudan with rice. In 2009, Uganda signed a partnership agreement with the Japan International Cooperation Agency to set up a rice research center. In Uganda, leadership is building a better future.

Another example of leadership is Will Allen, the CEO of Growing Power, a not-for-profit organization that produces food on three acres of land in the city of Milwaukee. The purpose is to feed the people of the disadvantaged neighborhood with a healthy diet from food produced locally. Growing Power is a successful enterprise that has received much-deserved attention. The organization is transferring its expertise. It is helping other communities in the USA and all over the world implement its methods. The Clinton Global Initiative founded by former President Bill Clinton has committed to helping Growing Power raise $1.9 million to build a model for local food systems in South Africa and Zimbabwe.

To transform Africa from traditional subsistence agriculture into a modern efficient food supplier is not a simple task. It will require strong leadership, resources and resourcefulness. It will also require the skills to manage change in a way respectful of cultures, social structures and of the environment. The African Green Revolution to be will be about much more than agricultural techniques alone.

Foreign farming investments are an opportunity, but no guarantee. After all, such deals do not differ much from those made by Western multinationals when they moved their manufacturing units to China and other developing countries. The purpose of these corporations was primarily to increase profits and not so much to help develop the countries they entered. It is unlikely that American corporations wished to make China more powerful than the USA. The host countries had the land available for the plants, they had the work force, but they lacked the capital. This should sound familiar. For the host nations, the relocations of factories were welcome investments that offered work to the locals. Jobs make an economy run. They provide families with the necessary money to buy food and clothes and pay for housing. The money can circulate and the economic machine can function. Without jobs, there cannot be any prosperity. African leaders must keep this in mind. Once there is stable employment, demand for goods and services increases and creates more jobs. Thus, the wheel is in motion.

One of the most effective ways of making such change happen is with financial incentives. In the past decades, the European Union granted many subsidies in order to develop certain productions. The subsidies were so efficient that the EU ended with huge inventories of products, such as butter or veal, because the production levels exceeded by far the demand. Nonetheless, subsidies have helped the EU to become self-sufficient, which was one of the objectives. Because of subsidies, wine producers have been encouraged to plant more vines, then to pull them out and then to plant them again. Without money incentives, these farmers would have never done that. Because of subsidies, Spain became a large producer and exporter of olive oil, because they ended up planting too many olive trees. This was good for consumers because olive oil became cheap.

132

Kazakhstan is increasing its production and it has new export possibilities. The country is now approved for the Chinese and South Korean markets, and it is aiming at developing new sales in other South Asian countries. Kazakhstan is planning to double its grain export subsidies to help its farmers achieve these goals.

When farmers are paid on volume, they find ways of increasing the volumes they produce. If they are paid on quality, they also change their strategy accordingly, which affects the whole production chain, starting with the genetics.

Money incentives do not have to come from government only. Corporations can contribute positively by having their own programs. McCain Foods developed a successful value chain in India by contracting farmers to produce for their French fries plant. The company brings its expertise and the technical support to the farmers so that they produce efficiently the right quality of potatoes. Farming in rural India is traditionally done manually, but after McCain Foods' arrival just 10 years ago, partner growers have learned the technology of sowing and reaping with machines and the value of applying fertilizers. The result has been record-breaking, with yields from one acre of land once averaging one to 10 tons of potatoes increasing to 15 tons today. McCain Foods also rewards the farmers by paying them a higher price than the one set on the *mandis*, the official government regulated marketplaces. This approach has benefited both McCain Foods, that gets the right type of product to process, and the contract farmers who make more money than they would otherwise. McCain Foods helped the farmers reduce their expenditure by 35% and increase their income by 104%. It also benefits the environment, as the contract farmers now use more efficient irrigation systems.

India has a subsidy system on agricultural inputs in place that appears to give mixed results. Subsidies on fertilizers, water or electricity help make these inputs cheaper for the farmer, which benefits the farmer, but the subsidy is not a good prediction of the efficient use of these inputs.

Subsidies on selected fertilizers has also led to fertilizer rations in many states, resulting in excess application in northern states (200 kg/ha) and sub-optimal application in many eastern and northeastern states (10 kg/ha). The subsidy system creates imbalanced fertilizer applications that affect productivity adversely and that causes higher incidence of pests and diseases. The subsidy system on fertilizers is very expensive and many doubt it will be sustainable. The cost jumped from US$ 5.8 billion in 2006-2007 to US$ 22 billion in 2008-2009. The free water program for farmers in many Indian states also needs to be looked at carefully, as it presents the risk of wastage of groundwater. Subsidies on production, as the ones the European Union has used could be useful, but in a commercial agriculture. The fragmentation of agriculture and the number of farms is high. India has more than 30 times as many farmers as the USA and the EU together. The extent of subsistence agriculture makes such subsidies rather difficult to administer, especially in a country where bureaucracy is famous for its slowness. A reason given to explain the woes of Indian agriculture is the lack of proper financing and insurance to farmers, although this varies a lot because of the diversity of India's farming structure. The access to better seeds will be critical. India still uses relatively low levels of hybrid plants. An increase in the use of this genetic material would help improving yields. There seems to be a consensus that reforms are necessary to improve Indian agriculture and food security. However, when the overwhelming majority of voters of the largest democracy in the world are active in agriculture, any attempt to reform agricultural structures and policies is rather delicate to carry out. It can affect the stability of the government. Regardless of the political cost, India's leaders will have to address the agriculture's weaknesses eventually and the sooner the better. This should happen in a gradual manner that does not disrupt the country's society too much, though.

Financial incentives on the wrong objectives can have unintended consequences. In late 2009, Argentina faced the possibility of becoming a beef importer while Argentina had always been an exporter. The reasons were financial. Soybean production increased strongly, which reduced the area available for grazing.

At the same time, the government, which fixes the price of beef, decided to maintain the price of beef at US$2 per pound, making beef more affordable than pizza. Considering the cost of the ingredients of pizza compared with the cost of production of beef, this will not be sustainable, but the attractive price of beef boosted consumption, and beef consumption hit a fifteen-year high.

Uruguay welcomes investments, even as low as US$20,000, and many large foreign companies are now present in Uruguay. In the agricultural sector, the government has encouraged the production of grass-fed beef without the use of hormones. In order to ensure full traceability, they have implemented a bonus system of up to US$0.30/kg of beef paid to producers who enter the program. This is a beautiful example of an efficient market-driven innovation supported by smart leadership.

In the USA and in Europe, there are some discussions about the possibility of implementing a system of taxes on fast food and soft drinks to influence the behavior of consumers, and to attempt to curb the problem of obesity and other food-related health problems.

Corporations know about financial incentives, too. They are always interested in going to places where their production costs are lower and where they pay less tax. During the 1990s, Ireland developed its economy largely because of attractive fiscal policies. All the manufacturing relocations and the outsourcing of services in developing countries are perfect illustrations of this attitude. Towards the end of 2009, the trading company Louis Dreyfus SA decided to stop buying grain from Ukrainian grain elevators, because Ukraine does not reimburse the VAT (Value Added Tax).

Financial incentives could support the transformation of agriculture towards more environmentally oriented production systems. Some proposals are already being investigated in the European Union.

Their purpose is to reform agricultural price systems. Some proposals suggest replacing the price support mechanism by a system of "environmental management payments".

According to T. N. Jenkins[20], the author of such a proposal, this would compensate farmers for the failure of the market to recompense them adequately for the environmental goods they produce.

Money is only a part of the equation, though. The contact point between agriculture and the consumer market takes place at the retail store level. It gives retailers a particular role. They have the ability to communicate with both sides and they have the power to pass on information and requirements.

This proactive role of retailers has developed the most in Europe, and especially in the UK, mostly because of food safety issues. Especially with private labels, the visible responsibility for food quality shifted from the producers to the retailers. They had no choice but to take the lead and inquire about product specifications and production practices. The gradual loss of trust in politicians to address and solve such issues contributed to the rise of the influence of retailers. They have become the spokespersons of the consumers and they started to question the way the industry was producing food, from the genetics to the store shelves. Their agricultural and technical specialists carry out regular audits that have greatly helped improve food quality, but it was not an easy process. Producers had to adapt. In many cases, it increased their production costs, which has always been the main reason behind their reluctance to change.

In North America, consumers have not been critical of their own food production until rather recently. Critical consumers, like the Europeans, help agribusinesses improve their practices. This has long-term advantages, too. With recurrent food poisoning, especially with E. coli in hamburgers, and the increasing criticism of animal husbandry about climate change, US agriculture has gained more and more negative publicity in the mainstream media.

---

[20] Department of Agricultural Economics, University College of Wales, Aberystwyth, UK, T. N. Jenkins, "Future harvests: the economics of farming and the environment: proposals for action".

The agricultural lobbies do what they are supposed to do and try to fight change. They will undergo similar changes as their European counterparts have over the last 20 years. They will face stricter government regulations, but the most impact will come from the retailers. In April 2010, Wal-Mart, the world's largest retailer, has taken the initiative by demanding its beef suppliers implement testing on E. coli and preventive measures according to internationally recognized standards.

Wal-Mart is also very active in increasing the sustainability of its supply chain. Although not everyone has perceived their change of approach, they have been instrumental in stimulating positive changes, such as in packaging and detergents. They have developed a "Sustainable Product Index", which has three main objectives. First, they will assess their suppliers in the field of sustainability. They will do this with a questionnaire of 15 items related to what they do about improving the sustainability of their products and of their processes. They also will ask them to carry out a similar assessment of their own suppliers, thus cascading back in the supply chain. Secondly, they will review the lifecycles of products together with a group of universities, retailers, suppliers, NGOs and government. Thirdly, they will develop information systems to inform consumers about environmental performance of the products offered, so that they can make informed choices. In the food sector, they are working towards developing more supplies from local farmers. They want to purchase socially and environmentally responsible foods certified for sustainability, such as coffee, wine, bananas and MSC-certified seafood.

Agribusiness will react to what retailers tell them. Food companies will have the choice to adapt or to lose business, and the recent delisting of some A-brand foods and beverages by retailers because of price disagreements are a sign of things to come.

Ten years ago, it would have been impossible to think that retailers could do without some of the food leaders, but with good quality private labels, retailers can now offer good value alternatives to the consumers.

The evolution of the agribusiness, however, will mostly be a voluntary one, as food companies have enough knowledge of the consumer trends and none of them wants to lose market share to their competitors.

At the beginning of 2010, Tyson Foods introduced its Open Prairie Natural Angus beef, which is grass-fed and produced without added antibiotics and hormones. This is a sign that something is changing. It is a different concept from the intensive feedlot beef.

Sustainable seafood is the hot item with many retailers and restaurants in North America and Europe. Because of this, many fisheries worldwide have already implemented changes and been certified by the MSC.

The American organic supermarket chain Whole Foods Market is growing at a strong pace as demand for organic products is growing, and organic food is available more and more at other retailers, too.

In France, the trend for local foods is so strong that the supermarket chain Carrefour has now introduced a new concept of stores dedicated especially to local productions. The stores, called "Carrefour City" and "Carrefour Montagne", are an answer to their losing market share to direct sales from farmers. In the USA, Wal-Mart is now sourcing food closer to its distribution centers, in order to reduce the carbon footprint of the food they sell, and to support regional farming communities.

In the UK, Marks & Spencer developed their "Plan A" with which the retailer aims at achieving sustainability in the next decade. This plan is quite extensive and covers all areas of their business. The plan also involves Marks & Spencer's suppliers, customers and personnel. In the agricultural sector, the plan includes programs for all vulnerable raw materials, such as wood, cotton, fish, palm oil, soya, cocoa, coffee and tea. Marks & Spencer has already started programs to reduce their impact on natural resources.

They moved towards 100% MSC or equivalent fish and 100% FSC-(Forest Stewardship Council)-certified wood that is recycled or otherwise protects forests and communities. The plan also includes actions to reduce food waste. All of Marks & Spencer's food suppliers will be assessed with a balanced performance scorecard that includes social and environmental issues as well as lean manufacturing. The objective is to have 25% of the suppliers achieve the very highest (Gold) performance standard by 2015. All 10,000 farmers who supply Marks & Spencer with fresh meat, dairy, produce and flowers will be part of the "Sustainable Agriculture Programme" by 2012. By 2015, Marks & Spencer aims at also engaging in this Programme the many thousands of farmers that supply them with agricultural ingredients used to produce the food they sell. Marks & Spencer works closely with the nongovernmental organizations Rainforest Alliance, Forum for the Future, Greenpeace, WWF-UK and the RSPCA that advise them on further actions. For the coming years, the list includes further improvements in the traceability of raw materials in the supply chains, the extension of the range of food commodities covered by sustainability standards, farmed fish as well as wild fish in their sustainability program, and water usage.

Sweden has started presenting the carbon footprint of food on the labels for food products sold in supermarkets and on some restaurant menus. The Swedish National Food Administration is managing this program. In the UK, Tesco has initiated label information about the carbon footprint of foods, with a first trial with dairy products.

In the Netherlands, the largest supermarket chain, Albert Heijn has announced it will stop selling traditional intensive pork by 2011. They will sell pork that follows animal welfare recommendations from the Dierenbescherming, an animal protection organization. Albert Heijn signed this agreement with the Dutch meat group Vion, one of the largest meat processors in Europe.

The trend is there, and retailers have not waited for government regulations to initiate the change towards a more sustainable agriculture.

Most of the issues that consumers raise about agriculture and food production are as much about trust as about technical matters. The best way to be successful in dealing with such issues is by taking the initiative and showing leadership. The only proper way forward with information is transparency. Only transparency can eliminate, or at least reduce to a minimum, negative publicity and stop the spread of untrue stories. The agricultural community will be able to inform the public properly only by being candid and open about the way food is produced. When dealing with bad publicity, the industry tends to react defensively. Defensiveness always puts the defendant in an awkward position. If this not handled properly, it can easily come over as suspicious, which reinforces the poor impression.

Issues about food production are highly emotional, as they deal with much more than just nutrition. Responding with rational arguments has very little effectiveness. Emotional concerns must be dealt with as emotions, not merely with cold scientific facts. Only once the emotional connection has been established, is it possible to communicate facts. The better informed the public is, the easier it is to discuss and address the problems that arise. Candor is only the first step; the clearly expressed will to improve the way food is produced is necessary. This does not stop with vague promises. It must come with an open agenda of issues the industry knows about and that it will be addressing without complacency. A clear commitment to a plan of action with defined timelines is the best way to create and restore trust with consumers. All the participants in the production chain, from breeding to retail, need to adopt this proactive approach to demonstrate to consumers that they do things right. This works significantly better than having to react to changes in legislation, which often are the result of pressure from the public opinion.

Information and knowledge contribute greatly to action. Good leaders take good care of the people they lead. One of the best ways to help them improve their lives is to give them education. People have gradually lost touch with Nature and they tend to take all their achievements for granted. It is simply stunning to read reports from polls among the city youth on food.

When asked where meat comes from, they answer that it comes from the supermarket. They do not see the connection with farms, and they do not really care. All they want is to eat.

As part of future education, there should be mandatory activities such as (re)discovering agriculture, working on farms, harvesting crops, dealing with farm animals, experiencing seasons and natural cycles, going fishing and hunting or learning how to make bread. Presentations in front of the class about reducing food waste and recycling, or about topics that help explain the relationship between water and agriculture and food would be helpful to create awareness for the future generations. They should get the basics to help them understand how to grow food while maintaining the necessary balance so that it is possible to keep on producing in the future. Humans can preserve only what they know, understand and respect. It is all interconnected.

The most efficient way to improve eating habits is by understanding nutrition and educating children at an early age about health, food, and diseases caused by either unbalance or excess. Food safety is not only about bacteria or residues. It is also about handling food properly at home and eating right.

Parents play a crucial role in teaching their children good eating habits. They have a very important leadership role. Teaching children about nutrition will help them eat properly. It is necessary to teach children about the basics of nutrition and of metabolism as early as possible, and education must include the parents, too. There is no big mystery behind what causes obesity, diabetes and other food excesses related ailments. It is easy to explain what functions the different food groups fill and how to compose healthy meals.

Parents also need to understand they have the duty to give their children a balanced diet, although it might mean that they, too, should have one. Most importantly, when it comes to decide what is on the table, children should not dictate what they want simply based on what they like.

To make people change their eating habits, information is necessary, but not sufficient. When it comes to food, there are many complex issues dealing with psychology, taste and a behavior people have acquired at a very young age. Further, marketing has used these psychological weaknesses very skillfully.

In many ways, eating habits are a reflection of the lifestyle and of the society. Therefore, trying to induce a change in eating habits can only succeed if people make broader changes in the way they live.

Consumer organizations, like the ones in Europe, are another great source of information. They are independent, and they provide many surveys and comparisons of consumer products. They have been very useful in helping consumers gain more awareness about what they consume. Unfortunately, such open and objective information is not directly available in all countries. This is a weakness in the fight for health.

Retailers, restaurants and the agribusiness need to co-operate more than they currently do, even though in this field, some are more active than others are. To solve a society-wide problem, the whole society must participate. It is rather typical to see how the meat industry in the USA is reacting to the proposal of a meat-free Monday in school cafeterias. The resistance to government intervention in telling how people should feed themselves is understandable in the land of free choice. Yet, when this leads to many health issues, one could argue that if the people cannot make the right choices, maybe someone else should set stricter rules to help them. Meat-free Mondays mean a little less business for the American meat industry in the short-term and maybe a little less in the longer term if it meant that the next generation might cut on meat consumption.

A survey carried out in the USA by Research Triangle Institute and the Centers for Disease Control and Prevention showed in 2009 that the annual medical cost of obesity reached $147 billion.

It is good to realize that the contribution of the meat and poultry industry to the US economy is $832 billion annually. Therefore, ongoing arguments between economic interests and health care costs will last for a while. Too many Americans do not eat a properly balanced diet. This should change. About two-thirds of American adults and one-third of the children are overweight. A similar trend is already emerging in developing nations, in China, for instance.

However, the meat industry in developed countries needs to realize that there are many people in other countries longing for meat. These new markets have more than the potential to replace the volumes lost in the domestic markets.

Efficiency: Producing More With Less

Efficiency is the ratio output/input. When resources are scarce, anything increasing this ratio is more welcome than ever before. In the years to come, reducing waste is the name of the game. The way the world deals with water, soil, fertilizers, feed and food will determine the population's level of well-being. The comparative performances of the plants farmers grow and of the farm animals they keep will determine how much the world can produce and eat. For plants and animals, performance will depend on the genetic potential and the environmental conditions.

Limited resources in land and water will have to be managed skillfully in order to meet demand. At the same time, the agriculture and food industry must not generate any harmful waste that would jeopardize the ability to continue to produce in the longer term. Efficiency must increase further. However, it is important to realize that efficiency and intensification are not the same.

Since World War II, much progress has been made to increase food production. Genetic improvement, new production techniques and mechanization, use of fertilizers, chemicals and pharmaceuticals, the development of animal nutrition, and government incentives have helped farmers to produce more efficiently and to manage well a previous doubling of the world population. Such progress has helped reduce costs and it has made food more affordable for more people, although unfortunately not for all.

Due to the development of manufacturing and later of services, the labor force moved to urban centers where they could find jobs.

This evolution caused agriculture to shift from a mostly labor-intensive food production to a mostly capital-intensive one. Mechanization and oil could help replace the workers and fewer people were needed to work on farms. Within 30 years, the percentage of the labor force working in agriculture dropped from over 50% to less than 5% in industrialized countries. As the economy became more prosperous, the standard of living improved and wages increased, labor costs also increased. This made a labor-intensive agriculture too expensive. The only apparent solution has been to further mechanize and intensify.

The development of manufacturing that went along with the rise of the consumption society also increased disposable income. At the same time, in constant currency, food became cheaper and more affordable. This led to a change of diet from mostly starch-based to protein-based, and a similar trend is happening in emerging countries.

The quality of life has improved, but at a cost to the environment. Intensification has caused soil erosion and loss of organic matter, loss of soil fertility and deterioration of ground water quality by manure surpluses, reduced genetic diversity and possibly lessened resistance to diseases, to name a few problems. Of course, for each of the problems, the first reaction is to come with a solution based on technology. This usually fits in and reinforces intensification. Unfortunately, Nature does not work that way. The environment needs time to process and eliminate problems through its cycles in the soil and in the water. Nature can handle a lot, but it can only handle so much. This is where the difference between intensification and efficiency becomes obvious.

Intensification tends to continuously load and overload the system, which explains why there is so much talk about sustainable agriculture nowadays. Food production cannot be sustainable if it does not allow its natural environment to process and eliminate the contaminants. Similarly, Nature cannot replenish on its own what people take out, unless they create the conditions for it to happen.

Efficiency goes beyond intensification. It integrates performance and sustainability. It allows having a high production by using inputs when needed, where needed and just as much as needed. This way, farmers can grow plants or animals with minimum waste while respecting the ecosystem. Efficiency also comes from optimization. In this regard, efficiency and intensification go hand in hand, but only up to the particular point when any incremental input does not produce more in the same proportion. More importantly, once production levels pass beyond the optimum, stress appears. This is very clear in animal production. When densities exceed a certain level, the animals' defense system becomes weak and makes them vulnerable to diseases.

In modern society, the common thinking is that technology is the only way to increase efficiency. Technology alone does not solve problems. People do. Money helps, too. The examples of the Dutch pig farmer with the old pig house and of Yacouba Sawadogo demonstrate this. They achieved great results with simple techniques. It does not take away from the usefulness of technology. Technology develops the tools of progress. However, the performance depends on the ability of farmers and workers to operate the machines and the systems. The key element in developing new technology is to train the users appropriately. Farmers and technicians need to have a solid basic education and training, and ongoing training is required as technology evolves. In industrialized wealthy countries, this is not a problem. Education and training is easily available and many farmers have degrees. In poor regions, where even children need to work to help feed their families, the situation is different. Parents have no money to provide their children with a proper education and the rates of illiteracy are high. The infrastructure of knowledge transfer is also different. In developed countries, governments and agribusiness have access to high-level research organizations, universities and technical extension services. They help farmers to be informed about the latest developments and to work continuously on further improvements.

Only once knowledge circulates does it become real power. Access to capital helps farmers to maintain and invest in equipment. In the countries lacking the funds to set up such a support structure for their farmers, the resources are more limited. These disadvantages explain the differences in yields and productivity between the rich countries and the less fortunate ones, next to natural conditions.

To move from the current situation to a new more productive food production, the current problems and limitations require reflection and creativity. The challenges will become opportunities. The solutions may not be easy, but they are not impossible. All the possible new developments and innovations are good reasons for optimism. By combining innovation and pragmatism, farmers will be able to develop new systems that will deliver strong results.

The three-R's approach (Reduce, Recycle, and Reuse) is an excellent starting point. By answering the question of how to eliminate waste, it is possible to start developing answers and defining strategies about what is produced, how it is produced and where it is produced.

The consumption of energy can be reduced by using more fuel-efficient machinery, by organizing and adapting logistics better or by better managing the distance between production areas and consumer markets. It is possible to reduce oil consumption by wasting less of the materials made from oil, such as fertilizers or plastics, or by using other materials for packaging, for instance.

The use of water can be reduced by having better irrigation systems, by using more water-efficient plants or keeping animals that consume less water. Farm management and water conservation techniques can help a great deal.

It is essential to reward financially people and companies that do the right things, so that they are motivated to improve their practices.

Financial incentives, such as lower taxes for better systems and practices, will encourage the development of more sustainable methods. Financial penalties for systems that have negative effects will support such an evolution. Such financial programs need to be implemented with a time schedule to execute the planned action to eliminate bad practices.

It is necessary to educate and train all the people involved in food production about how they can use resources more efficiently. Continuous education will help farmers and food producers to understand and use new systems with better results faster. It will also provide innovators with the tools to develop the systems of the future. The human element is the most important one for a proper use of all the tools and systems that have been developed or that will be developed in the future.

Leaders need to foster a mentality of innovation. To meet the increasing demand, the current methods are not sufficient. Higher efficiency will come from improvement of existing systems and from the development of entirely new ones. As there is not much time to achieve the objectives, the leaders in government, business and all organizations need to create dynamic conditions to stimulate research and development.

Measuring progress is a crucial part of efficiency. At all stages of the food supply chain, there is a need to define "efficiency indicators", so that all the people involved know what their mandates are, and what parameters they can influence, control and improve. They need the right tools to measure their progress and they need to know what they are doing.

To succeed, all the players in food production will become, directly or indirectly, managers of the living resources of the planet.

PART III

Taking Action to Feed the World

Future Evolution of Markets

The demographics are evolving and economic power is shifting. This will have consequences on consumption markets. Until recently, the largest share of consumption took place in the West and especially in the USA, but with the emergence of new economic powers, there will be a redistribution of wealth and new consumption markets. In the coming 40 years, the world will count 2.5 billion more consumers. This offers plenty of business opportunities for farmers and food producers. The main difference with today is that business opportunities will grow in developing countries, not anymore in the West.

The aging and increasingly health-conscious West will not show any increase in consumption per capita. Western consumers already eat more than they actually need. They do not have much potential for more consumption. They will shift from quantity to quality. Individual consumption will likely drop, actually. Older people need less food than the young and the shift from quantity to quality will continue. Immigration policies in these countries might offset this somewhat, but producers are going to have to look for alternative markets for their agricultural products. They should not have to worry too much, as there will be plenty of people to feed in other regions.

With half of the world population in Asia, and a growing young population in Latin America, Arab countries and Africa, the bulk of the demand will shift to these countries. As developing countries grow a middle class, the needs for food will change in a similar manner as it did in the West. As people have more money, they will replace the starch part of their diet, be it bread or rice, by protein of animal origin, mainly meat.

A good indication of the potential for change is the percentage of disposable income dedicated to food. In many underdeveloped countries, this number exceeds 50%, and in emerging countries, it has already substantially decreased. It is slightly below 40% in India and Russia, while in China it is around 28%. Western countries and developed nations are below 15%, with the lowest of all in the USA with 9.9%.

The consumer demand for animal products will increase dramatically. Presently, the USA consumes 20% of all the beef consumed worldwide, while Americans represent only 5% of the world's population. According to a recent study from the research company GIRA, world meat consumption should increase by 21.3% between 2005 and 2015. They expect the consumption of poultry to increase by almost 30%, while pork consumption should increase by 20% and beef by only 13%. A third of the increase should take place in China alone.

The growing Asian population will inevitably increase the demand for rice, as it is their main source of carbohydrates. Unless farmers develop new production areas for rice, which requires specific growing conditions, the balance between supply and demand will be difficult to achieve, and switching to other grains might be difficult as culinary traditions can be stubborn.

The competition between the need to feed people with basic commodities, and the need to feed farmed animals and possibly for some time the need to produce biofuels will be aggressive. Since it takes more than one and even several kilograms of animal feed to produce one kilogram of meat, the FCR will affect by which factor the price of the various animal products will increase. Efficient productions like chicken meat and eggs will be successful and the price will remain competitive against other sources of animal proteins, due to its low FCR, to its low water use and to the good agricultural value of its manure.

Less efficient species such as pigs and beef cattle will see the price of their products increase relatively much more. Pigs also have the disadvantage of producing low quality manure from an agricultural point of view. This will limit the possibilities of increasing pig production. Pork, however, is a traditionally important food in some cultures, for instance in China. Therefore, pig production will still have a reasonable volume growth, with geographical variations. A high FCR species, such as beef cattle will have a relatively lower increase in production. Higher feed costs, linked to a relatively high capital need will probably push a number of farmers to shift to other more efficient productions. Highly intensive systems such the feedlots will also undergo major changes, as mentioned earlier. The US$0.99 beef burger will not be here for much longer. Hamburgers will continue to exist, but they will be more expensive. There are also increasing possibilities for specialty beef products, such as grass-fed beef, but customers will have to pay the right price for it. Grass covers vast areas of fragile soil, and cattle are one of the few species that can transform grass into high value protein.

Demand for stricter food production standards and a higher demand will influence another very important aspect of food: the price. The law of supply and demand indicates that agricultural prices will increase in the future. It will be true for all agricultural products, but the increase will be even stronger for animal products, such as meat, poultry, dairy and fish, than it will be for grains.

The price always influences the level of consumption per capita. The price increase to come will reduce the level of consumption and the price differential between the types of protein. Together with health concerns, higher prices will cause a shift between the respective consumption of the different types of food. In Western countries, people consume quantities of animal products that are substantially higher than what they actually need, and this has led to health issues. The decrease in consumption will help make people healthier, and lighten somewhat the burden of health costs in that part of the world.

Emerging countries will experience a different evolution. They are in a situation comparable with the Western world of post World War II. Their economies are growing strongly, they have their own baby boom, with a young and growing population, except for China, and their middle class is expanding and it is getting wealthier. In developing countries, consumption trends show an increase of consumption of animal products, from rather low levels, though. In these countries, consumption per capita will increase, but will not reach the levels Western countries have shown, simply because prices will be too high for consumers to reach such individual consumption levels. They will choose affordable meats and fish, before looking for other environmental or ethical considerations. Unfortunately, except for Brazil and a few other countries in South America, they do not have the land or the water to produce all the meat they want. Therefore, they will need to find reliable suppliers for these products. If meat is more of a challenge to produce and to source, Asian and African countries in particular have a tremendous opportunity to develop aquaculture much further than the current levels, especially with marine species.

Less average consumption per capita in the West will be more than compensated by the growth in emerging countries, where population numbers are significantly higher. The consumers will be distributed geographically rather differently than they are today. Productions will be located and distributed in different areas than today.

The Water Challenge

Although most of Earth is covered with water, only 1% of all the Earth's water is fresh water. With an increasing population that needs more food and more water to live, water is going to become a highly strategic resource. As climate changes, the current rain distribution and geographic availability of water is likely to change dramatically, too. Estimates for 2040 indicate that at least 3.5 billion people will run short of water. This is almost 10 times as many as in 1995.

The water situation varies around the globe. The Comprehensive Assessment of Water Management in Agriculture[21] reviews the situation of water availability – or scarcity – around the world. The group conducting the survey defines three types of water scarcity.

Physical water scarcity happens when "*Water resources development is approaching or has exceeded sustainable limits. More than 75% of the river flows are withdrawn for agriculture, industry and domestic purposes. This definition – relating water availability to water demand – implies that dry areas are not necessarily water scarce.*"

Approaching physical water scarcity happens when "*More than 60% of water flows are withdrawn. These basins will experience physical water scarcity in the near future.*"

[21] More at http://www.iwmi.cgiar.org/Assessment/index.htm

Economic water scarcity happens when *"Human, institutional, and financial capital limit access to water even though water in nature is available locally to meet human demands. Water resources are abundant relative to water use, with less than 25% of water from rivers withdrawn for human purposes, but malnutrition exists."*

Brazil is the country with the world's largest reserves with 19% of the world's total, while the Brazilian population represents only 2.7% of world population. Russia, with 2% of the world population, comes second with 10% of the world's reserves. Canada is third with 7% of the reserves while Canadians represent only 0.5% of the world's population. Yet, this does not mean that there are no water scarcity issues. Drought affects the Canadian prairies regularly and affects the production of both crops and cattle.

Most of the northern hemisphere has sufficient water reserves. The combination of economic development, enough precipitation and a relatively low population density is an advantage.

In contrast, all the regions with a growing population happen to be in a rather dire water availability situation. For instance, China has similar water reserves as Canada with 7% of the total, but with 21.4% of the world's population, the imbalance is quite clear. Traditionally arid regions, such as deserts and sub-deserts show physical scarcity. There is hope, because many countries suffer mostly from economic scarcity, not from physical scarcity. These countries are in sub-Saharan Africa, Central America, large parts of India and of South Asia. The problem is mostly a lack of infrastructure development that requires funding and political will.

The whole Middle East, from Turkey to Pakistan, is in a difficult situation. The region is approaching physical water scarcity, which will increase an already vulnerable food security situation. The fast growing young population in these countries is already frustrated by difficult economic and political conditions, and the region presents many elements of some major conflicts in the making.

Countries in the Black Sea region, like Kazakhstan and Ukraine, which have the potential to increase their food production, also present a vulnerable situation. Water scarcity in the region could affect the future wheat markets and prices. The situation is not irreversible, but it will require a better management of water, and especially of rivers. In the past, when these countries were part of the Soviet Union, the central power made the decisions. This time, the decisions need to be made between states that might have different views on river management and irrigation strategies. This adds to the complexity.

Mexico and the southwest of the USA also show an increasing risk of desertification. The region faces a water scarcity situation similar to the countries of the Mediterranean region, and it needs to rethink its production model to avoid a disaster. Because fresh produce has a high water content, export of fruit and vegetables actually means exporting water, which goes against the environmental interest of the region. California, Mexico, Texas and, to a lesser extent, Arizona represent a large part of the fruits and vegetables produced on the continent. A worsening of the situation could threaten the economy of California. Since Americans tend to give a preference to technological solutions, the use of humidity sensors, nanotechnology, drip irrigation systems and desalination will fit in the future approach of their agriculture. However, this might not be sufficient to overcome the problem. Other regions of the USA, with help of the change in climatic conditions, will develop alternative production areas to supply produce to the large markets of the East Coast.

Water availability and regional differences have the potential to reshape the food map. It can also reshape the economic and even political map. It will require good management and leadership to be successful in transforming opportunities into food and water security.

According to some research, the maximum of human population the Earth could sustain with the amount of water available, ranges from 6 billion to 15 billion, depending on how it is used.

Food production will become more and more focused on water efficiency. The main action points will be about using only what is needed and about collecting, conserving and recycling water. The need to use water efficiently will have consequences on what will be produced and where. In countries where water is scarce, the focus will have to be on water efficient crops. Water availability will drive the specialization of regions.

Fewer people can be supported if less water is available for agriculture. This is particularly true when the share of meat in the human diet increases. Meat production requires about 10 times more water per calorie than grain production does. During the World Nutrition Forum held in 2009, Mr. Osler Desouzart, of OD Consulting from Brazil, indicated that water consumption would be a limitation for animal production in the future. According to his research, it takes 2,828 liters to produce 1 kg of poultry, 5,900 liters of water to produce 1 kg of pork and 16,000 liters to produce 1 kg of beef.

The location of animal productions will change as well, and factors such as the availability of fresh water, the distance to market and the type of presentation, fresh or frozen, will increasingly have an influence. Since farm animals consume a lot of water with differences between species, countries where water is scarce might have to rethink their animal protein sourcing policies and prioritize the use of water between productions. This will affect where meat is produced and how it is transported to consumer markets. Animal production, especially beef production, will increasingly shift to countries where water is abundant. South America, especially Brazil, will become the uncontested world leader, in production and in exports. Some parts of Northern America will remain competitive, although water scarcity in the West and the increasing use of corn for ethanol will have a negative effect. Europe will still be a large producer, but it will produce mostly for its domestic market. Regions with water scarcity, such as Arab countries and India will focus more on poultry production.

160

Some plants have such high needs for water that their production systems will have to be altered. In some cases, there might not even be any other choice but to limit their production to small selected areas. The use of combined crop productions on the same field is likely to gain back some popularity, because it is a way of saving water and protecting the plants and the soil from excessive evaporation. This will mean a different look at yields and harvesting systems. There is a need for new and more efficient irrigation systems and for systems aimed at collecting and conserving water. Computerized systems are already in use in wine production, using sensors for humidity and temperature, to determine how much water the plants needs at the most optimal time of the day and deliver it at the exact spot. Such an optimization approach will prevail.

The production of genetically modified wheat that needs only a third of the water needs of regular wheat varieties is an exciting prospect. Yet, contrary to natural mutations, genetic engineering does not undergo natural selection. Therefore, nobody can predict what possible side effects, if any, it might bring. Nonetheless, it is an attempt to deal with future water shortages. Hopefully, there will be other less controversial solutions to deliver similar results. Once again, continuing innovation will shape the future.

Food processing plants, such as slaughterhouses or washing stations for produce, use large quantities of water. In these sectors, new and more efficient systems will have to be designed to reduce water use. They will have to meet hygiene and food safety standards. Water treatment and recycling have already been in use for years and they will continue to gain momentum.

Further, there is a need for political action to address water shortages and water quality problems that expand far beyond local operations. Many agricultural areas suffer regularly from drought. Other areas have seen the flow of rivers drop dramatically. Many rivers such as the Yellow River in China, the Colorado River in the USA and other river systems in Northern and Western India, or in North Africa have great difficulties reaching the sea.

In other areas, such as the Arabic Peninsula, the countries realize that traditional irrigation systems are facing serious limitations because of the competition between the need for drinking water and the need for irrigation.

These problems affect the availability, the quality of the water and the environment. Failure to address and, more importantly, to solve such problems properly would have catastrophic consequences for large populations. A balanced plan to have water available for people, agriculture and industries is necessary.

Water and food production are linked very closely. Water is necessary to plants and to animals, but also the type of production will determine how much water is used, what the efficiency is and how much is left for human consumption and other uses.

Of all activities, agriculture is the main consumer of water, accounting for about 70% of all water use. The amount of water used for agricultural purposes has increased sharply. Over the period 1990-2000, FAO numbers show a five-fold increase.

Yet, data about water use has to be looked at carefully because most of it focuses on what is called the "blue water", which is river discharge and groundwater. By taking into account the "green water", which is water coming directly from rainfall, the picture changes. From a current estimated number of over three billion people suffering from water scarcity, this number falls to about one billion when the green water is considered.

The cycle of water is very simple. Rain falls and some of the water filters through the ground to replenish groundwater reserves. Some of the rainwater also runs on the land and it partly evaporates or it joins groundwater at a later stage. Some of the rainwater is also used directly by plants for their growth.

Plants also produce water that evaporates into the air. All the humidity contained in the air eventually falls again as rain when the climatic and geographic conditions allow it.

The "blue water", as described earlier is the type of water most widely used in agriculture. The plants do not use a large part of the precipitation immediately. The rainfall water (the "green water") continues its cycle on and through the ground, sometimes causing severe soil degradation, such as when a heavy monsoon washes precious soil into the river systems and eventually to the sea. Another major area of water loss for agriculture is through evaporation on the fields because of a warm and dry climate.

A new analysis including both blue and green water gives a new and more representative idea of the actual situation. A group of researchers from Stockholm Resilience Centre at Stockholm University, Stockholm Environment Institute and Potsdam Institute for Climate Impact Research, led by Johan Rockström, has used the latest modeling tools to assess the future situation[22]. From their results, it appears that future scenarios are not as bad as originally anticipated. For 2050, their scenario indicates that 59% of the world population will face blue water shortage, and 36% will face green and blue water shortage. Even under climate change, good options to build water resilience exist without further expansion of cropland, particularly through management of local green water resources that reduces risks for dry spells and agricultural droughts.

Collecting rainwater is a good way of conserving water for dry periods. It increases the volume of water available for the crops and it reduces the demand on the existing blue water. By combining both sources of blue and green water, farmers have the ability to produce more because of the extra green water. Investment in tanks and reservoirs is all that is required. The return on investment is high and the payback time short.

Another approach is to develop a system of canals and drains to channel the excess rain, for instance during a monsoon, and channel the water to more reservoirs for later use. Another advantage of developing such a system is lower risk of soil degradation.

---

[22] Water Resources Research, Johan Rockström et al., Future water availability for global food production: The potential of green water for increasing resilience to global change, 14 February 2009

Water would not be able to gather momentum as freely and as erratically as it does when no channeling is in place. Such a project does not need to collect all the rain at once, but save what is possible for later. As time goes by, more projects that are similar can be developed and more green water can be stored. Collecting water is not just for the regions with a dry climate. It is a useful approach in all climates, because there are always dry periods. Moreover, it can take some time for groundwater reserves to rebuild to acceptable levels. Storing rainwater makes the water available on request. Another possibility could be to import water from areas with a surplus, but it is a costly and physically difficult solution because water is not compressible. Since many people think water is the new oil, a future network of aqueducts could be an option. The Romans used to build such systems to bring water to cities, centuries ago.

Next to the actions to collect and store water from precipitations, it is important to limit the losses due to evaporation and transpiration. Eliminating weeds not only increases crop yields, it helps in keeping water only for food production.

Evaporation depends on climatic conditions, but it also depends on how the surface of the soil is protected. A bare soil directly exposed to sunlight, heat and wind will dehydrate much faster than if it is covered or if it is in the shade. Techniques that will protect the soil from direct exposure to sun and wind will help retain water in the soil longer and reduce the quantity of water farmers need. Mulching is a way of creating an insulating layer on the surface of the soil, which reduces evaporation. It also limits the growth of weeds, which makes this technique even more useful. It can be done by leaving plant debris on the ground, but it can also be done by light tillage. As an old French saying tells, "*A good hoeing is worth two watering*". It sums up the advantage of this technique. It also means that more labor is necessary in some situations.

From all agricultural areas, Asia, with 73% of the world irrigation volume, uses the most irrigation for food production.

164

About 34% of the arable land in Asia is irrigated, which is a sharp contrast with North America, where only 10% of arable land is irrigated, or Africa, where this number is only 6%. In Africa, the low number is the result of a lack of development, as many areas could use more water to improve crop yields.

In a report published by IWMI (International Water Management Institute) and the FAO, resolving the water crisis in Asia is crucial for preventing major food shortages. According to the authors *"Asia's food and feed demand is expected to double by 2050. Relying on trade to meet a large part of this demand will impose a huge and politically untenable burden on the economies of many developing countries. The best bet for Asia lies in revitalizing its vast irrigation systems."*[23]

In Asia, the old surface irrigation systems are in bad shape and suffer from a lack of proper maintenance. The old system, which also has brought problems of increased soil salinity and water clogging, is being replaced by groundwater pumping. To face the future challenges of food and water demand in Asia, better systems, and especially a better management of the water resources, will need to be implemented. The demand for water increases not only because of a growing population, but also because of a changing diet. Food supply will need to meet the demand for more fruit, more vegetables and more meat.

An innovative system for rice-growing areas is the MIRI (Multiple Inlet Rice Irrigation) system, developed by the USDA Agricultural Research Service. This system consists of a disposable, thin-walled, polyethylene irrigation tubing to connect rice paddies when the fields are flooded with water, instead of the current system that floods fields by discharging water.

---

[23] Adity Mukherji, Thierry Facon et al., Revitalizing Asia's Irrigation − To Sustainability meet tomorrow's food needs, 2008

For their research, the USDA Agricultural Research Service used the same variety of rice, soil type, planting date, and management practices on 14 paired fields over the growing seasons from 1999 until 2002. The MIRI method required an average of 24% percent less irrigation water than conventional paddy flooding. Since rice fields often share a water supply with other crops, the MIRI system goes beyond just saving water and energy for the rice crop. The amount of water available to irrigate these other crops usually depends on how much water is used to first adequately irrigate the rice. The reduction in the rice's water usage has the potential to increase yields for the other crops.

Food production will meet demand in Asia only through increased water efficiency and increased yields. Better irrigation systems and especially a "more crop per drop" approach are necessary. The irrigation of the future will be about delivering to the plant the quantity of water it needs when it needs it, and use all other possible techniques of moisture conservation to reduce water wastage. Precision agriculture techniques will also help increase yields while reducing the use of fertilizers. Future crop production will require plant varieties that are also more efficient than today's. The development of drought-resistant varieties or of varieties that can grow in soils with a higher salinity will improve the food supply in the region. For instance, the purpose of Atash Seeds, the joint venture signed in 2009 between the French seed company Limagrain with the Indian biotech company Avesthagen, is to provide farmers with varieties that produce higher yields in dry and saline soil. In Australia, the CSIRO (Commonwealth Scientific and Industrial Research Institute) has introduced a salt exclusion gene through non-GM methods into durum wheat. The improved wheat can grow better on soils with high salinity. The yield of the salt tolerant wheat is 25% higher than the regular variety on saline soils.

According to a 2009 report[24] of McKinsey, "*Agricultural measures could help fill 80% of the gap between the current situation and the situation in 2030 in India and the remaining 20% required to close the gap, would be delivered mostly through the rehabilitation of existing irrigation districts and the completion of earlier projects such as canals*". According to their projections, "*The total annual cost for the combined set of supply and agricultural levers is approximately $6 billion per annum—just more than 0.1% of India's projected 2030 GDP*".

Water scarcity is not the only problem. The quality of the water is an even more essential aspect because it affects the actual availability of water for drinking and for irrigation. In many areas, water is available, but it is not usable. It is contaminated and improper even for irrigation purposes. As an example, here is an excerpt from an article published in November 2008 in the UK newspaper The Guardian about the Yellow River situation[25]:

> "*Much of it is now unfit even for agricultural or industrial use, the study shows.*
>
> *The survey, based on data taken last year (2007), covered more than 8,384 miles of the river, one of the longest waterways in the world, and its tributaries.*
>
> *The Yellow River Conservancy Committee, affiliated to the ministry of water resources, said 33.8% of the river system's water sampled in 2007 registered worse than level five. That means it is unfit for drinking, aquaculture, industrial use and even agriculture, according to criteria used by the UN Environment Programme.*
>
> *Only 16% of the river samples reached level one or two, the standard considered safe for domestic use.*

---

[24] McKinsey, Charting our Water Future, 2009

[25] The Guardian, Tania Branigan, One-third of China's Yellow river 'unfit for drinking or agriculture'

The Yellow River is China's second longest after the Yangtze, flowing west to east across the country through areas with high concentrations of factories.

The report said waste and sewage water discharged into the system last year totalled 4.29bn tonnes. Industry and manufacturing made up 70% of the discharge into the river, with households accounting for 23% and just over 6% coming from other sources."

The problem of water contamination in China is not limited to rivers. The coastal seawaters are polluted, too. A recent report of China's State Oceanic Administration showed that most shellfish contain unacceptably high levels of the insecticide DDT and of heavy metals such as cadmium and lead. The contamination covered an area of 147,000 square kilometers (59,000 square miles) of coastal waters in 2009. This was 7.3% higher than the year before.

Although agriculture is the main user of water, the problem reaches far beyond this sector. Future water management will have to include a comprehensive water strategy to reduce water use, water wastage, work on water quality and the impact of agriculture, industry and urbanism on the environment. The example of the Yellow River demonstrates how important this is.

Solving the water challenge will be neither easy nor cheap. By doing something about the problem, the cost will be labor and capital. By doing nothing, the cost will be water scarcity, poverty, food insecurity and conflicts. Most of the systems that bring improvements are either labor intensive or capital intensive. Water scarcity is the highest in regions where poverty is also widespread. The local farmers lack the resources to invest in better systems. This is why government and businesses must participate actively.

As crops and farm animals consume a lot of water, any food loss is a waste of water. It is true in India with post-harvest losses and it is true in the USA with meat recalls. This problem is particularly serious in countries that suffer from water scarcity. Reducing food waste also reduces water waste!

In the food production chain, saving water goes beyond blue and green water management. Food processing companies, which are also large users of water, can take action to reduce waste. For instance, Kraft Foods showed a saving of over 20% of water in their operations over the period 2006-2008.

Hydroponics can be helpful in producing more food with less water. By producing in a computerized controlled environment, it is possible to manage water distribution to the plants, and to recover the water that evaporated. In Kuwait, the Wafra Faisaliya Farm produces fresh produce for several supermarkets. According to Mamhoud Nammas, the head of the farm, *"hydroponic production helps saving 90% of the water compared with the conventional soil production"*[26]. In a country like Kuwait where water is scarce, this system offers large benefits to the population. Hydroponic production has the disadvantage of requiring a high initial investment that not every farmer can afford. It has proven to be competitive, especially in challenging climatic conditions.

Another technique is desalination of seawater. With 70% of the surface of the planet covered with oceans, it is a tempting solution. Desalination, however, is expensive because it requires a lot of energy. There is more research being carried out in several countries to find better ways of removing the salt from the water at a lower cost than it is currently. According to the World Future Society, *"Water desalination may soon become one of the world's largest industries"*. Some projects are in the works to desalinate seawater to save groundwater reserves. For example, The United Arab Emirates have requested a huge project of floating islands covered with solar panels in order to produce electricity and at the same time desalinize seawater. Other research projects focus on mobile and local systems. For instance, researchers at MIT and in Korea are working on developing portable desalination units powered with solar cells or batteries. The electrostatic process would separate the salt and the contaminants from the water.

---

[26] Kuwait Times, 'Hydroponic saves 90% water over conventional soil based farming', 28 March 2008

Water treatment will be critical, because wasting is not an option. The treatment needs to happen at municipalities' level, but individuals can also manage it. For example, this is what the many "water refill stations" in Indonesia and in The Philippines offer. These stations use some rather simple and low-cost systems to purify water and they sell it to city dwellers. There are attempts, for instance by The Aquaya Institute, to export this model into East Africa.

How to Increase Agricultural Production

Substantially increasing food production can be done in two ways: by increasing the area in production and by increasing yields.

The FAO estimates the total area of arable land at 1.4 billion hectares. This represents only 11 % of total land area, which means that every human being has only 0.2 ha (less than half an acre) to grow food. Therefore, each person is the tenant of a rather small garden. Pastures cover a total of 3.4 billion hectares, which represent about 27 % of total land. The majority of the land is not fit for agricultural or pastoral purposes. Land is unsuitable for arable farming because of several reasons: there is no source of fresh water, the climate is too hot or too cold, too rainy or too snowy, the land is too rocky or too mountainous, or the soil is too salty, too polluted or too poor in nutrients.

The percentage of arable land varies between countries. This affects their ability to produce food and their level of food security. Some countries stand out when it comes to potential.

Western Europe is in a very good position with most countries having more than 30% arable land. Central and Eastern European countries have more potential than they currently show because of their high percentage of arable land. In Poland, Ukraine, Moldova and Hungary, this percentage is higher than 40%. The Black Sea Region with Russia, Ukraine and Kazakhstan has high potential to expand wheat production. Since 2004, the region had added 7 million hectares to the production of grains. It has the potential for tens of millions of hectares of additional and accessible arable land for grains, legumes and oilseeds.

Their biggest challenge is infrastructure, as the poor condition of rail links to ports keeps supply chain costs high.

In the Middle East, a group of countries has good potential to develop agriculture further. Turkey, Lebanon, Syria, Armenia and Azerbaijan have between 20% and 30% arable land.

A number of African nations have good areas of arable land, especially in the Ivory Coast-Niger-Nigeria-Cameroon region. Nigeria has more than 30% arable land and Togo more than 40%. The surge in investment in Africa is still at an early stage, but already the signs are positive. In recent years, according to FAO data, Africa has been recording a 3.5% rate growth in farm production compared to 2% population growth, putting an end to decades of stagnation.

Brazil has still some potential to develop more agriculture and a commodity that deserves more attention is rice. The country's acreage in rice has decreased in the past few years, although the production level remained stable due to yield increases. Brazil has a favorable climate for rice production. Today, they have two regions where rice is produced. In the Rio Grande do Sul, water is available and production levels are high. In the Nordeste, water is less available and yields are lower. The type of rice produced did not meet the need of the Brazilian consumer, which explains to some extent why rice production has not expanded. Instead of looking only at the domestic demand, Brazil should look at Asian markets where demand keeps increasing. Brazil could become a major rice supplier to these countries. There are similar climatic and agronomic conditions between some of Brazil's regions and some of the African countries where Asian countries are buying land to produce rice. Compared to Asia where water is scarce, Brazil does not have this problem.

War-torn Iraq and Afghanistan both have about 15% arable land and perhaps agriculture could be a way of bringing them back into the world economy. A solid program for agricultural development would certainly help, if it includes the necessary infrastructure for water and power.

Early in 2010, the USA started a program to encourage the development of fruit production such as apples and grapes with the intent of offering a better income to Afghan farmers than what they receive for opium. The production of fruit might work if the financial incentives are good enough, but there is no guarantee they will replace the poppy production. An unusual mixed crop system could develop.

Pakistan, with close to 25%, and especially India with more than 40% arable land should achieve more, and so can South East Asia. India is blessed with its land, although the Green Revolution has caused significant soil degradation. India's agriculture is very dependent on the monsoon. The rule of thumb is that if the monsoon is good, the agriculture –and the economy- will be good, too. The aging infrastructure, or the lack of infrastructure in some cases, is a serious limitation for an increase in food production. The human factor, especially politics, will be central to change this situation.

According to FAO projections, by 2050, the planted area in developing countries will have expanded by 120 million hectares while it will be reduced in developed countries by 50 million hectares. It represents a net increase of 70 million ha compared with 2009. They expect Sub-Saharan Africa and Latin America will show all of the net increase.

Agricultural development is more than just agricultural activities. It creates and improves a cluster of many economic activities necessary for the proper functioning of a community. It goes far beyond farms and fields. Agricultural development cannot be separated from urban development.

By developing agriculture, the very first farmers created the conditions for settlement. Human settlements always have been linked to drinking water and sufficient food supplies. In these sedentary communities, other activities developed later to fulfill the needs of the locals.

The famous pyramid of needs defined by Maslow[27] is a good tool to identify the needs to be met. The basic essential needs are food and water, shelter, physical safety and health. Once these needs are met, adding other activities becomes more natural and simple.

Developing large urban centers is no guarantee of prosperity. Like many things in life, the key is balance. Originally, the role of cities was to offer safety and protection for the population, as people could come for shelter behind the city walls. By then, cities and countryside were interconnected. The function of cities has evolved through time to the point where urban centers and rural areas now seem two separate entities.

Over the last 150 years, the focus has been about growing industrial capabilities. Industrialization has been the engine for the migration of population from the countryside to the cities. In the early stage of industrial development, many companies were providing their employees with housing. Although the social condition of workers was far from optimal, companies were showing some level of social responsibility. Despite social inequalities, there was a social fabric. With the increasing size of cities, this sense of community has gradually disappeared and cities have faced a growing problem of poverty. Industrialization and urbanization have also affected the rural areas and the agricultural world. Many rural areas have faced and are still facing isolation and poverty. There have been many efforts made to improve this, but the situation has not always improved.

Too often, policies tend to restrict rural development to agricultural development. Instead of focusing on integrating agriculture in the development of the local as well as the global economy, agriculture remains separated from the economy at large and projects do not have enough chances for success. Large urban centers have problems and remote and depopulated rural areas have problems. This is the clear sign that the current economic model is out of balance.

---

27 A.H. Maslow, *A Theory of Human Motivation*, Psychological Review 50(4) (1943):370-96.

In order to have successful agricultural development, it is essential to have visionary leadership that makes the resources available to achieve the goals. Money incentives are important, but at the same time, it is necessary to develop education, research and knowledge transfer. Education is paramount to eliminate poverty because it is the best way to gain the necessary skills for a successful life. Developed countries have an important role to play in the transfer of expertise and in the training of farmers in less fortunate regions. These elements have been the basis of the success of agriculture and of the economy in the West. They have contributed to the Green Revolution of the 1960s that made crop yields increase to such levels that agriculture could help meet the needs of the population.

Poor leadership, on the other hand, can be very damaging to the prosperity of a nation. For instance, Zimbabwe used to have a strong agriculture and it could have been a beacon for other African nations. In 2000, Robert Mugabe's government decided to redistribute land to small poor black farmers and remove more than 4,000 large commercial farms run by white farmers. The situation resulted in conflicts and sanctions from the EU and the USA. The government's poor management caused a lack of fertilizer supplies, of equipment and seeds. This affected food security negatively. Between 2000 and 2009, agricultural production dropped by 70%. This example shows how fragile and how dependent on the actions of a few men food supply is.

To rebuild the necessary social fabric in rural areas, development projects must create the conditions to have balanced and complementary activities. Some see the future of agriculture as urban farming, but it will be about urbanizing the countryside with human size settlements just as much. Isolated farmers with no direct connection with their markets are not getting the value for their products to make a decent living. They will look for alternatives. To have more people involved in food production, they must make enough money.

By creating a proper infrastructure around agricultural areas, farmers can serve the market better. This, in turn, will drive production up. It is important to remember that the main purpose of agriculture is to feed people. Producers and consumers must be able to meet one another. To do this efficiently, governments need to create the proper network of roads, railways and waterways to bring the products to market. Infrastructure also includes proper storage facilities. For many developing countries, infrastructure is the weak link in the supply chain. In these countries, as is the case in Brazil and India, most of the food losses happen post-harvest. If India could reduce the post-harvest losses to the levels of Western countries, it would be able to be comfortably self-sufficient.

A market-driven approach to agriculture is crucial for effective agricultural development. This approach goes beyond just feeding the population. It also creates value for the ones who produce the food. A profitable market for the farmers' products also means more money in their pockets, which creates more spending power to develop demand for other businesses, be it for products or services. That way, local economies and communities can grow and develop. It is a thorough and integrated process embracing modernity. It is not about an idealistic back-to-nature movement or about creating local farmers markets purely for marketing purposes. In the current rural areas and in other regions, the successful future will be about bringing the economy to the people before bringing people to the economy.

In South America, agricultural development policies have had various levels of success.

Chile has developed a strong export-oriented agriculture –and aquaculture- thanks to a large variety of climatic conditions that have allowed the country to provide northern hemisphere countries with the produce they lack off-season. It is now one of the major exporters of fruit, wine and seafood. Their success is the result of a favorable policy framework together with an entrepreneurial and innovative spirit.

From the beginning, Chileans have understood that their agricultural exports would be successful only by being efficient and by delivering top quality products. They have delivered just that. Moreover, Chilean agriculture receives strong support through many private as well as public agencies to open and conquer new markets.

Argentina has been in an economic slump for many years and is having trouble emerging from this situation. Considering the climatic conditions, the water availability, the soil conditions and the quality of the grassland in the Pampas, Argentina should be one of the most prosperous nations on Earth. Argentina is the second world producer of soybeans behind the USA. It is the fourth producer of corn behind the USA, China and Brazil. It is the third largest beef exporter behind Brazil and Australia. Agriculture could be one of the drivers to rebuild the Argentinean economy. Unfortunately, the recent agricultural policies have been more disruptive than productive. The dialogue between government and farmers is difficult.

Uruguay, their close neighbor, benefits from better government policies. It is expanding its agricultural production. The focus of Uruguayan producers is on quality and on market-driven export. This approach is successful.

Brazil is the new agricultural giant. Over the last few decades, Brazil has undergone a spectacular transformation. The country is now one of the world's leaders in agriculture and food. In particular, the sectors of meat and poultry have been booming. Brazil is now home for some of the largest agribusiness companies. Brazilians have passed the USA as the number one exporter of chicken meat since 2006 and their expressed objective is to become the largest producer of beef in the world.

The expansion comes with a consolidation of the industry. JBS is now the largest meat company in the world after their acquisition of Bertin. It came only weeks after Sadia and Perdigão merged to create Brasil Foods that was temporarily the largest Brazilian meat and poultry company in late 2009.

The other dominating sector in Brazilian agriculture is the sugar business. This sector has grown strongly because of the production of sugarcane ethanol, which is a competitive biofuel alternative that helped Brazil to compensate for its lack of oil reserves. In 2009, the Brazilian unit of the French group Dreyfus Commodities, Bioenergia, bought Santelisa Vale to create the world's second sugarcane processor behind the number one Cosan, from Brazil. Shortly after, the American-headquartered company Bunge bought Moema to expand its presence in the sugar processing business. In February 2010, Cosan and Shell have decided to co-operate in the development of biofuels. Brazil is gaining an increasingly strategic position in global agribusiness. If foreign companies acquire Brazilian businesses, Brazilian companies are active buying foreign companies as well. Marfrig has grown its poultry business with acquisitions in Europe, such as Northern Ireland's Moy Park, formerly owned by OSI Industries from Chicago. In 2009, JBS bought Smithfield Beef and completed the purchase of Pilgrim's Pride, the largest but bankrupt US chicken processor. In 2010, they acquired Rockdale Beef of Australia.

While the other continents were growing and developing, poor leadership, corruption, famines, AIDS, malaria and armed conflicts plagued Africa. Economically speaking, a number of African countries now show impressive results. For instance, Angola is now one of the world's fastest growing countries and their revenue from oil is driving a complete transformation. African growth does not come only from oil. The information and communication technology sector is growing very fast. The use of cell phones is growing, in particular among farmers who can use it to get market information. The GSM mobile phone system covers 94% of the population. Africa is marching, but it needs more money to achieve its development.

In agriculture, the continent has lagged behind the rest of the world. The larger part of the African agriculture still is subsistence agriculture with a fragmented rural structure. In most African countries, agriculture employs between 60% and 80% of the active population. Progress has been slow because of the lack of funds for agricultural development.

However, there is no shortage of agricultural land in Africa. According to the FAO, there are 700 million hectares of unexploited arable land on that continent. This is almost the size of Australia! In particular, the Guinea Savannah region offers great potential. It stretches from the south of Senegal and Guinea to the south of Sudan, from the south of Sudan to Mozambique and the south of Madagascar, and from western Tanzania to Angola. This region covers 600 million hectares, which is twice as large as the current total world wheat area, but only 10% of this area is cultivated.

Many African farmers need the basics in order to succeed. Access to good quality seeds, applying techniques that enhance soil fertility, developing irrigation, education and technical support are the basis for further development. Aggressively trying to implement immediately large-scale farming, a high level of mechanization, high-tech equipment and genetic engineering might not be the best priority. Compared to other continents, the use of water reserves for irrigation is low.

African agriculture produces far below its potential. The Green Revolution that has helped Asia cope with its food shortages has not taken place in Africa. There are lessons to be learned from the past. The Indian case provides many examples of possible consequences. First, the Green Revolution helped increase food production and feed the population. This is an important and positive fact. Secondly, the Green Revolution has also created problems, such as soil degradation and salinity. It is also an important and, unfortunately, negative fact. Thirdly, 40 years later, Indian agriculture is still struggling to feed the people, largely due to insufficient infrastructure, government policies and lack of financing for farmers. Learning from the past and developing strategies to have the positive results without the negative consequences will be essential in this time of active investments by foreigners in Africa.

The continent can use all the help it can get. The population is young and it is growing fast. They need food, education and health care. Africa needs to accelerate its development. Agriculture and food will play a major role. The dynamics are changing, too.

On a continent used to depending on foreign help, many African countries have already taken the lead and initiated reforms. The example of Uganda with its spectacular rice production boost and the example in Burkina Faso show what people achieve when they focus on solutions and take proper action.

Developing more land for crop production will offer only limited possibilities. The best strategy to improve food security is to grow more food per hectare. Yields depend on two things: the genetic potential of the plants and the environmental conditions in the field. These conditions will influence how much of their potential the plants can express. The African average yields are lower than in the rest of the world. For instance, the Sub-Saharan average for cereals is 1.2 ton per hectare while the world average is at 3.1 ton per hectare. The following table shows data from the FAO on yield variations for wheat produced from 2006 to 2008.

Country	Wheat yield (tons/hectare)
USA	2.6 – 3.0
Canada	2.3 – 2.9
Australia	0.9 – 1.6
Argentina	2.0 – 2.6
Brazil	1.6 – 2.5
Kazakhstan	1.0 – 1.3
Russian Federation	1.9 – 2.4
Ukraine	2.3 – 3.7
France	6.3 – 7.1
Netherlands	7.1 – 8.8
Germany	7.0 – 8.1
UK	7.2 – 8.3
China	4.6 – 4.8
India	2.6 – 2.8
Pakistan	2.5 - 2.7
Turkey	2.1 – 2.4
Egypt	6.4 – 6.5
Kenya	2.2 – 3.1
Madagascar	2.4 – 2.5
Mozambique	1.1 – 1.3
South Africa	2.8 – 3.1
Zimbabwe	3.0 – 3.6

Yields may vary between years, but the table clearly shows that performance varies substantially between countries. The world's largest exporters such as the USA, Australia or Canada are not the top yield performers. Climatic conditions explain some of the variation, but higher yields are possible. The data also offers a lot of hope because it means that plants are not expressing the maximum of their genetic potential.

All countries have potential to achieve higher yields. The top performers give an indication of what the potential might be. At least, it is close to 10 tons per hectare.

A large part of the solution to improve yields lies in creating a better growing environment for the plants through water management, fertilizer management, soil preservation, weed control, and pest management. These practices are far from optimal in many regions. Africa lags behind the other regions, but there are strong regional differences within the continent. Some of these nations already achieve good yields. They have good potential for the future if they receive the necessary support in capital and equipment.

While in 2007-2008, the average worldwide wheat yield was at 2.8 tons/ha, the objective of the FAO for 2020 is to reach 4 tons/ha, and for 2050 to achieve 5 tons/ha.

Next to wheat, another vital grain crop, especially for Asia, is rice. This continent produces 90% of the world rice. Asia is struggling to feed its population and it has to cope with water scarcity and soil degradation. Less than 6% of the rice production is traded internationally. Saving water can reduce domestic water conflicts, especially in poor rural areas where water is the scarcest. The demand for rice is expected to increase by 38% by 2040. Considering the volume of water needed in the current production system, increasing production to such levels will have serious consequences on water availability in the region. Efficient water management and innovative cultivation techniques will be the key to improve yields and production.

Research carried out by IWMI[28] compared two possible scenarios for the production of grains in 2050. One scenario is based on expanding the cultivated area and the second scenario is based on yield improvement by using better irrigation systems.

The first scenario predicts that yields will increase by 52% in South Asia and by 40% in East Asia. The second scenario, which focuses on yields, predicts a yield increase potential of 100% in South Asia and of 70% in East Asia.

Another interesting technique is the SRI (System of Rice Intensification). According to its supporters, which include the World Wildlife Fund, the SRI presents the advantage of using 25% to 50% less water. Compared with the traditional method, yields are about 30% higher, and some people mention even 50% to 100%. It also uses less seeds because the plant population is reduced. This can save farmers up to 80% to 90% on the costs of seeds. The SRI technique is not new. It was first developed in Madagascar in the early 1990s and since then farmers in 28 other countries in Africa and India have used it. In the SRI, the soil is kept moist, but not flooded as in traditional systems. This improves root growth and allows the development in the soil of aerobic organisms that enhance growth. The rice plants are spaced widely to allow the leaves to collect the maximum amount of sunlight, grow stronger roots and maximize photosynthesis. The rice seedlings are transplanted at less than 15 days, which is at a younger age than in the traditional system. This minimizes transplant shock and root damage. Although this production method has many critics, governments in several Asian countries support its development. They are interested in investigating this technique further. In India, the state of Tripura has committed to the SRI and more than 70,000 farmers of that state are using this system. India has set the objective of cultivating five million hectares of rice with SRI as part of the government's National Food Security Mission.

---

[28] FAO, Adity Mukherji, Thierry Facon et al., Revitalizing Asia's Irrigation — To Sustainability meet tomorrow's food needs, 2008

China is also expanding the area cultivated with the SRI, although not as aggressively as India. The Indonesian President, S.B. Yudhoyono, who has a PhD in Agriculture, has publicly endorsed the SRI and he has asked the Ministry of Agriculture to promote the system. Cambodia and Vietnam are also promoting the SRI as a way of making advances in food production and food security. The supporters of SRI are not only governments, but also companies.

For instance, Syngenta, through its subsidiary in Bangladesh, has expressed its support for the method. The SRI is now under review at Cornell University in the USA and at the Agricultural University of Wageningen in the Netherlands. If the outcome of this research is positive, the SRI will indeed revolutionize rice supplies in Asia and in other parts of the world.

The recent introduction in India of flood-tolerant rice varieties that can survive up to two weeks under water is promising. These varieties are the result of precision breeding and are not considered GMOs. According to IRRI (International Rice Research Institute, based in the Philippines) estimates, they could help increase rice production by up to four million tons in flood sensitive regions of India and in Bangladesh, where 20% of the land is subject to floods. The development and the introduction of drought-tolerant varieties through genetic engineering and non-GM procedures offer reasons for optimism, too. The introduction of hybrid varieties has also resulted in increased yields. Although the development of varieties of hybrid rice has been slow since the 1990s when they were introduced, it is now gathering momentum. From 10,000 hectares in 1995, the area has grown to 1.3 million hectares in 2009. This growth is expected to continue as the Indian government has committed to expanding the area to three million hectares by 2011 and because better quality seeds are offered by the suppliers.

Technology will also help farmers improve their yields. For instance, Pakistan is launching a subsidized program to develop the use of mechanical rice transplantation. One of the problems rice farmers face is a shortage of labor, which affects production negatively. The current average yield of about 280 kg per hectare is low.

The Pakistani government expects that the use of mechanical transplanters will increase the yields by 25%. Further, this development program also includes the introduction of better techniques in rice nurseries. The combined effect of the new technology will improve the quality of the rice and increase the farmers' income.

Even if the growing conditions are usually sub-optimal for the plant to express its full potential, increasing yields will require further genetic selection. This will be largely achieved with traditional breeding methods, by selecting the best performers and breeding a better next generation. Of course, improving yields also raises the controversial topic of GMOs. Genetic engineering programs can actually contribute to enhance the potential of the plant to grow better and more efficiently, even in adverse conditions. They need to solve practical agricultural problems and produce better plants. Yields are the priority.

More developments are taking place with rice. At the IRRI, researchers are using genetic engineering to modify the way the plant builds tissue so that it becomes more efficient in warmer and drier climates. To achieve this, the research team needs to determine which genes regulate the more efficient leaf anatomy to make the enhanced rice more productive. Once they have discovered how to engineer such modifications, similar projects could be developed with other plants to turn them into what they call "turbo crops". Such an approach might be useful to improve the production of wheat in sub-Saharan African regions.

Another environmental factor influencing yields is weeds. Effective weed management could theoretically increase yields and production to substantially higher levels. This problem is especially sensitive in Africa, where yields have stagnated. Many small farmers do not have access to much mechanization or herbicides for financial reasons. They must weed the fields manually. This technique is not efficient and it limits their ability to manage large cultivated areas.

Eliminating weeds will need to go beyond the use of herbicides because resistant weeds are becoming a bigger and bigger problem. For instance, in the USA, 13 species of weeds are now resistant to glyphosate. For small farmers in poor countries, simple solutions such as educating the farmers on how to clean their seeds of weed seeds can have a dramatic impact on weed reduction and yield increase.

Another technique called "solarization" also offers some possibilities. Solarization is the use of plastic films to cover the soil or to use polymers as mulch. Weeds cannot grow, as the temperature at the soil level reaches high levels that are lethal to them.

Proper soil management is crucial for future food supplies and for the environment. A number of innovative techniques are being tested to improve soil protection and preserve the fertility of the soil. For instance, the USDA is carrying out a test for a new harvesting system for grain. A recent study from the USDA ARS suggests that using a stripper header during grain harvests could boost profits and have conservation benefits. The idea of this system is to strip away the grain and leave as long stubble as possible, so that it protects the soil from erosion and enhances precipitation storage. For wheat, the stripper header leaves 2-foot tall (60 cm) stubble, compared to 6 to 8 inches (15 cm to 20 cm) left by the usual sickle bar header. The stripper header has been tested on millet and wheat, and so far, the results tend to indicate this harvesting method does not affect yields.

A nice illustration of how the innovation process develops and succeeds is the use of no-tillage techniques. In a recent book, the International Food Policy Research Institute (IFPRI) describes the cases of no-tillage agriculture in Argentina and in India and Pakistan.

Farmers developed no-tillage, or zero-tillage, techniques to address soil degradation after it took place in the USA's Dust Bowl in the 1930s and in the Soviet plains of Kazakhstan in the 1960s.

In these regions, the use of tillage with heavy machinery combined with intensive monoculture and dry and windy climatic conditions caused a rapid erosion of the soil and a significant loss of fertility. The no-tillage techniques have been applied successfully and they have restored soil quality and improved crop productivity. To explain it simply, no-tillage consist of planting seeds directly in the soil without further soil preparation. In a no-tillage system, farmers have other preparation issues to deal with, such as dealing with weeds and the vegetal debris of the previous crop.

In Argentina, these techniques have been used on soybean, which is a major export crop for the country. Argentina was facing the same risks of soil degradation in the 1990s because of damaging agricultural practices for two decades. In two regions of the Pampas, soil degradation had reached a level of 47% in one area and up to 60% in another. The combination of factors that helped restore and improve soybean productivity has been the use of the herbicide glyphosate on genetically modified glyphosate-tolerant soybean. The herbicide broke down the plant residue and the weeds, which allowed the farmers to plant the soybean earlier. However, this technique requires using a different type of machinery and drillers were developed and used, replacing the previously used machines. Combined with other positive political and market developments, the production of grain and oilseed crops on no-tillage land increased to amazing levels. From about 300,000 hectares of land in 1990/91, production reached more than 22 million hectares in 2007/08[29].

In the Indus-Ganges Plains, agriculture also faced soil degradation and yield stagnation. It was the result of unsustainable intensive agricultural practices developed in the years of the Green Revolution in the 1960s. No-tillage techniques have been introduced in the rice-wheat system with very good results in the late 1990s and early 2000s. The farmers' income increased using zero-tillage, mostly because of lower costs due to less need for machinery and fuel in this system.

---

[29] IFPRI, Chapter 8, Eduardo Trigo, Eugenio Cap, Valeria Malach, and Federico Villarreal, Innovating in the Pampas, 2009

Zero-tillage appears to increase wheat yield by 5-7%, which adds positive sales revenue to the farms. The rise in yields is closely associated with the timing of planting the wheat. By allowing farmers to plant wheat more quickly after the rice harvest, zero-tillage can reduce yield losses because heat stress at the end of the wheat season can reduce the yields by 1-1.5% a day[30].

As in Argentina, farmers needed new equipment and a drilling machine had to be developed. Zero-tillage is an example of how governments play a role in innovation and progress. In India, the government and the Rice-Wheat Consortium were supportive, and the farmers implemented zero-tillage rather quickly. In the Pakistani part of the Plains, similar actions went more slowly, mostly because of bureaucratic infighting.

Actions to enhance soil fertility are needed in all countries. Managing both organic matter and minerals is of the highest importance. The objectives are to enhance and to preserve soil fertility, as well as to protect the water from pollution.

The organic matter, be it plant residues from crops, manure from farm animals or "black water" from humans, actually belongs to the soil that produced it in the first place.

Composting is one way of enriching soil with organic matter, but it is not the only way. The production of compost is one of the basics of organic farming, of subsistence agriculture and of urban farming as well. When there is little soil and no possibilities of throwing away waste, people have no other choice than to do what is right and recycle the organic matter.

---

[30] IFPRI, Chapter 9, Olaf Erenstein, Leaving the Plow Behind, 2009

Another technique that has been drawing attention recently is the production of biochar. Biochar is the product obtained by slow burning of agricultural waste in anaerobic conditions. The process creates a highly porous charcoal that helps soils retain nutrients and water. It has the capacity to capture and store carbon dioxide, which makes it an attractive solution for environmental reasons. Its ability to retain nutrients helps reduce the use of mineral fertilizers. Biochar is nothing new. Populations in the Amazon region used such a process some 2,000 years ago, and the carbon-rich soils of this area are known as "*Terra preta*". This product seems of interest especially for regions where the soil has been severely degraded and where there would be little alternatives but deforestation and burning. The IBI (International Biochar Initiative) based in Washington, DC, organizes conferences around the world to increase awareness about the potential of the product.

Depending on the origin, organic matter consists of three types of components: gases, liquids and solids. These components need to be dealt with in different ways because all three of them have their own useful potential applications.

The solids present in the manure will be used after most of the free water has been removed, mostly by gravity.

Biogas comes from methane present in the manure and from anaerobic digestion of organic matter. It can be used as an energy source to produce electricity for the local community. Biogas is considered a renewable source of energy and its production will increase by collecting as much of the methane produced as possible. There will be digesters set up on more farms and sewage treatment facilities.

There is no such thing as an excess of organic matter in the soil, but bringing minerals on the land requires a more prudent attitude. The most difficult part of the manure to deal with is the liquid fraction. The minerals dissolved in the liquid part are not easy to separate and remove. There is no cheap and fast way of evaporating water in most climates. Manure must be kept in a watertight containment to avoid any leakage of harmful substances to the environment.

The different fertilizing elements have different behaviors in the soil and organic matter has the ability to fix minerals to some extent. Phosphorus is not mobile, and if brought in too high quantities, it accumulates. This eventually threatens the fertility of the soil. Potassium has a limited mobility and in normal conditions, it will not accumulate nor will it leach in large quantities into the groundwater. Nitrogen is much more difficult to manage because it is very mobile once dissolved. It escapes the binding forces from soil and organic matter rather easily. If the plants do not use it almost immediately after application, the nitrogen will travel through the soil at the first rain and it will go into the groundwater. When this happens continually, the level of nitrates in the water increases to harmful levels. The high level of nutrients in the water enhances the growth of algae in rivers with potentially severe risks to the aquatic fauna.

Because nitrogen is so mobile, replacing organic matter by mineral fertilizers on soil has led to huge losses of nitrogen. These losses also represent a huge waste of the large amounts of energy required to produce those fertilizers. Estimates are that half of the nitrogen spread on crops leaches, and half the use of fossil fuels in agriculture is used for the production of mineral fertilizers. Such losses increase the carbon footprint and the emission of harmful gases of agriculture. The debate on nitrogen fertilizers tends to be biased, though. It should not be about using them or not at all. Once more, pragmatism is the most efficient attitude. Nitrogen does enhance plant growth. The pragmatic solution that will prevail and end the debate is to bring as much organic matter and nitrogen from the manure as reasonably as possible, first. The second step is to estimate how much nitrogen it brings and to compare it with the nitrogen requirement to obtain the desired yields. Then farmers can complement with mineral fertilizer if needed and use a precision farming approach. There are many sources of fertilizers for crops, coming from plant waste, from plant residues, from manure or from human feces in sewage waiting for a use in agriculture. Optimizing fertilization means using these sources first to complete the cycle, and then using synthetic fertilizers to fill the gap only when needed.

Managing nitrogen is a challenge. Nitrogen represents 79% of the air but plants do not have the ability to use this nitrogen directly for their metabolism. Yet, legumes for instance, can store some nitrogen in their roots where nitrogen-fixing bacteria have a symbiotic relationship with the plants. Rotating crops and using the root bacteria is a commonly used technique for reducing fertilizer consumption. Biology will bring solutions to the nitrogen challenge. Genetic engineering will find ways for plants to absorb or fix the nitrogen from the air to reduce the use of mineral fertilizers. The University of Illinois is studying ways of designing and building new biological functions in a plant, the so-called synthetic biology. At Stanford University, researchers identified a gene in alfalfa that stimulates the symbiotic bacteria living in the roots to fix nitrogen that the plant uses for its development and growth.

They introduced the gene into mutant plants that did not have the ability to get bacteria to fix nitrogen and the function appeared. Understanding this mechanism opens the possibility to introduce a similar ability in other plants.

There are new developments to find alternatives to mineral fertilizers. In particular, the culture and production of cocktails of bacteria populations that can fix nitrogen from the air and store it in the soil for the plant to use "on demand" might present potential. The idea is to replace most of the mineral fertilizers by these living bacterial cultures. They also would increase the amount of organic matter in the soil. These products could also protect plants against pathogens. Unlike mineral fertilizers, which require regular applications, these bacterial populations would sustain themselves. Trials carried out on different crops such as rice, barley, corn, soybean, tomatoes, cucumber and fruit show strong increases in yields. The challenge for these products is to compete economically against the current fertilizers on large-scale operations. As the price of oil increases, the economics of fertilizers will change, too.

Developing more food production on the land goes beyond arable land. Grassland covers almost 2.5 times the area of arable land. The only limitation, and it is an important one, is that cellulose is not digestible by humans. The irony is that cellulose is the most common organic compound on Earth and it is a chain of glucose molecules. Although people cannot digest cellulose, herbivores can. Until now, the best use farmers have been able to make of grass is by keeping ruminants. From cattle, sheep and goats to horses and water buffalo, grasslands support large numbers of domestic animals. They become the source of meat, milk, wool, and leather products. Until someone can invent a process to transform cellulose in a digestible food source for humans, the use of grassland will not change much.

Grasslands are complex ecosystems. They not only feed farm animals but they also are the habitat for a wide array of plant species and for many sorts of animals, ranging from insects to birds, rodents and other mammals. Grasslands usually have developed on rather poor and vulnerable soils.

The grass provides protection and structure, which preserves the stability of these lands. Cautious management is required to ensure the continuity of the grasslands and the possibility of producing food. Proper management of grasslands includes many parameters that go beyond production yields only. Many rural communities and nomadic populations, often poor, depend on pastoral production. Therefore, management of grassland must integrate many socio-economic factors. A long-term vision of a sustainable farming activity is necessary in these regions. In many cases, grassland farming must go hand-in-hand with the management of the ecosystem as a whole. This prevents loss of soil and water wastage that could result in loss of output potential, which could cause the beginning of a desertification process. This is true under any climate, but it is even more critical in tropical and sub-tropical regions. Properly managed grassland can lead to a better and higher production of forage for livestock. The use of grains or commercial feed can be reduced in the production of animal products. It frees land for the production of food directly aimed at human consumption.

Grassland could also be used for the production of biofuels. A team of researchers from the University of Minnesota sees many advantages in producing biofuels from grass. They estimate that the production from prairie biomass would yield 51% more energy per acre than ethanol produced from corn on arable land. An added benefit is that biofuels made from grassland biomass are carbon negative, as the plants store more carbon in their roots and in the soil than is released by the fossil fuels used to grow and process the grass. According to the research team, making biofuels from prairie biomass would help remove and store between 3 and 4.5 tons of carbon per hectare per year. The production of both corn ethanol and biodiesel from soybeans are carbon positive. Further, the researchers estimate that growing mixed prairie grasses on all of the world's degraded land could produce enough bioenergy to replace 13% of global petroleum consumption and 19% of global electricity consumption[31].

Producing biofuels from mixed prairie grasses could not only provide stable production of energy, but it also could enhance soil fertility, preserve wildlife habitats and offer recreational opportunities, while keeping ground and surface waters cleaner. Biofuels made from cellulose also deliver a better yield performance. According to USDA data[32], the yields of biofuels vary widely. They reach 100 gallons per acre for rapeseed in the European Union, 400 gallons per acre for US corn and 660 gallons per acre for Brazilian sugarcane. Cellulosic ethanol could raise ethanol yields to more than 1,000 gallons per acre, which would significantly reduce land requirements.

The competition for corn and oilseeds between biofuel production, human consumption and animal feed will become fierce and influence policies.

---

[31] National Science Foundation, Press Release 06-171, Mixed Prairie Grasses Better Source of Biofuel Than Corn Ethanol and Soybean Biodiesel, 7 December 2006

[32] USDA, Economic Research Center, Amber Waves, The Future of Biofuels: A Global Perspective, November 2007

For instance, when the prices of agricultural commodities skyrocketed in 2008, the Chinese government put a moratorium on expanded use of corn for ethanol and promoted other feedstocks that do not compete directly with food crops, such as cassava, sweet sorghum, and jatropha.

Although it sounds attractive to produce ethanol from cellulose, the technology to produce it needs to be developed further. This production needs to be economically viable, which is currently not always the case. Except for Brazilian ethanol made out of sugarcane, other biofuel processes are financially disappointing. Without subsidy from the US government, corn ethanol plants would lose money and not have a place in the market. By producing ethanol from cellulose, the demand for crops like corn or soybean for biofuel purposes would drop, keeping prices for both human food and animal feed more acceptable. In April 2010, a group of American associations of livestock, meat and poultry producers sent a letter to the US House of Representatives to ask for the removal of corn ethanol subsidies and protective tariffs. The higher demand for corn causes an increase of their cost of production.

The economics of food and of energy are changing, and this will change the way the world must look at both. The scarcity of resources will affect the price of commodities in such a way that solutions not financially sensible today may become attractive tomorrow. Grassland management will evolve towards more efficiency and more production.

For the future, policies need to consider more than arable land and grassland. Since pragmatism is one of the pillars of the future of food production, it is only legitimate to wonder why not consider producing without soil on a large scale. Soilless production is not new, but development has remained relatively modest. Hydroponics is a growing activity that offers possibilities for the future. Considering the extent of the water challenge, hydroponics in one form or another will gain more interest as a production method.

For many small farmers the capital requirement is a deterrent because the initial investment for hydroponics is high. Further, producing crops without soil requires a different set of expertise than field production. There are many technical parameters involved in the proper management of the climate conditions, as well as for the fertilizer applications. Despite these technical and financial hurdles, hydroponics is a solution for areas where fertile soil and water are scarce resources. The example of the vegetable farm in Kuwait proved it.

Another country where this technique has been developed on a large scale is Israel, where the level of technology is advanced. Because of its geographical location and because of its political situation, Israel needs to have highly efficient food production. Ben Gurion, the founder of modern Israel, quickly realized that the natural conditions were adverse to food production. He strongly encouraged the development of hydroponics, which once more illustrate the importance of visionary leadership to a successful food policy. Using a high degree of automation and robotics, Israelis are able to grow fruits and vegetables with high yields. Israelis have also become quite skilled at desalination of water and at the management of salt water in fertilization programs.

Next to the highly efficient use of water, yields are one of the main advantages of hydroponics. The yield performance is the result of a controlled environment in which the plant density is higher than in fields and where the growth is substantially faster than in the open air. The farmer can set the right temperature, the right air humidity, the right level of light, and the right level of nutrients for the plants. There are also lower risks of diseases and pests, which contributes to a much higher production per surface unit.

Japan' agriculture is very innovative because it needs to find constantly new ways of supplying enough food to the population. In Japan, they have been working on producing hydroponic rice, and they have been able to obtain four harvests in a year, while there is only one in open field production.

In Saudi Arabia, an 18-acre greenhouse farm has been set up to produce vegetables such as tomatoes, cucumber and lettuce. In open fields with traditional irrigation, the yields would reach 5 tons per acre. In the hydroponic facility, the yields are as high as 200 tons per acre.

Considering the lack of arable land and the population growth in Arab countries and in the Middle East, hydroponics is an attractive solution. Farming the desert must be considered. One company from the UK, Seawater Greenhouse Ltd, is working on exactly this. They build light-structure greenhouses that fit in warm arid climates. They have already a number of projects running in The Canary Islands, Oman, Abu Dhabi and Australia. According to them, the energy requirements to operate the greenhouses are modest, which makes the system very efficient.

Here is the description of their process as described on their website[33]:

> "The Seawater Greenhouse uses the sun, the sea and the atmosphere to produce fresh water and cool air. The process recreates the natural hydrological cycle within a controlled environment. The entire front wall of the building is a seawater evaporator. It consists of a honeycomb lattice and faces the prevailing wind. Fans assist and control air movement. Seawater trickles down over the lattice, cooling and humidifying the air passing through into the planting area.
>
> Sunlight is filtered through a specially constructed roof, the roof traps infrared heat, while allowing visible light through to promote photosynthesis. This creates optimum growing conditions - cool and humid with high light intensity.

---

[33] At www.seawatergreenhouse.com/theprocess.html

Cool air passes through the planting area and then combines with hot dry air from the roof cavity. The mixture passes through a second seawater evaporator creating hot saturated air, which then flows through a condenser. The condenser is cooled by incoming seawater. The temperature difference causes fresh water to condense out of the air stream. The volume of fresh water is determined by air temperature, relative humidity, solar radiation and the airflow rate. These conditions can be replicated in the thermodynamic model and, with appropriate meteorological information, the detailed design and performance of the Seawater Greenhouse can be optimized for every suitable location and environment."

The company is also involved in the "Sahara Forest Project"[34] that aims at developing a large-scale system for the production of freshwater, energy and food in arid regions. It combines the Seawater Greenhouse system with concentrated solar power (CSP) and extraction of nutrients from seawater. The facility will be powered with the CSP solar panels. Orchards will be planted along the greenhouses to create more humid microclimatic conditions.

Native drought-resistant plants, such as jatropha, an oil-bearing plant originally from South America, will be grown to produce biofuels and organic matter to enhance the soil fertility. The purpose of this project is to rebuild a fertile ecosystem where food can be grown again on tens of thousands of hectares. It is also worth mentioning that Bellona, a Norwegian environmental organization, is a partner in the project. This is an example of innovative and sustainable agricultural projects that can be created when businesses and not-for-profit organizations join forces.

---

[34] At www.saharaforestproject.com

Urban Farming

Since the beginning of urbanization, human settlements have developed around the bare necessities, which are water and fertile ground. Today's major urban centers have been growing from their original core, and they cover a lot of fertile land. One of the dilemmas for the future will be to accommodate the increasing concentration of population in cities and to keep arable land available.

Urban farming is not a minor activity. The United Nations estimates that it represents 15% to 20% of all the food produced in the world.

Inevitably, there will come a time when all apparent arable land will be in use for agricultural production, and there will be a need for more. A vast area of good agricultural land is inaccessible because it is located under cities and roads. The loss of arable land under cities is even more worrying as the world population will increasingly live in urban areas. For instance, China's agricultural land is shrinking by 1% a year because of urbanization. In the urban area of the Beijing-Tianjin-Hebei region in China, 74% of the new urban land came from the conversion of arable land between 1990 and 2000. In the USA, urban areas grew almost a million hectares between 1992 and 2003.

In a report published in 2000, the Brookings Institution mentions that 70 major cities in the USA averaged 15% vacant land area.

In the future, urban farming is going to be an increasingly relevant topic in the discussions of how to increase food production. There will be not just more people on the planet but the size of urban consumption markets will double by 2050.

A number of universities have added urban farming to their curriculum. For instance, Ryerson University from Toronto in Canada includes it as part of its work on food security. The University of Georgia in the USA now hosts the Georgia Center for Urban Agriculture in the Faculty of Agriculture. The Xavier University College of Agriculture in the Philippines now teaches and conducts research on the topic.

Although urban farming is getting more publicity, it is far from being a novelty. In the not so distant past, cities used to grow along with agriculture. There were farms in the cities to provide food for the local residents. Most cities still have a "Market Square" in the town center. This is reminiscent of the farmers markets and livestock markets that were held at least a couple of times a week. There were orchards and gardens, and in the early stages of industrialization, most fresh vegetables were still produced at the periphery of the cities. There used to be small gardens used by workers to grow their own vegetables, and many houses had a small garden for the same purpose. In the West, after World War II, the economy drew increasingly more people to manufacturing and services jobs and the agricultural population decreased to levels as low as 3% of total working population. At the same time, with the development of car traffic, most of these farming activities become about impossible to keep in the core of the town because access became more and more difficult. With the rise of the supermarkets, society evolved a bit further. Their buying power made them look beyond the city limits and procurement became international. The relevance of local farms tended to disappear. Cities and agriculture segregated into areas with little interaction. This contributes to the ignorance of city dwellers about food and farming. The rift was created, but in many developing nations, this process did not go as far or it took other forms. This has allowed farming to stay in cities. Usually, the reason is poverty.

According to the FAO, one-third of the world population lives in slums or informal settlements, where they have become highly dependent on affordable food supplies.

Food insecurity and potable water scarcity adds to poverty. Therefore, most urban farming projects have been the result of necessity.

An interesting example of development of urban farming can be found in Cuba. The country used to depend heavily on the Soviet Union for its food production and supply. Cuba used to receive subsidized oil, chemical fertilizers, pesticides and other farm products, in exchange for the sugar they produced. About half of Cuba's food was imported. After the collapse of the Soviet Union, the Cuban economy contracted by 35% between 1989 and 1993 and their foreign trade dropped by 75%. The toll on the population was high. The average daily calorie intake per capita fell from 2,900 in 1989 to 1,800 calories in 1995. During the same period, protein consumption dropped by 40%. The Cuban population had no other choice but to learn how to grow their own food. This was done though small private farms and thousands of tiny urban gardens. Because there were no chemicals or fertilizers available anymore, food production became organic. Previously, Cuba used more than one million tons of mineral fertilizers and up to 35,000 tons of herbicides and pesticides per year. The new economic situation created the emergence of thousands of new urban individual farmers who set up and developed cooperatives and farmers markets, under control of the government. These urban farmers found the support of the Cuban Ministry of Agriculture, who provided university experts to train volunteers in the use of organic pesticides and beneficial insects. Without the fertilizers, the old hydroponic units from the Soviet Union were no longer usable, until they were converted for organic gardening. The original hydroponic units were filled with composted sugar waste. "*Hydroponicos*" (hydroponics) became "*organopónicos*". In the early 1990s, the rapid expansion of urban farming was accomplished by putting abandoned land into production. In Havana, *organopónicos* were developed in vacant lots, old parking lots, abandoned building sites, and even between roads. Currently, more than 7,000 such farms produce about a million tons of food per year. The Cuban government, however, is omnipresent with about 200 government centers spread over the country.

The government provides the land, the water, the organic compost, the seeds and irrigation materials. The results have been impressive. In Havana, more than 200 gardens supply more than 90% of the fruit and vegetables the inhabitants need. Over the period from 1994 to 1999, the yields have increased from four to 24 kilograms per square meter. The city of Havana produces enough food for a daily serving of 280 grams (about 10 ounces) of fruits and vegetables per inhabitant. All garden crops such as beans, tomatoes, bananas, lettuce, okra, eggplant and taro are grown intensively within the city. Farmers use only organic techniques since these are the only methods permitted in the urban parts of Havana. Another positive side effect of urban farming is job creation. In the city of Havana, the urban agricultural workforce has increased from 9,000 in 1999 to more than 44,000 in 2006.

In the city of Shenzhen in China, urban farming is included in urban development. As part of an "open economic zone", this city has been growing rapidly from a village into a large urban center. The Chinese government supports urban food self-sufficiency programs. Because of new agricultural progress, Shenzhen's urban planning has been developed to include farming. Farms are located about 10 km away from the city center. One group of farms produces perishables such as lettuce, and a second group of farms, located a bit further away from the city core, produces other vegetables such as potatoes, carrots and onions.

In order to deal with water, waste recycling and soil fertility, local farmers have developed integrated productions systems such as the mulberry-dyke fishpond system. The mulberry tree is used to grow silkworms.

The waste of the silkworms is used to feed the fish held in ponds, and the fish are fed with waste from other farm animals. The ponds generate mud that is used to grow crops. The farm animals are fed with the crops produced with the mud. The fish and other animal proteins are eventually brought to market.

As economic growth and pollution are threatening some of the urban farms, the city of Shenzhen plans to invest large amounts of money in agricultural projects to preserve the typical Shenzhen characteristics and sustain the levels of urban farming. These projects cover various activities, such as a safe agricultural base, an agricultural high-tech park, agricultural processing and distribution, forestry, eco-agricultural tourism, as well as the expansion of the local produce wholesale market. By investing money in farms around the city, Shenzhen's goal is to have these farms provide 60% of the meat, vegetables and aquaculture products needed by the local population.

In Bangkok, 39% of the land is vacant. This creates a favorable situation for the development of urban farming. In 2000, the Thailand Environment Institute initiated a large project of urban gardens. The purpose goes beyond food production only. The project is aimed at reducing poverty, developing an urban green plan and educating the local communities about urban food production.

In Mumbai, India, Dr. Doshi has developed an urban food production project. The methods use simple tools and equipment, and are low cost. Food is produced on terraces and balconies. The purpose is to develop an organic farming system that provides food self-sufficiency for households. Dr. Doshi's concept uses the entire domestic household's waste and provides a daily quantity of 5 kg of fruit and vegetables, such as mangos, figs, guavas, bananas, and sugarcane for 300 days per year.

Although there are many urban farming projects in many cities in developing countries, this trend is not limited to these countries.

The City of New York supported a number of urban farming initiatives in low-income neighborhoods. The city also has a composting program available to gardeners and urban farmers.

The result has been positive and from a subsistence level of crops, a number of these farms have evolved into commercial operations that sell their surpluses to the local market for city residents. Similar projects have been developed in other US cities, including Philadelphia, West Oakland, Detroit, Chicago and Milwaukee.

Growing Power from Milwaukee demonstrates that urban farming goes far beyond the production of food. It has a social and educational function. It provides healthy food for people who have no access to the rather expensive organic foods found at specialized retailers. All that is available in the neighborhood are fast food restaurants. The closest grocery store is several miles away from the neighborhood where the Growing Power farm is situated. It is a practical vertical farm equipped with affordable material. In a greenhouse, they have combined several layers of vegetables in pots with the production of yellow perch in tanks. The system recycles the water from the fish using the fish waste as fertilizer. The compost pile is the only heat source for the greenhouse. Although this is not a high-tech farm, it serves its purpose quite efficiently. On this farm of 3 acres, they are able to produce one million pounds of food, an equivalent of 375 tons per hectare, which they sell in the farm store.

Further, urban farming can help rehabilitate a neighborhood. It can create a new use for abandoned old factories. It can recreate the fabric of a local community by involving and training the residents around one purpose. Neighborhoods with community gardens and green areas are more attractive to home buyers. The price of real estate in these neighborhoods is higher.

In Detroit, where the economic crisis and reduction of population over decades has left large stretches of land unattended inside the city limits, Hantz Farms, a subsidiary of the Hantz Group, founded by Detroit financier John Hantz, is working with the City and the State to acquire large acreage of abandoned land. The actual area to be farmed is still unknown, but the idea is to develop farming on a large scale. Hantz Farms plans to start small with a pilot project of 40 acres (16 hectares) and the lots will be allocated to specific crops.

Eventually, the farmed area could cover 5,000 acres (2,000 hectares). They take a futurist look at farming, though. Their business plan calls for the deployment of the latest in farm technology including hydroponic and aeroponic growing systems.

As demand for food increases, it will be useful to find ways of recovering or compensating for the lost arable land. In order to conserve arable land from further housing and infrastructure development, it will become necessary to think vertical. It could mean the end of the individual house, and the further development of multifamily dwelling as the typical home. Agricultural activities will likely develop in the cities themselves, by allocating some area for gardens, both at ground level and suspended on top of buildings, and farms will return to the cities. The vertical solution is to build farms and organize food production in a vertical layout. So far, infrastructure had chosen the easy, cheapest and most obvious solution, which was to lay cities and transport on the ground. An increased redevelopment of roads and transport lines on elevated structures, such as the bridges and the train lines, will take place. This can free a huge area of land for food production. Of course, it sounds like a costly solution, but food scarcity will make food prices skyrocket even more.

The idea of vertical farming is gaining popularity, which makes sense because of the limited ground area available to food production in cities. Rooftop gardens are also getting more attention, as the area of roofs covers up to 30% of urban centers. This is not a new idea. The hanging gardens of Babylon built around 600 BC had the same purpose.

In 2001, during a study project of New York rooftop gardens, a group of students from the Columbia University under supervision of Dickson Despommier received the assignment to study the possibilities of vertical farming. They developed a fascinating concept of a 30-storey building for the production of fruit, vegetables and even fish and chickens in highly robotized and climate-controlled facilities[35].

---

35 At www.verticalfarm.com

The building would cover the ground area of a city block. The ground floor is a supermarket where the food produced would be sold to the city residents. The farm would produce potable water through evaporation of sewage. Energy would be provided by solar panels, wind energy and from methane produced in the farm by plant and animal waste. Since all the food would be produced with hydroponics, the needs for fertilizers would be much lower than in open-field agriculture. Since all the production is indoors, the risks of diseases or pests would be reduced to almost zero. Further, since the climatic conditions are controlled, there is no fear of drought or flood. The old fear of weather conditions does not apply in the vertical farm. Such a building could provide food for 50,000 consumers year-round, according to the research group. In this farm, the crop yields per acre would be four to six times higher on average (even up to 30 for strawberries) than outdoor farming. Because such a farm is a closed system, there would be no runoffs from the farm, meaning that there would be no risk of contamination of soil or water by chemicals or minerals. Another advantage that the research group indicates is the simplified logistics. With such a structure, there is no storage space needed, and almost no transport involved from the farm to the consumer. Such a project is not cheap, though. They price the required investment at US$ 200 million for one vertical farm, which would mean US$ 4 billion for a city of one million residents. Of course, this concept is different from the more usual small-scale urban farm, but it has already gotten the interest of some investors in Abu Dhabi and in South Korea. The US cities of Seattle and Las Vegas are also considering such a project, but on a smaller scale.

The vertical farming approach is not about agriculture only. Architects are involved in developing new designs to make such projects feasible, from a construction point of view. Their approach also includes esthetic elements to blend vertical farms in the urban landscape. For example, the concept of "Massive Agricultural Urbanism"[36] presented by Greg Chung Whan Park is a vertical system of terraces laid out in curves to optimize the use of sunlight.

---

[36] Massive Agricultural Urbanism at www.yankodesign.com

Such a farm would produce soybeans, green beans, tomatoes, cucumbers, eggplants, lettuce, carrots, spinach and strawberries. Agriculture will become part of urban development.

The urban planning of the future will find more harmonious ways of organizing settlements, logistics and quality of life. Over the last few decades, much of urban development was organized around transportation and mobility. The current traffic nightmare that the inhabitants of most large cities experience is not sustainable. It causes severe air pollution and the hours spent in traffic jams as well as the delays they cause represent a high financial cost to the economy. In a couple of decades from now, there is little chance the Suburbia model with long commutes will still be considered. Remote working will have become usual and the economic activities will be located more harmoniously than they are today. Cities will integrate housing, business, transportation *and* agriculture, too.

As the economy, the demographics and the environmental issues are going to bring some deep transformations, the respective places of urban centers and of rural areas will change, too. Today, people look at urban farming mostly from the point of view of the necessity of feeding the urban poor, but it needs to be part of a larger picture. Activities such as agriculture, economic development in general and urban planning will be integrated and they will be closely linked. The economy will become more and more about strategically managing the planet, its resources and its space. Some areas will be developed around manufacturing, others around services, and others dedicated to agriculture and food. Cities will be developed to enable easy interaction between different purposes, be it residential or business. Transportation and logistics will be designed to allow an efficient flow of goods and persons.

Urban farming will become an integral part of the economic activity of the city. Energy and environmental concerns will stimulate the setup of an efficient supply chain with freshness, health, waste reduction, recycling and short distance to the consumers' markets as the main reasons to locate farms within the cities.

The transition between city and countryside will become more gradual than it is today. It will happen naturally, as cities will have to grow beyond their current borders and spread over rural areas.

In the mixing of urban and agriculture, one activity will require special care, though. As the risks of epidemics and of transmission of viruses between humans and farm animals exist and increase, local governments will need to set up appropriate measures to prevent diseases and their spreading. A high density of people, together with a high density of animals, could have catastrophic consequences.

Urban food production will also help create more and new jobs in cities. Many of the urban poor are the same people who left the countryside because of rural poverty and they did not find work in the cities, either. Considering the increasing density of population in cities, there is no successful future in further urbanization unless the problem of poverty is solved. By integrating the urban world with the necessity for agriculture, many new jobs can be created in the cities. These jobs will go beyond farming only. They will also include all direct and indirect activities in the supply chain, such as processing, packing, transportation, wholesale, distribution and retail.

Developing and Cultivating the Sea

Although some people still think the next frontier is outer space, there is a whole new world on Earth available for further economic development. Water scarcity and the increasing competition between animal feed and human consumption will limit the possibilities of increasing animal production on the land. This is why the prospects of developing protein production in the sea gains momentum and interest.

The oceans could be the additional Earths that are required to produce more food. About 70% of the planet is covered by water and most of that volume is left largely unexploited, with the exception of fisheries. Unfortunately, fisheries have done a poor job at managing their supply source and fish stocks have been dramatically depleted.

The only past timid colonization efforts are mostly limited to coastal regions. Yet, when reviewing all the economic possibilities of the oceans, it appears that there are opportunities to develop and to integrate a number of activities.

Tremendous energy potential is available in and over the oceans. They contain huge reserves of hydrogen. Of course, producing hydrogen will also require producing the necessary energy to split the water molecules. Using fossil fuel cannot be an option, as the gas emissions would defeat the purpose. The advantage is that the energy needed can be found in the oceans themselves.

Large wind farms located in the oceans or floating solar energy farms could be used to split water and produce hydrogen and oxygen.

The hydrogen could be used as fuel and the oxygen could be used to allow people involved in underwater activities and settlements to breathe. Further, more electricity can be produced by using the strong currents to run through turbines. In such a scenario, almost all energy requirements could come from clean emission-free electricity.

Access to clean drinking water is one of the biggest challenges facing humanity. Although there is plenty of water in the oceans, the main problem will be to make it drinkable. Using the sources of renewable energy just described, desalinating seawater would be a viable possibility.

On the land, the need for more and more acreage has caused deforestation, which is undermining the natural capacity to capture CO_2. It is time to consider replacing these lost trees by cultivating the oceans with large vegetal populations. It is possible to grow aquatic meadows and forests. Such a development is complex because ocean life is three-dimensional. Depth plays a significant role in marine ecosystems. Another area of attention when developing such vegetal populations is to make sure they do not get out of control and affect the oceans' ecology as many other species will interact with them, creating complete ecological systems and food chains.

By looking at aquaculture from its literal meaning, there should be possibilities to cultivate the water and develop it in a similar way as agriculture on the land. There are also lessons to be learned from the mistakes made in agriculture. The only way the current aquaculture production can survive in the long term is by producing, or cultivating the feed ingredients in the oceans as well. The current supply of raw materials for aquaculture feed has a limited future, as the need for fishmeal and fish oil will exceed by far the current production possibilities. Exhausting the wild stocks used to produce fish oil and fishmeal is not an acceptable option.

Further, replacing these foodstuffs by vegetal protein and oils from agricultural crops can work in the short term, but as demand for food and animal products increases, there will be too much competition for raw materials to serve both animal husbandry and aquaculture. Growing the feedstuff in the sea is a tremendous endeavor. Choosing which feedstuffs to produce in the sea, how to manage them, how to ensure the sustainability of the new aquaculture, and at the same time ensure that the marine ecosystems will recover and function properly as well is far from simple. It will require an aquaculture of plankton, of algae, of aquatic plants, of fish, of shellfish, of marine mammals and maybe more. So far, humans have depleted the food chains in the sea. Now is the time to restore them and increase the ocean-based food supplies.

Fish stocks have been depleted to unacceptable levels. It is the result of short-term thinking combined with highly efficient but damaging fishing methods. The damage is two-fold. It reduces the availability of a high value food source, and it endangers the sustainability of marine and terrestrial ecosystems. For instance, wild salmon contributes to the ecosystem of the temperate rainforest in the Pacific Northwest. Over there, salmon is an important food source for bears before they go into hibernation. After spawning, the salmon carcasses also produce organic matter used for the renewal of the forest. Although aquaculture claims to be the way to compensate for the lack of supply of wild fish, it is only true within limits. Some aquaculture species are fed with fishmeal and fish oil. Replacement of these feed ingredients is also limited by the quantities agricultural crops can supply, and consequently their price.

Researchers Boris Worm of Dalhousie University and Ray Hilborn of the University of Washington have studied the state of world fisheries and reviewed the possibilities to rebuild fisheries. Their conclusions are encouraging as they notice a number of regions where fisheries have recovered by applying a number of measures, such as California, New England, Iceland, New Zealand and Kenya.

In half of the ecosystems they studied, exploitation rates have declined. On the less positive side, they still note that the pressure on fisheries is in many cases too high. Sixty three percent of assessed fish stocks worldwide require rebuilding to reverse the collapse of vulnerable species. In an earlier, though contested report, Boris Worm had estimated that if nothing happened, all fisheries would collapse completely by 2048. Among the measures that help, they mention the reduction of catches, gear restrictions, catch shares, protected zones and community-based management.

Another recent report published in 2009 by the Pew Charitable Trusts reviewed the possibilities and the economic impact of rebuilding fisheries in the Mid-Atlantic Ocean for four species: summer flounder, black sea bass, bluefish and butterfish. They also reviewed what the downside of doing nothing would be. They then compared status quo management scenarios with scenarios where populations would have been rebuilt by 2007. Here are their conclusions[37]:

> "If the four species had been rebuilt by 2007, commercial landings would increase by 48 percent, resulting in an additional $33.6 million per year (in 2007 dollars) in direct economic benefits in perpetuity. In the recreational sector, rebuilding these four fish populations would increase landings by 24 percent more per year than status quo management, with an economic value of approximately $536 million per year (in 2007 dollars) in perpetuity.

> In sum, for both commercial and recreational fishing sectors, rebuilding populations of black sea bass, bluefish, butterfish and summer flounder by 2007 would have generated an additional $570 million per year in perpetuity in direct economic benefits. During a 5 year period, the accrued total would total $2.85 billion in economic benefit, a substantial contribution to the Mid-Atlantic economy and its coastal communities."

---

[37] The Pew Charitable Trusts, Investing In Our Future: The Economic Case for Rebuilding Mid-Atlantic Fish Populations. 23 July 2009

Although the situation is serious, such reports show that there is hope. Rebuilding wild fish stocks requires the will and the organization to make it happen. All parties involved, from whichever country concerned, will have to act in a coordinated manner. A report presented in early 2010 by IFM-GEOMAR (Leibniz Institute of Marine Sciences) and by the University of Kiel indicates that the objectives of the European Union to restore their fisheries by 2015 will not be met. They actually estimate that it will take at least another 30 years to achieve this goal.

Governments will set up programs to rebuild wild fish stocks to bring volumes back to sustainable levels. Proper fishing methods and quotas will help provide more secure supplies. Such programs will have to be drastic and negotiations will be tough, because the fishing industry is at overcapacity and some of the equipment used is no longer acceptable. There will be an increasing number of protected species. There will be quotas on allowed commercial species. Some fisheries will close down while others will have to reduce their fleet substantially. Until fisheries are rebuilt, the sector will go through difficult times and deep restructuring. Many jobs in the fisheries will be lost and they will not return. This is a harsh but true fact. The choice will be between having fewer fishermen and lower catches versus business as usual for a while and then have eventually no fishermen and no catches left at all. Dealing with this situation will require some sort of a stimulus plan for seafood with all stakeholders involved, such as government, fishermen, aquaculture industry, retailers, food service and consumers.

Fisheries and aquaculture will evolve towards ecosystem-based management, in the same way as land-based agriculture will. It will happen through further marine zoning and planning with the distinction between economic zones, protected sanctuaries and recreational areas. They all will be dedicated to specific activities that will ensure an efficient exploitation and the long-term sustainability of the oceans. The demand for seafood is strong, but because wild fish are scarce, they are expensive. Aquaculture is unlikely to be able to fill the gap of demand for seafood in the near future, but it has the long-term potential to fill the huge gap left by depleted wild fish stocks.

In the aquaculture sector, efficient low-cost species such as tilapia and pangasius have a good future ahead. They grow fast and their cost of production is low. They can help feed a large population for an affordable price. However, aquaculture will have to solve some environmental issues of its own to be successful. Growing a carnivore species such as salmon will also meet its own limitations. Although, salmon feed has shifted from mostly fish oil and fishmeal to a much more complex and more price competitive mix of vegetal oils, farmed salmon production will see its production costs increase, as agriculture will have difficulties meeting the demand for vegetal oil, too. Salmon cannot remain a commodity. It will become a luxury product again.

In 2009, a group of researchers from the CSIC (Consejo Superior de Investigaciones Científicas, the Spanish High Council for Scientific Research) published a report on the potential for marine aquaculture. This report presents how marine aquaculture could be the most efficient way to meet the demand for animal protein in the future. The authors of the report do not see fisheries as a significant option anymore. The time needed to replenish the stocks will be too long for fisheries to be able to meet the needs of the population. They are much more optimistic about aquaculture. In the last three decades, aquaculture has grown rapidly. In the 1970s, it accounted for about 6% of fish available for human consumption. It has now represents more than half. The rate of growth of aquaculture production volume has started to slow, though. This is normal considering the recent growth rate. Aquaculture is expanding in all regions, but Asia is the uncontested leader with 87% of global production volumes. It is the fastest growing food supply activity and the projections for future growth are optimistic.

Land-based farm animals are large consumers of grains, legumes, oilseeds, animal protein and water. This limits seriously the possibility of growth for meat and other terrestrial animal products.

The Spanish researchers think marine aquaculture could multiply its production by a factor of 20 by 2050. Aquaculture would play a major role in providing the world population with animal protein.

Another point raised by this group is the nitrogen efficiency in animal production. According to their sources, it is slightly more than 10% for land animals with variation between species. The nitrogen efficiency of beef is low with only 5%, while pork does better with 15%. The low nitrogen efficiency means that these land animals release a major amount of nitrogen in the environment. In contrast, marine animals have much greater nitrogen use efficiency, with numbers reaching about 20% for shrimp and 30% for fish. Marine aquaculture culture releases two to three times less nitrogen in the environment than livestock production does.

Output of aquaculture is another advantage compared with land-based animal husbandry. A 2009 report from the Brazilian Ministry of Fisheries and Aquaculture indicated that in the Amazon region, aquaculture is now more profitable than livestock production. In particular, the farming of Black Pacu, an indigenous species that can grow to 25 kg, reaches amazing yields. In net tanks, this species produces 120 tons per hectare, which is 400 times higher than the yield obtained with livestock, and the profit per hectare was 300 times higher.

From a nutritional point of view, replacing meat and dairy by seafood rich in healthy components such as omega-3 fatty acids is attractive. From an environmental point of view, the idea of shifting the production of animal protein from the land where it uses scarce resources to the ocean where space and water are not limitations makes sense. Freshwater aquaculture represents 57% of total aquaculture, but it faces similar limitations as land-based animals because of water scarcity. The limited access to water creates the worst constraints on freshwater aquaculture in tropical and sub-tropical regions because of the population growth. Northern temperate regions still have growth potential, as they do not face the same pressure on water demand.

There is an untapped potential with marine aquaculture because it does not use fresh water. The FAO estimates the overall growth potential for marine aquaculture at 7.5% per year, as well as an increase of the number of species produced.

The main challenge to execute such a development of marine aquaculture production is to find the proper quality and quantity of feed. The researchers do not see the use of fishmeal and fish oil as an option anymore. They predict that the species used to make these products will not be available in sufficient quantities anymore. According to the FAO, marine aquaculture could exhausts all fish feed sources by 2040. More alternative feed sources are necessary. Replacement by protein and oils from agriculture crops is an option for the short term, but as aquaculture volumes would increase, the competition for these ingredients with meat production will make them too expensive, and for the reasons explained above, depending on land agriculture to feed marine species will face crop production limitations.

Aquaculture could provide economic development for emerging countries in Latin America, Asia and Africa.

Peru could have a booming food sector in the years to come. The coastal region offers good potential for the production of seafood. The main asset of the country when it comes to food production is the sea. Peruvian fisheries have experienced some difficult times in the past, but they have been able to restore the anchovy's fisheries rather rapidly. Peru produces a lot of the raw materials necessary to develop marine fish farming. They can learn from the experience of their neighbors Chile and Ecuador about this industry, and especially about how to prevent pushing it to the limits and creating major disease problems. The Peruvian government released in the beginning of 2010 the National Aquaculture Development Plan for 2010-2015. The plan aims to increase private investment in the sector by 50% to increase production, domestic consumption and export of aquaculture products.

The Aquaculture Network of the Americas was created in March 2010 after 34 years of discussions. The organization will encourage intergovernmental cooperation to develop a sustainable aquaculture, increase food security and reduce poverty.

The FAO will provide technical support and funding will come from the member countries. The nations participating in this network are Brazil, Uruguay, Paraguay, Argentina, Bolivia, Colombia, Ecuador, Peru, French Guyana, Panama, Costa Rica, El Salvador, Guatemala, Belize, Cuba, Trinidad and Tobago, Dominican Republic, Mexico, Haiti, and Canada.

The sea will be a major element in the future of South East Asia's food production. Thailand and Vietnam are already large players in aquaculture, and other countries will join. The Philippines and Indonesia have ideal conditions to cultivate the sea, due to the climate and their geography. The Philippines have more than 7,000 islands and Indonesia has more than 15,000 with a total coastline of 90,000 km (this is more than twice the Earth's circumference at the Equator). Indonesia, with a marine area four times the size of its land area, has already expressed its objective of becoming the world's largest producer of seafood by 2015. The region's fisheries have been already seriously damaged because of overfishing, but aquaculture, including the production of algae, shows potential. The South Eastern Asian aquaculture sector will undergo dramatic changes, though. The sector is fragmented with many small family-run operations. The organization of value chains needs to be improved to ensure the viability of aquaculture farms because the farmers do not generate much cash. Their suppliers as well as the buyers have a stronger bargaining position. The restructuring will probably happen because of farmers failing. It is likely that seafood processors will take over and expand the farming operations.

Kenya offers a nice illustration of the potential aquaculture can offer the regional economy. The Ministry of Fisheries Development has carried out a survey and the preliminary results show an enormous potential for fish farming in Kenya. The government is supporting financially the construction of fishponds. In order to increase fish production, 140 constituencies have received government money for the construction of 200 fishponds per constituency. According to the Minister, if the potential is fully exploited, fish production could be increased to 11 million tons per year.

Such a production level would represent about US$ 10 billion in earnings. In 2008, the total production was only of 4,220 metric tons. Such an explosive growth will create many jobs for fish farmers, feed manufacturers, fish processors and traders. The development of aquaculture in Kenya would also ease conflicts in Lake Victoria between Kenyan fishermen and Ugandan authorities. This is a welcome side effect.

Developing the future of aquaculture is not just a matter of growing fish in pens. It requires broader thinking that includes not only the oceans but agriculture on land, too.

Aquaculture is a young industry. High demand for seafood has been the engine of the strong growth that now raises a number of concerns about its sustainability. Fish farming has adopted similar intensive systems as land-based animal husbandry. Therefore, aquaculture faces similar challenges and criticism as livestock production.

There are many lessons to be learned by the modern intensive aquaculture industry from livestock production. Most companies involved in this sector have been inspired mainly by the evolution, and the success, of the chicken industry. Fish farms have high densities of animals. Even if the surface at the sea level is rather limited, each farm goes deep. The biomass they contain would make many chicken farms actually look like small operations. Moreover, they are very exposed to the natural environment, as the pens are open nets. Farmed fish is sensitive to disease and disease spreading. The problems of white spot disease, which have plagued the shrimp farming industry in Ecuador and Central America in the late 1990s, or the ISA crisis that hit Chilean salmon farmers in 2009 just shows how sensitive and vulnerable aquaculture farms can be.

Aquaculture will be confronted with situations as bad as swine fever or avian flu. Producers and lawmakers will have to reconsider the level of intensification and the location of farming sites, including rotation of sites with fallowing periods as a standard procedure. Further, navigation rules will be tightened to reduce the possibility of cross-contamination from one marine zone to another.

The experience and knowledge that has been gathered in land-based animal production can be useful for aquaculture to be able to be competitive and to offer the proper quality to consumers. Like the more mature agricultural productions, aquaculture must adopt a market-driven approach, even though the markets are eager for seafood. As part as the food industry, seafood farmers must realize that consumers have similar expectations for their products as they do for other animal products. They want a consistent quality that meets their expectations, predictable supplies and safe food.

Marketing and processing of seafood have definitely improved, but farming is still struggling with natural conditions affecting growth and mortality numbers. One area of aquaculture still in its infancy is genetics. For many species, farmers still depend on brood stock collected from wild fish. The lack of structured genetic selection programs and the lack of large enough gene pools are potential threats to the future of some productions. An example is the production of tilapia in the Pacific region, where the stock used by farmers originates from Mozambique tilapia introduced some 60 years ago. That line has lost so much of its genetic variation that genetic improvement programs do not work anymore.

The industry will also sharpen its veterinary procedures further and increase its control on prevention and on medication. Aquaculture companies will develop new systems to prevent feces from entering the ecosystem. Currently, it is flushed into the ocean. This is a controversial practice because undesirable substances may enter the water. Considering the number of fish held on farms and their densities, the volume of feces produced can reach substantial levels. There will come a time when it will not be allowed anymore. Fish farms will have to be equipped with feces collection systems and they will have to find a use for the "manure".

In order to address the environmental risks, a number of systems have been tested or are being tested as possible alternatives. From a technical point of view, land-based farming in close containment is the safest way to avoid any interaction between the farm population and the sea. However, such a system requires land and it requires a high investment that, so far, does not seem financially viable.

Other floating large close containment bags are also available, but they do not seem to be competitive from a cost point of view, yet. AgriMarine Industries, from Canada, is working on developing floating closed containment systems for fish farming. These cages would have a supply for oxygen, a recirculation system for water and a fish waste collection system. The purpose of this design is to be able to farm on the sea instead of on the land. In this system, there is no interaction between the farmed fish and the marine wildlife. Another advantage is that there is no requirement to purchase or lease land and build expensive facilities. The system is now on trial in China and a project is underway in British Columbia, where the company is based.

Another approach being investigated is IMTA, or Integrated Multi-Trophic Aquaculture. It consists in re-creating a local ecosystem around the farms by growing other marine species near the pens. A combination of farmed salmon with mussels, scallops, sea urchins and sea cucumbers is under review in the Bay of Fundy, New Brunswick, Canada. Shellfish are grown to use organic matter and seaweed species will use inorganic wastes, such as nitrogen.

For shrimp production, a research project on a new land-based system has started at the AgriLife Research Mariculture Laboratory in Texas. The system has a water recirculation, or zero water exchange system. There is no release of feces or potential pollutants into the environment and there is no risk of bringing pathogens to the farm, unlike the current farming systems. This presents large benefits from an environmental and from a health point of view. The results also show excellent production results, with yields about 10 times higher than those of the current open pond systems used in the USA. Considering the price of feed and its share in the production cost of farmed fish, farmers will need to develop genetic programs to improve the feed conversion ratio, in addition to growth and flesh quality. The feed industry has been diversifying it sources of raw materials for some time to cope with the rising price of fish oil and fishmeal, which is the result of higher demand from the fast growing aquaculture sector. They carry out research to find the right profiles of oil to meet the fish flesh quality requirements, especially the omega-3 content, by using vegetal oil.

This is not a sustainable approach for the long term. There will be a completely new industry to produce "farmed" fish oil and fishmeal to meet the feed industry needs. A new approach to aquaculture feeds will see the development of a feed value chain based on aquatic ingredients, such as plankton, algae and seaweed. However, the timelines for completion are unknown for this very new area.

As Jacques Cousteau once said, "We must plant the sea and herd its animals. Using the sea as farmers instead of hunters. That is what civilization is all about - farming replacing hunting. "[38] Human consumption and aquaculture have started the movement. Both the pharmaceutical and the biofuels industries are seeing potential in this sector, too.

Another possible source of food in the future could be algae and seaweed. The typical Asian diet consists of as much as 20% algae. A country active in the farming of seaweed is Indonesia, where three species of seaweed are cultivated for food, feed and biofuels. The Indonesian production was 910,000 tons in 2005 and estimates for 2010 are of 1.9 million tons. Seaweed is an affordable production that delivers good profit to the farmers. According to the Indonesian Minister of Maritime Affairs and Fisheries, it costs only US$200 per hectare to produce seaweed, but due to its fast growth, the seaweed can be harvested up to 10 times per year. The profit per harvest is about US$500. One or two families can cultivate one hectare of seaweed.

Brazil is investigating the farming of algae, too. A company in the State of Ceara, in the northeast of the country, is planning to plant several farms with algae originating from The Philippines.

In order to exploit this potential and meet future demand for human food, animal feed or biofuels, it will be necessary to increase production of all algae species that have benefits for humans. China is one of the countries boosting production and the farming area now expands offshore as well.

---

[38] In an interview on 17 July 1971

In the field of nutrition and pharmaceuticals, a micro alga[39] has a high content of lutein, which is an antioxidant, also present in egg yolks, with great commercial possibilities. When added to foods, lutein can help slow down the degeneration of eyesight or the appearance of cataract.

Spirulina, an alga from Lake Chad in Africa, is now being exploited. The algae contain 70% protein, which is about five times as much as meat and it is rich in vitamin A and B12. The market pays a high price for Spirulina. Local harvesters, mostly poor villagers, make a good income from Spirulina, but they are harvesting the algae at too high a rate to keep this production sustainable.

There are many trials to produce biofuels from algae. So far, the cost of production does not make them an attractive alternative, in spite of their amazing productivity, up to 20 times higher than agricultural crops. As progress is made, current cost forecasts for a barrel of algal oil are more optimistic, with estimates as low as US$20. The productivity of algae is simply amazing and oil yields could be as 250 times as high per hectare as they are for soybean oil. Growing algae is also water efficient and producing biofuels from algae would help reallocate water for food production on the land. Once the oil is removed, the by-products are still of high nutritional value and can be used for animal feed.

Unfortunately, a recent study from the University of Virginia reached the conclusion that producing biofuels from algae consumes more energy and has higher emission of greenhouse gases than other sources of biofuels. The challenge goes on. Science and technology will find ways of growing and producing food and fuel efficiently from algae.

As the young aquaculture industry matures, it will evolve in similar directions and develop similar growth strategies as the ones in agricultural productions.

---

[39] The micro alga's Latin name is *Scenedesmus almerienses*

Fish farmers will need to develop more farming areas. They will go further away from the areas that have already been developed. In regions where aquaculture is in its infancy, the industry will receive incentives to develop and grow. It will gradually become integrated in other value chains, especially because fish can use, consume and produce by-products from and for other food productions, such as in aquaponics or the example of the mulberry tree–fish ponds combination.

Developing aquaculture will lead to the integration of marine aquaculture into the overall ecosystem management. The current tensions between fisheries and aquaculture will slowly disappear, as fisheries will undergo changes and restructuring. Aquaculture will offer job opportunities to seafood professionals. It will become an active player in rebuilding fisheries, by offering services in the areas of breeding and multiplication of fish stocks to be released in the sea. This is already the case in Alaska. In 2009, 19% of all salmon catches had been raised and fed in hatcheries before being released into the ocean. This practice increases the sustainability of the fisheries and secures employment in the local communities.

Another development to expect is offshore aquaculture. Aquaculture operations located in coastal areas, although they are easier to access and generally situated in quieter waters, are often located in zones where there are local issues to deal with, such as interaction with wild fish or recreational activities.

Moving offshore can reduce these problems. A number of projects are already in the works, such as Open Blue Sea Farms, a producer of cobia in Panama. Cobia is a rather new aquaculture species. This fish can reach a body weight of 6 kg in one year. The company uses the Aquapod system developed by MIT together with Ocean Farm Technologies, a company based in the state of Maine in the USA. The huge cages will have the ability to move and change location, using solar energy. Having the ability to change locations has several advantages. It allows moving to areas where water quality is better because it varies with seasons and climate conditions.

It also can allow farms to move away from the routes of wild fish and substantially reduce risks of disease and parasite contamination and spreading. Having the ability to move closer to markets also has the advantage of reducing the time to transport time the fish to market, and therefore offer a fresher product. Another innovative fish containment system is the Oceansphere developed by Hawaii Oceanic Technology Inc. It consists of large deep-water aluminum and Kevlar spheres that can contain up to 24,000 tons of fish. Offshore fish farming is getting more and more attention as the next step for aquaculture. The US government has now approved the development of offshore farming in the Gulf of Mexico. In Chile, a deepwater salmon farming project is now under development by Acuicola Tripanko, backed by a group of Norwegian banks. This project aims at offering a solution to the kind of problems the Chilean industry faced with the ISA crisis. Going offshore brings some organizational difficulties, such as rotating the crews working on farms, dealing with rough weather, organizing feed deliveries and ensuring proper maintenance, at an acceptable cost, of the equipment.

Before going offshore in such high-tech projects, many countries will first develop their own aquaculture industry with small farmers as the cornerstone of the system. This is part of agricultural development and it should help many communities to create activity and grow the economy at the local level.

If going offshore is a trend for the future, the opposite trend to eliminate interactions between farmed fish and the environment will happen, too. It can happen by using close containment systems, aquaponics and recirculation systems, or by creating artificial isolated ecosystems under complete supervision and management of the farmers. Such systems are new and they need to be developed further. Aquaponics is among the most promising techniques, especially with fast-growing species. It uses relatively little water, does not reject any contaminant in the environment and can be put in place inside cities, near the consumer markets. Moreover, high growth species allow high yields on a limited farm area, which means a faster payback time on the initial investment.

CONCLUSION

Can We Feed Nine Billion People?

Towards a maintenance society

We are living in a period of transition. The economic crisis of the last couple of years is the consequence of an unsustainable financial model. The economy will now follow a different course than it did over the last 60 years. The shift in economic power, the demographics and a different set of values will create new conditions, challenges and opportunities.

The consumption society that has brought so much comfort in developed countries is ending. The economic crisis has been the result of an imbalanced economy. Consumption goods, their parts and their packaging are stacking up in landfills. The frenzy of industrialization has caused pollution and degradation of the environment. The obsession of more profit and greed has moved factories around the planet. As manufacturing moved to developing countries, the environmental impact in developed nations disappeared locally, but it has caused great damage in emerging nations. Globalization has actually exported pollution. Easy credit and the excessive use of home equity, which has only a virtual value has been used to pursue always more growth. Marketing has done its share and it has convinced consumers they needed more and that they had to have it now. Stock markets are not about long-term investing anymore, but about fast trading on news as they come. People wanted too much too fast. Even if the word credit comes from the Latin for "believe", the economy does not function on wishful thinking and delusion forever.

If the consumption society is dying, another model will replace it. The stimulus plans developed by most countries focus on infrastructure. Everywhere in the world, there is a need for the expansion and the maintenance of energy infrastructure and of transportation infrastructure. It will happen with government money, but it will involve businesses as well. There is also a huge need of stimulus money for agricultural infrastructure and financing, although this sector seems to have been somewhat neglected. The next society will be a maintenance society.

The increasing economic weight of NGOs is a sign. The economy will focus more on keeping the house in order. This kind of activity will be at least as important as consumption and retail. Agriculture and food will play a major role in that area. There will be more so-called green jobs created in the future.

The era of excess is over. Of course, a percentage of the population will still overindulge, but it will become less common. The era of cheap goods is over, too. Resources are already depleted and there are more people to come on Earth. This evolution will make saving and recycling essential. Maintenance is the future and many jobs lost during the years of recklessly throwing away will reappear in some form. A maintenance society also means a responsible society. Responsibility will become a central value that political and business leaders will have to embrace. The areas of accountability will shift and performance contracts will include more diversified objectives.

In the maintenance society, agriculture will participate in preservation. This description is reminiscent of the farms at the beginning of the 20th century. However, the efficiency of production as well as the efficiency of preserving the environment will be much higher, due to new technologies. The new market situation will lead to an agriculture with high yields, with highly efficient systems to use water, to recycle waste, to preserve the fertility of soils, and to protect ecosystems on the land and in the oceans.

The balance between supply and demand will be fragile and many inputs will become scarce. There is no alternative to being efficient. Learning the lessons from the past will help avoid repeating the same mistakes again.

The need for efficiency and sustainability will require going back to the basics. The world will have to manage the economy, and agriculture in particular, by focusing on the three fundamental elements that land, labor and capital are. In this case, the land includes the sea and the fresh water as well. Allocating labor will bring businesses to rethink the workforce not only in numbers, but also in jobs and salaries. The labor situation varies widely between countries, but it will also evolve in the years to come.

Different local models that will help optimize food production are possible. The need for money will be critical as usual, but it must not be reduced to investments. Training the farmers of tomorrow is an essential component of this investment. Funding will be essential for developing agriculture and the critical infrastructure such as education, health services, roads, railways, waterways and proper storage.

The purpose in the coming years and decades will be to avoid waste, be it of food, of water, of land, of soil, of energy, of organic matter or any other input necessary for production. Efficiency will be about food production per hectare in a sustainable manner in order to be able to produce indefinitely. It will have a major impact on which production will be developed and where. For instance, in regions with physical water scarcity problem, animal productions or crops that consume a lot of water will be affected negatively. Similarly, the competition for crops between human consumption, animal feed and biofuels will inevitably change the economics of food, feed and energy. The resulting price increase will have a different magnitude between the crops and their use. Diets will become more balanced and excesses will not be affordable anymore. Consumers will redistribute their food budget accordingly to the new market situation.

Next to working on improving further efficiency of production, there will be more programs to reduce food losses in the supply chain from farm to consumer. They will include action in the areas of logistics, storage, processing, retail, food service and recycling. This will determine how far from market food will be produced, processed, packed and preserved. It also will influence how commercial relationships will evolve between producers and retailers. Governments will also play their role by introducing new legislation as well as new taxes.

The next agricultural revolution

The world is changing rapidly, and it will keep doing so. By 2050, the economic, environmental and demographic conditions will look quite different.

The next agricultural revolution to feed nine billion people will be different from the previous one. After World War II, agriculture advanced because of petroleum and chemistry. This time, biology and renewable energies will lead progress. It will not be just a revolution in science and technology. It also will be a different way to think about the economy and the environment. Knowledge and communication will become increasingly important, even more so than today.

Agriculture is a life science. Biological solutions will gradually replace chemical applications. All sorts of organisms will be involved to improve the way farmers and the food industry will produce. After having thought big for decades, the future will involve the very small.

Bacteria and viruses will help fight pests and diseases. They will help reduce the use of chemical herbicides and pesticides dramatically. Genetic engineering will evolve and, as a business, it will mature. DNA science will focus on eliminating flaws and on increasing the metabolic efficiency of living organisms. Genetic engineering cannot continue to be about intellectual property and patents. Soon, seed companies all over the world will know how to do the same. Competition and market forces will determine which model will survive. Governments will not allow a select few to control food. They will get involved in genetic engineering programs and they will break monopolies. Genetic improvement will become collective property again.

Ecology will be a part of food production. Agriculture will manage ecosystems, and economy will become the management of the planet. Living organisms on land and in water will assist food production.

Farmers will think in terms of systems and cycles. Instead of isolating the field, they will integrate environmental parameters as well.

Organic matter will become central in the future agriculture. Farmers will recreate the cycles to improve the structure of the soil and its fertility. Agriculture will aid in fixing carbon. The use of mineral fertilizers will decrease sharply. Composting will become a key element of agriculture again.

The economics of agriculture will be different, because the economics of energy will be different. With oil resources shrinking and oil prices increasing, new technologies will dominate. Solar power and wind energy will become common sources of energy. The economics of water will change, too. The management of water will reshape food production. Water will become substantially more expensive and only systems that save and preserve water will survive.

Information technology will help make decisions faster than ever before. Portable computers will give the farmer the ability to get data almost instantly about the status of the crops, markets, health status and conditions of production. It will allow them to optimize inputs and outputs better and faster. It will save time, inputs and money. Knowledge and information will be the best tool to act efficiently and to improve food production.

Transparency will become the rule. There will be no secret because consumers will be better informed and because there will be nothing left to hide.

Agriculture will regain its place in the economy as the most important activity. A change in the attitude towards funding and investments will also be part of the revolution. More players will engage in agriculture because returns will be higher for all. To achieve food security, the world will need farmers. In most discussions about the future of agriculture, one question seems to be left aside, although it is a very important one: who will be the farmers of the future?

As mentioned before, the forecast of nine billion people on Earth by 2050, of which 70% living in cities, means a decrease of the rural population by about 25% from the current numbers. A consequence of this will be fewer farmers in the future. Who will they be and where will they be?

A lot of the good agricultural land is in the northern hemisphere in areas where the population numbers are stagnating. These are regions where the average age of the population is increasing from an already rather high level of about 50% of the population older than 37. The average age of farmers in the USA is 58. The European Union shows a similar picture, with 34% of farmers being 65 or older, while only 6% of EU farmers are younger than 35. In Japan, young people do not show interest to become farmers. The Japanese are working on developing robots that would do the farmers work.

With an aging population and a low percentage of the active population being in farming, the northern hemisphere will face some difficulty in replacing the existing farmers when they retire. Further, farmland has become attractive to investors, and land prices are increasing strongly. One can wonder whether young farmers will be able to afford to buy farms in the future. This could lead to a situation where the people working the land no longer own the land.

It could have an effect on how to structure agriculture in the future, because if labor becomes scarcer, agriculture will have to require even more capital and mechanization than today. The countries of the northern hemisphere already have large commercial farming structures.

Unless they can find many new farmers, the concentration trend will continue. There will be fewer and larger farms than today. A new type of farmer will appear in urban centers. Many future farmers will come from cities. They will run small operations and produce locally, either in rural areas or in cities.

The surge in urban population will happen mostly in Africa, Asia and Arab countries. In many of these countries, the agricultural infrastructure is fragmented and farms are small. There is a need to rationalize and modernize production to increase yields. This is necessary to feed a population with little possibilities to grow food where they live. Although urban farming will develop in these regions, too, this means a revolution of how agriculture will have to be organized and structured. Asia and South America have already engaged in such a process for a few decades. Different countries will face different challenges, mostly about access to water and about ensuring the sustainability of their environment. In developing countries, there will be a consolidation of farms, too. Subsistence farming does not produce enough food efficiently enough. The speed of the consolidation process will depend on how fast the economies of these countries will grow. This will require a lot of capital that many farmers alone cannot afford, especially considering how their income situation usually is. More capital will come from large corporations, investors and governments.

The revolution will not just be for farmers and the other players in agriculture to carry out, but consumers will have their share to deliver. A change in mentalities is necessary. Wasting food is not acceptable. Selfishness will not work anymore. Food security is not a given, it is a work in progress.

Making it happen with pragmatic visionary leaders

There are enough resources to boost food production to the desired levels. There is also enough capital in the world to make it work. The sums of money made available to banks, carmakers and the other stimulus programs following the Great Recession of 2008 prove it. To save the world economy, governments found trillions of dollars as if they were growing on trees. Maybe the way to get the money flow into agriculture is for the wealthy to become hungry, too. The future will tell if this will be the case.

The most needed resource in order to cope with the food production of the coming decades is strong, visionary, pragmatic leadership. Mentioning that agriculture production needs to grow by 70% by 2050 does not go far enough. The world needs to develop a plan that goes beyond the rhetoric from politicians and international organizations.

The plan needs to detail how much of what productions are needed to feed the world. The plan must go beyond global numbers and investigate what the world's needs for rice, wheat, corn, beans, cotton, chickens, fish, etc... will be. It will require processing the demographic forecasts by including the eating and cultural habits. Then it becomes possible to develop the production plan to meet the demand. Such a plan is not only global, but it has to be broken down to local levels such as regions, countries, provinces, cities and villages. This is the market-driven approach the world needs to execute the plan by going back into the food production chain to farm level.

The plan must follow the SMART approach. It has to be Specific and detailed per production. It has to be Measurable, in order to be able to monitor progress and respond appropriately to stay on target. Further, it must be Ambitious. The best of all objectives is to feed all human beings a balanced diet. However, the plan needs to be Realistic in order to gain acceptance and support from the ones who will have to execute it. Last but not least, it will have to have Timelines, as farmers will need to know when to deliver what is expected from them.

A market-driven agriculture is much more efficient than a production-driven one, but efficiency is required at all levels. An important part for the success of such a global plan is in the allocation of the productions where they are the most efficient to grow. This is not necessarily the same as being the cheapest to grow in the short term. This time, it is necessary to consider the externalities in the production cost.

The most critical part of the next agricultural revolution is leadership. Having a responsible long-term vision is critical, but it will not be enough. The world will need leaders who will make the right things happen. In all sectors of the society, there will be a need for such leaders who can muster the energies and who make the general interest and the long term come first. The need for food security will alter governance systems, in government and in business ethics. A challenge will be to manage greed and fear. First, there will be greed. Then, there will be fear. Until this day, humans have done a poor job of feeding the world. Famines have come and have gone and there still are hungry people. Humans have done a poor job at preserving their environment, too. With nine billion people, such a poor performance will have much heavier consequences than with six billion. Procrastination and sloppiness are attitudes the world cannot afford anymore. The proper leadership will come, but the change will not take place easily. There will be a major crisis first.

The road to feeding nine billion people will not be easy. Many dangers are lurking. Of course, natural conditions will keep playing a role. Natural catastrophes are always a risk and climatic events, diseases or pests can disrupt food supplies. The structure and the regulations of financial markets and especially of agricultural commodities are very important. If countries fail to set the right policies, the actions of a few speculators can have as dramatic consequences as a swarm of locusts. Actually, the human factor has the most influence on what will happen. This is the worst danger, too. Humanity's attitude will determine its fate.

We must fear complacency, for it leads to inaction. There is a lot of work to do to succeed and every minute lost will have a cost eventually. We must fear partisanship and lobbyism, because they both work for only half of the world at best. They contribute to make the issues more opaque and delay change, while what is needed is flexibility, even agility, and transparency.

With all the science and knowledge available, it is possible to feed nine billion people in the coming decades. To improve infrastructure and train the farmers, it would take less than the amount spent on bailing out the banks. There is a huge potential to reduce food losses and increase food security. Many regions produce under their potential. Just imagine how much food Africa could produce by increasing production yields to the current world average. It is possible to increase the yields in almost all countries. People in rich countries can change their diet and free incredible quantities of food. If it does not happen voluntarily, market forces will make it happen. The future higher food prices will result in consumption that is more responsible. The answer to "Can we feed nine billion people by 2050?" is "Yes!" Technically, it can be done much earlier than 2050. SIMPLE and SMART will go a long way.

Will we feed nine billion people by 2050? That is a different question! It will all depend on everyone's attitude. Making it happen will require effort from all.

APPENDICES

Appendix 1: World population distribution per continent (Source: United Nations)

A major shift is happening in the location of the world population. North America and Europe will represent a smaller part of the population, while the percentage of Asia and Latin America will remain stable. Africa is the continent where the next baby boom will take place. Managing food and agriculture in Africa is crucial for the future.

Distribution of the world population among continents

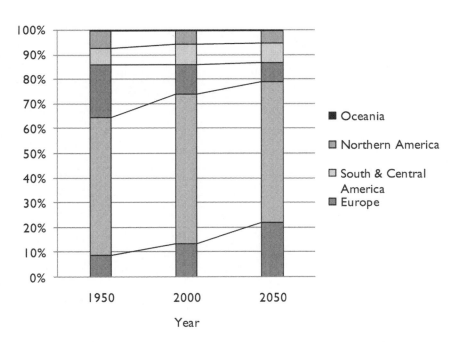

Appendix 2: Concentration of the world's population

The 16 most populated countries account for two-thirds of the world population. Most people are not aware which countries are on this list. Considering the economic and political situation of a number of the countries belonging to this group, there are reasons to worry about future stability. The median age of these countries is also an indicator of possible unrest.

Country	Population	% of world population	Median age
China	1,337,320,000	19.6	34.1
India	1,180,220,000	17.3	25.3
USA	309,199,000	4.5	36.7
Indonesia	231,369,500	3.4	27.6
Brazil	192,860,000	2.8	28.6
Pakistan	169,410,000	2.5	20.8
Bangladesh	162,221,000	2.4	23.3
Nigeria	154,729,000	2.3	19.0
Russia	141,927,297	2.1	38.4
Japan	127,530,000	1.9	44.2
Mexico	107,550,697	1.6	26.3
Philippines	92,226,600	1.4	22.5
Vietnam	85,789,573	1.3	27.4
Germany	81,882,342	1.2	43.8
Ethiopia	79,221,000	1.2	16.9
Egypt	78,200,000	1.2	24.8
Total	4,531,656,009	66.7	

(Source: government data from these countries)

Appendix 3: Five top producers of agricultural products, per product per country

Product	Country #1	Country #2	Country #3	Country #4	Country #5	
Wheat	China	India	USA	Russia	France	1
Rice	China	India	Indonesia	Bangladesh	Vietnam	1
Corn	USA	China	Brazil	Mexico	Argentina	1
Potatoes	China	Russia	India	USA	Ukraine	1
Cassava	Nigeria	Thailand	Brazil	Indonesia	Congo	1
Soybeans	USA	Brazil	Argentina	China	India	1
Sugar beet	France	USA	Russia	Germany	Ukraine	1
Sugarcane	Brazil	India	China	Thailand	Pakistan	1
Cow milk	USA	India	China	Russia	Germany	1
Beef	USA	Brazil	EU-27	China	Argentina	2
Pork	China	EU-27	USA	Brazil	Russia	2
Chicken meat	USA	China	Brazil	EU-27	Mexico	2
Aquaculture*	China	India	Vietnam	Indonesia	Thailand	1
Aquatic plants	China	Indonesia	Philippines	South Korea	Japan	1

1: 2007, Source FAO

2: 2009, Source USDA

*: production of fish, crustaceans, mollusks

References

Advantage Environment, Satellites controlled agricultural machines create environmental benefits, http://advantage-environment.com/livsmedel/satellite-controlled-agricultural-machines-create-environmental-benefits/

Agence France Presse, Calorie switch the key to feeding future billions: researchers, 7 October 2009, http://www.google.com/hostednews/afp/article/ALeqM5gpulRj-fsEKE69LHQW9CV0HK_Efw

AgriLife News, Rod Santa Ana, New shrimp-farming method could revitalize the U.S. industry, 5 January 2010, http://agnews.tamu.edu/showstory.php?id=1625

AgriMarine, Inc., http://www.agrimarine.com/web/pages/technologies.html#

Algae Alliance, Algae Foods, Robert Henrikson, 27 October 2009, http://www.algaealliance.com/algaebiofood.html

America's Heartland – Solar poultry, http://www.americasheartland.org/video/304_5_solar_poultry.htm

American Association for the Advancement of Science, The Last Wild Hunt: Deep-Sea Fisheries Scrape Bottom of the Sea, February 2007, http://www.mcbi.org/what/what_pdfs/LastWildHuntPR_FinalFeb14_2007.pdf?ID=150

Anchorage Daily News, Laine Welch, Fishing Crew Data Program Stalls, 27 March 2010, http://www.adn.com/2010/03/27/1202080/fishing-crew-data-program-stalls.html

Applied Robotics, Solutions in reach | Meat Gripper,
http://www.arobotics.com/products/grippers/Pneumatic/meat_grippe
r.aspx

Asian Institute of Technology, H. C. Warad & J. Dutta,
Nanotechnology for Agriculture and Food Systems – A View, 2005,
http://www.nano.ait.ac.th/Download/AIT%20Papers/2005/Nanotechn
ology%20For%20Agriculture%20And%20Food%20Systems%20_%20A
%20View.pdf

Beijer Institute Workshop, Geoffrey Heal et al., Genetic diversity and
interdependent crop choices in agriculture, 12 September 2002,
http://www.beijer.kva.se/PDF/95031744_Disc170.pdf

BiobasedNews.com, Barney DuBois, Biopesticides: the future of pest
control?, 17 September 2009,
http://www.biobasednews.com/node/23593

BioScience, Vol. 59 No 11, Carlos Duarte et al., Will the Oceans Help
Feed Humanity?, December 2009, http://www.aibs.org/bioscience-
press-releases/resources/Duarte.pdf

BNET.com, E. J. Henten, Robot picks cucumbers in a greenhouse,
September 2005,
http://findarticles.com/p/articles/mi_qa5409/is_200509/ai_n21378645
/

Canadian Institutes of Health Research, Novel Alternatives to
Antibiotics Research Initiative, 27 July 2007, http://www.cihr-
irsc.gc.ca/e/31302.html

Center for World Food Studies SOW-VU, Vrije Universiteit
Amsterdam, Brief no. 3, China' rapidly growing meat demand: a
domestic or an international challenge?, December 2005,
http://www.sow.vu.nl/pdf/Brief%20Feed%20for%20China.pdf

CIMMYT, Hans Joachim Braun, Socioeconomic factors determining
the supply and demand of wheat, 10-13 November 2009,
http://www.cimmyt.org/english/wpp/rainf_wht/yieldWorkshop/docs/
HBraun.pdf

References

CNBC.com, Jim Rogers Buys Land, Starts Farming, 3 March 2009,
http://www.cnbc.com/id/29477080

CNBC.com, Which Oil Producers Are Making Money?, 2009,
http://www.cnbc.com/id/27355967

CNN, Matt Ford, In-Vitro Meat: Would lab-burgers be better for us
and the planet?, 8 August 2009,
http://www.cnn.com/2009/TECH/science/08/07/eco.invitro.meat/inde
x.html

CNNMoney.com, David Whitford, Farming: one way to try and save
Detroit, 29 December 2009,
http://money.cnn.com/2009/12/29/news/economy/farming_detroit.for
tune/index.htm?cnn=yes

Cornell International Institute for Food, Agriculture and
Development, http://ciifad.cornell.edu/sri/

Cornell University, NANOSCALE SCIENCE AND ENGINEERING
FOR AGRICULTURE AND FOOD SYSTEMS, 18-19 November
2002, http://www.nseafs.cornell.edu/web.roadmap.pdf

Department of Agricultural Economics, University College of Wales,
Aberystwyth, UK., T. N. Jenkins, Future harvests: the economics of
farming and the environment: proposals for action,
http://www.cababstractsplus.org/abstracts/Abstract.aspx?AcNo=1991
1887330

Dickson Despommier, The Vertical Farm: Reducing the impact of
agriculture on ecosystem functions and services,
http://www.verticalfarm.com/essay2_print.htm

Ecological Society of America, Ransom A. Meyers et al. Why do fish
stocks collapse? The example of cod in Atlantic Canada, 1997,
http://as01.ucis.dal.ca/ramweb/papers-total/why_do_fish.pdf

European Commission, Adapting to climate change, The challenge for
European agriculture and rural areas, 2009,
http://ec.europa.eu/agriculture/climate_change/workdoc2009_en.pdf

European Commission, Joint Research Centre, Soil Erosion, 22
January 2010, http://eusoils.jrc.ec.europa.eu/library/themes/erosion/

European Environment Bureau, EU soil policy, "From neglect to
protection" The need for EU level legal protection,
http://www.eeb.org/activities/Soil/documents/EEBpositionpaperonaSo
ilThematicStrategy_002.pdf

European Food Safety Authority, Public consultation on the welfare
aspects of genetic selection in broilers, April 2010,
http://www.efsa.europa.eu/en/consultations/call/ahaw100330.htm

European Nanotechnology Gateway, Nanotechnology in Agriculture
and Food, May 2006,
http://www.nanoforum.org/dateien/temp/nanotechnology%20in%20ag
riculture%20and%20food.pdf

FAO Water, Natural resources and Environment Department,
http://www.fao.org/nr/water/infores_maps.html

FAO, Adity Mukherji, Thierry Facon et al., Revitalizing Asia's Irrigation
– To Sustainability meet tomorrow's food needs, 2008,
http://www.fao.org/nr/water/docs/Revitalizing_Asias_Irrigation.pdf

FAO, Biochar: A Strategy to Adapt/Mitigate Climate Change?, 2009,
http://www.fao.org/fileadmin/templates/rome2007initiative/NENA_F
orum_2009/Factsheets/FAO_CCFactsheet_Biochar.pdf

FAO, Food and Agriculture Statistics Global Outlook, 2006,
http://faostat.fao.org/Portals/_Faostat/documents/pdf/world.pdf

FAO, Food For The Cities, 2009,
ftp://ftp.fao.org/docrep/fao/012/ak824e/ak824e00.pdf

FAO, Food, Agriculture and Cities: Where do we stand?, September
2009,
http://km.fao.org/fileadmin/user_upload/fsn/docs/Food%20Agricultur
e%20and%20Cities.pdf

FAO, Grasslands of the World, 2005,

ftp://ftp.fao.org/docrep/fao/008/y8344e/y8344e00.pdf

FAO, How to Feed the World in 2050, High-Level Expert Forum, 12-13 October 2009, http://www.fao.org/fileadmin/templates/wsfs/docs/Issues_papers/HLEF2050_Africa.pdf

FAO, Media Centre, The lurking menace of weeds, 11 August 2009, http://www.fao.org/news/story/en/item/29402/icode/

FAO, Physical and Economic Water Scarcity, http://www.fao.org/nr/water/art/2007/scarcity.html

FAO, Protecting genetic diversity for food and agriculture, http://www.fao.org/Ag/magazine/pdf/angr.pdf

FAO, Soils Bulletin, Alexandra Bot, José Benites, The Importance of Soil Organic Matter, 2005, ftp://ftp.fao.org/agl/agll/docs/sb80e.pdf

FAO, The State of World Fisheries and Aquaculture 2008, Part 4: Outlook, ftp://ftp.fao.org/docrep/fao/011/i0250e/i0250e04.pdf

Farm Industry News, Kurt Lawton, In the year 2013, 1 March 2003, http://farmindustrynews.com/mag/farming_year_3/

Financial Times, Javier Blas, G8 shifts focus from food aid to farming, 6 July 2009, http://www.ft.com/cms/s/0/60720902-6992-11de-bc9f-00144feabdc0.html

Financial Times, Javier Blas, UN to regulate farmland grab deals, 18 November 2009, http://www.ft.com/cms/s/0/be986784-d3a4-11de-8caf-00144feabdc0,dwp_uuid=a955630e-3603-11dc-ad42-0000779fd2ac.html?nclick_check=1

FIS.com, Analia Murias, Amazonia fishery – aquaculture output gains momentum, 15 December 2009, http://fis.com/fis/worldnews/worldnews.asp?monthyear=12-2009&day=15&id=34933&l=e&country=0&special=&ndb=1&df=0

FIS.com, Analia Murias, Microalgae, a promising source of lutein, 14

December 2009,
http://fis.com/fis/worldnews/worldnews.asp?l=e&ndb=1&id=34901

FIS.com, Denise Recalde, Pacific nations establish tuna cartel, 25
February 2010,
http://fis.com/fis/worldnews/worldnews.asp?l=e&ndb=1&id=35669

FIS.com, Denise Recalde, Millions earmarked for fish farms, 12 January
2010,
http://fis.com/fis/worldnews/worldnews.asp?l=e&ndb=1&id=35142

FIS.com, Ocean pollution contaminating China shellfish: report, 12
March 2010,
http://fis.com/fis/worldnews/worldnews.asp?l=e&ndb=1&id=35848

FIS.com, P. Jimmycho, Seaweed farming takes prominence, 30
October 2009,
http://fis.com/fis/worldnews/worldnews.asp?l=e&ndb=1&id=30303

Food Business News, Erik Schroder, Medical cost of obesity
approaching $147 billion a year, 28 July 2009,
http://www.foodbusinessnews.net/news/weekly_enews.asp?ArticleID
=104515

Food Business News, Erik Schroder, U.S.D.A. launches nutritional
web tools, 24 September 2009,
http://www.foodbusinessnews.net/news/weekly_enews.asp?ArticleID
=106129

Food Love: Growing Power,
http://www.youtube.com/watch?v=k39D2myzRFQ&NR=1

Foodstuffs Foodlink, Tim Lundeen, Can corn learn to fix its own
nitrogen? 14 March 2010,
http://www.feedstuffsfoodlink.com/ME2/dirmod.asp?sid=&nm=&type
=news&mod=News&mid=9A02E3B96F2A415ABC72CB5F516B4C10
&tier=3&nid=9BC2B2A411D2439F9060DDE6C2DCBF9E

Friends of the Earth, Out of the Laboratory and on to our Plates,
March 2008,

http://www.foeeurope.org/activities/nanotechnology/Documents/Nano_food_report.pdf

Government of India, Ministry of Agriculture, Department of Agriculture & Cooperation, National Food Security Mission, Operational Guidelines, August 2007, http://www.indg.in/agriculture/rural-employment-schemes/nfsm-operationalguidelines.pdf

Government of Saskatchewan, Bio-Pesticides – The Future of Pest Control?, January 2008, http://www.agriculture.gov.sk.ca/bio-pesticide

Growing Power, http://www.growingpower.org/

Hawaii Oceanic Technology, http://www.hioceanictech.com/

Hilmur Saffell, Ideas From Abroad, Some Old, Some New, 2009, http://www.mayhillpress.com/ideal2.html

Hilmur Saffell, Saudi Arabia: Hydroponics in the middle of the desert, 2009, http://www.mayhillpress.com/arabian.html

How Stuff Works, Bambi Turner, How Hydroponics Work – Hydroponics Growing and the Future of Agriculture, 2008, http://home.howstuffworks.com/hydroponics7.htm

How Stuff Works, Maps of world agricultural employment, http://maps.howstuffworks.com/world-agricultural-employment-map.htm

IDRC (International Development Research Center), Mark redwood, Agriculture in urban planning, 2008, http://www.idrc.ca/en/ev-135185-201-1-DO_TOPIC.html

IFPRI & WorldFish Center, The future of fish – Issues and trends until 2020, 2003, https://idl-bnc.idrc.ca/dspace/bitstream/123456789/29758/1/121861.pdf

IFPRI, Chapter 7, Re-greening the Sahel, Chris Reij, Gray Tappan, and

Melinda Smale, 2009,
http://www.ifpri.org/sites/default/files/publications/oc64ch07.pdf

IFPRI, Chapter 8, Eduardo Trigo, Eugenio Cap, Valeria Malach, and
Federico Villarreal, Innovating in the Pampas, 2009,
http://www.ifpri.org/sites/default/files/publications/oc64ch08.pdf

IFPRI, Chapter 9, Olaf Erestein, Leaving the Plow Behind, 2009,
http://www.ifpri.org/sites/default/files/publications/oc64ch09.pdf

IFPRI, The Other Green Revolution, 30 October 2009,
http://www.youtube.com/IFPRI#p/c/FD9E0158B368FC9C/0/_0FEuGF
XkMw

International Biochar Initiative, http://www.biochar-international.org/

International Energy Agency, Energy Technology Essentials, Biofuel
production, January 2007, http://www.iea.org/techno/essentials2.pdf

International Energy Agency, Statement,
http://www.iea.org/journalists/arch_pop.asp?MED_ARCH_ID=417

IRRI, Press release, 26 July 2006,
http://www.irri.org/media/press/press.asp?id=137

IRRI, Rice Today, Dr. Samarendu Mohanty, Rice Facts – A Look At
India, July-September 2009,
http://beta.irri.org/news/images/stories/ricetoday/8-3/Rice_facts.pdf

IRRI, Rice Today, Savitri Mohapatra, Uganda's Rice Revolution, July-
September 2009, http://beta.irri.org/news/images/stories/ricetoday/8-
3/Uganda's_rice_revolution.pdf

ISRIC, World Soil Information,
http://www.isric.org/NR/exeres/545B0669-6743-402B-B79A-
DBF57E9FA67F.htm

ITIM International, http://www.geert-hofstede.com/

Kraft Foods, Kraft Foods Reduces Global Plant Water Use By More

Than 20% In Less Than Three Years, 10 August 2009,
http://phx.corporate-ir.net/phoenix.zhtml?c=129070&p=irol-
newsArticle&ID=1319159&highlight=

Kuwait Times, Ben Garcia,'Hydroponic saves 90% water over
conventional soil based farming', 28 March 2008,
http://www.kuwaittimes.net/read_news.php?newsid=NTY0NzU3MzE
z

Les Echos, La spiruline, une algue salée "produit miracle" du lac
Tchad, 21 December 2009,
http://www.lesechos.fr/depeches/medecine-sante/afp_00215638-la-
spiruline--une-algue-salee--produit-miracle--du-lac-tchad.htm

Les Echos, Razzia sur les terres agricoles, 18 October 2009,
http://www.lesechos.fr/journal20091019/lec1_1_enquete/0201719412
97-razzia-sur-les-terres-
agricoles.htm?utm_source=twitterfeed&utm_medium=twitter

MacArthur Fellow: Will Allen, 2008,
http://www.youtube.com/watch?v=3EpTWQWx1MQ&feature=playe
r_embedded

Marks & Spencer, Plan A – Doing the right thing – Our Plan A
commitments 2010-2015, March 2010,
http://plana.marksandspencer.com/media/pdf/planA-2010.pdf

McKinsey, Charting our Water Future, 2009,
http://www.mckinsey.com/App_Media/Reports/Water/Charting_Our
_Water_Future_Full_Report_001.pdf

Meat & Poultry, Steve Bjerklie, The evolving role of robotics, 25
September 2009,
http://www.meatpoultry.com/news/weekly_enews.asp?ArticleID=106
172

Meat International, Evegen Vorotnikov, Russian grocery stores face
criticism over quality of meat products, 3 December 2009,
http://www.meatinternational.com/news/russian-grocery-stores-face-
criticism-over-quality-of-meat-products-id2114.html

Meat International, Meat consumption up by 21.3%, 4 December 2009, http://www.meatinternational.com/news/world-meat-consumption-up-by-21.3%25-id2119.html

Meat International, The Netherlands: "Lab" pork created for the first time, 1 December 2009, http://www.meatinternational.com/news/the-netherlands-lab-pork-created-for-the-first-time-id2107.html

Meatpoultry.com, Bryan Salvage, Argentina may have to import beef soon, 11 December 2009, http://www.meatpoultry.com/news/weekly_enews.asp?ArticleID=107935

Milbank Quarterly, Lisa M. Powell and Frank J. Chaloupka, Food Prices and Obesity: Evidence and Policy Implications for Taxes and Subsidies, Volume 87 No 1, 2009, http://www.milbank.org/870109.html

Milwaukee-Wisconsin Journal Sentinel, Karen Herzog, Growing Power will take ideas to Africa, 30 September 2009, http://www.jsonline.com/news/milwaukee/62766677.html

Mint Map: The World's Resources by Country, Ross Crooks, 6 December 2009, http://www.mint.com/blog/finance-core/mint-map-the-worlds-resources-by-country/?display=wide

MITERRA-EUROPE, Assessment of nitrogen flows in agriculture of EU-27, http://eea.eionet.europa.eu/Public/irc/eionet-circle/water/library?l=/copenhagen_freshwater_2/presentations_day2/miterra-europe_2008ppt/_EN_1.0_&a=d

Monterey Bay Aquarium, Seafood Watch Ocean Issues, http://www.montereybayaquarium.org/cr/cr_seafoodwatch/issues/wildseafood_overfishing.aspx

National Geographic, Brian Handwerk, Giant Robotic Cages to Roam Seas as Future Fish Farms?, 18 August 2009, http://news.nationalgeographic.com/news/2009/08/090818-giant-robotic-fish-farms.html

References

National Science Foundation, Press Release 06-171
Mixed Prairie Grasses Better Source of Biofuel Than Corn Ethanol
and Soybean Biodiesel, 7 December 2006,
http://www.nsf.gov/news/news_summ.jsp?cntn_id=108206

New York Times, Astrid Scholz, Ulf Sonesson, Peter Tyedmers, Catch
of the freezer, 8 December 2009,
http://www.nytimes.com/2009/12/09/opinion/09scholz.html?_r=1&src
=tptw

New York Times, Tracie McMillan, Urban Farmers' Crops Go From
Vacant Lot To Market, 7 May 2008,
http://www.nytimes.com/2008/05/07/dining/07urban.html?_r=1&ex=1
210824000&en=9d6a23b0418d45a4&ei=5070&emc=eta1

New Zealand Ministry of Agriculture and Food, Chapter 4 –
Megatrends affecting the sector, 2009,
http://www.maf.govt.nz/mafnet/publications/meat-the-future/mss-
report-09-chapter4.pdf

Norman Uphoff, The System of Rice Intensification (SRI) as a System
of Agricultural Innovation, http://www.future-
agricultures.org/farmerfirst/files/T1c_Uphoff.pdf

Nouvel Obs, Fillon veut-il vraiment vaincre l'algue verte? 21 August
2009,
http://tempsreel.nouvelobs.com/actualites/20090821.OBS8341/?xtmc
=A_levages_intensifs&xtcr=1

Pig333.com, Prashant L. Shinde Byung Jo Chae, Antimicrobial peptides
as an alternative in pigs nutrition, 20 Octobre 2009,
http://www.pig333.com/nutrition/pig_article/1917/antimicrobial-
peptides-as-an-alternative-to-antibiotics-in-pigs-nutrition

Popular Science, Cliff Kuang, Farming in the Sky, 4 September 2008,
http://www.popsci.com/cliff-kuang/article/2008-09/farming-sky

Popular Science, Hilary Rosner, The Future Of Farming: Eight
Solutions For A Hungry World, 7 August 2009,
http://www.popsci.com/environment/article/2009-07/8-farming-

solution-help-stop-world-hunger

Rebecca Chung, Beyond Scarcity: Global Water Crisis, 2008, http://phsj.org/wp-content/uploads/2009/01/beyond-scarcity-global-water-crisis-chung-2008.pdf

Rebuilding global fisheries, 30 July 2009, http://www.youtube.com/watch?v=ZIsl-AkrPmo

Reuters, Jack Daniel, Sardine cannery nationalized, 15 May 2009, http://www.reuters.com/article/idUSTRE54E5P620090515

Reuters, Jack Daniel, Venezuela temporary seizes Cargill plant, 15 May 2009, http://www.reuters.com/article/idUSTRE54E5P620090515

Reuters, Raymond Colitt, Climate change threatens Brazil's rich agriculture, 1 October 2009, http://www.reuters.com/article/environmentNews/idUSTRE59100M20091002?pageNumber=1&virtualBrandChannel=11604

Robotics News, Applied Robotics Announces New Meat Gripper Achieves USDA Acceptance, 22 January 2009, http://www.robotics.org/content-detail.cfm/Industrial-Robotics-News/Applied-Robotics-Announces-New-Meat-Gripper-Achieves-USDA-Acceptance/content_id/1258

Robotics News, Carnegie Mellon Developing Automated Systems To Enable Precision Farming of Apples, Oranges, 20 November 2008, http://www.robotics.org/content-detail.cfm/Industrial-Robotics-News/Carnegie-Mellon-Developing-Automated-Systems-To-Enable-Precision-Farming-of-Apples-Oranges/content_id/1022

S.K. Wall, J. Zhang, M.H. Rostagno, P.D. Ebner. Phage Therapy To Reduce Preprocessing Salmonella Infections in Market-Weight Swine. APPLIED AND ENVIRONMENTAL MICROBIOLOGY, 2010; 76 (1): 48 DOI: 10.1128/AEM.00785-09

Science Daily, Asia Faces Food Shortage by 2050 without Water Reform, 28 August 2009, http://www.sciencedaily.com/releases/2009/08/090817143558.htm

Science Daily, Basque Research Chitosan as alternative to growth-promoting antibiotics for cattle and other ruminants, 18 March 2010, http://www.sciencedaily.com/releases/2010/02/100226093215.htm

Science Daily, Large Reductions In Agricultural Chemical Use Can Still Result In High Crop Yields And Profits, 8 May 2008, http://www.sciencedaily.com/releases/2008/05/080508091947.htm

Science Daily, Massachusetts Institute of Technology (2010, March 23), New approach to water desalination could lead to small, portable units for disaster sites or remote locations, 24 March 2010, http://www.sciencedaily.com/releases/2010/03/100323161505.htm

Science Daily, MIRI Method Reduces Water Use In Rice Field Tests, 23 January 2009, http://www.sciencedaily.com/releases/2009/01/090120143617.htm

Science Daily, Organic Farming Beats No-Till?, 24 July 2007, http://www.sciencedaily.com/releases/2007/07/070722162434.htm

Science Daily, World Wildlife Fund (2007, October 18), Growing More Rice With Less Water, 18 August 2007, http://www.sciencedaily.com/releases/2007/10/071014202450.htm

Science, Worm et al., Rebuilding Global Fisheries, 31 July 2009, http://www.sciencemag.org/cgi/content/full/325/5940/578?ijkey=Pqb NYLoANJflg&keytype=ref&siteid=sci

ScienceDirect, Minghong Tan, Xiubin Li and Changhe Lu, Urban land expansion and arable land loss in China – A case study of Beijing-Tianjin-Hebei region, July 2005, http://www.sciencedirect.com/science?_ob=ArticleURL&_udi=B6VB0 -4CMJCP5- 3&_user=10&_coverDate=07%2F31%2F2005&_rdoc=1&_fmt=high& _orig=search&_sort=d&_docanchor=&view=c&_searchStrId=119097 3608&_rerunOrigin=google&_acct=C000050221&_version=1&_urlV ersion=0&_userid=10&md5=6ce1a3d2a6c1c7e59d0d991cfe040cc3

Seawater Greenhouse Ltd, The Process, http://www.seawatergreenhouse.com/theprocess.html

SIWI, Lundqvist, J., C. de Fraiture and D. Molden. Saving Water: From Field to Fork – Curbing Losses and Wastage in the Food Chain. SIWI Policy Brief. SIWI, 2008, http://www.siwi.org/documents/Resources/Policy_Briefs/PB_From_Filed_to_Fork_2008.pdf

Soil Erosion Site, http://soilerosion.net/

The Comprehensive Assessment of Water Management in Agriculture, 2007, http://www.iwmi.cgiar.org/Assessment/index.htm

The Economist, Agriculture and Satellites: Harvest Moon, 5 November 2009, http://www.economist.com/research/articlesBySubject/displayStory.cfm?story_id=14793411&subjectID=348924&fsrc=nwl

The Economist, Green shoots, Private investment is helping India's farmers in a way government support cannot, 11 May 2010, http://www.economist.com/displaystory.cfm?story_id=15663767&fsrc=nlw|hig|03-11-2010|editors_highlights

The Guardian, Juliette Jowit, Call to use leftovers and cut food waste, 28 October 2007, http://www.guardian.co.uk/environment/2007/oct/28/food.foodanddrink

The Guardian, Tania Branigan, One-third of China's Yellow river 'unfit for drinking or agriculture', 25 November 2008, http://www.guardian.co.uk/environment/2008/nov/25/water-china

The Observer, Richard Wachman, Water becomes the new oil as world runs dry, 9 December 2007, http://www.guardian.co.uk/business/2007/dec/09/water.climatechange

The Pew Charitable trusts, Investing In Our Future: The Economic Case for Rebuilding Mid-Atlantic Fish Populations. 23 July 2009, http://www.pewtrusts.org/our_work_report_detail.aspx?id=54271&category=614

The Sahara Forest Project, www.saharaforestproject.com

TR News 221, July-August 2002, Measuring the Service Levels of Inland Waterways Alternative Approaches for Budget Decision Making, David V. Grier, http://onlinepubs.trb.org/onlinepubs/mb/TRNews221Features.pdf

Trends in Japan, Rice-planting robot, 14 October 2005, http://web-japan.org/trends/science/sci051014.html

UNEP/GRID Arendal, Biodiversity loss: state and scenarios 2006 and 2050, 2007, http://maps.grida.no/go/graphic/biodiversity-loss-state-and-scenarios-2006-and-2050

UNEP/GRID Arendal, Maps and Graphics, 2007, http://maps.grida.no/go/graphic/biodiversity-loss-state-and-scenarios-2006-and-2050

UNEP/GRID Arendal, Philippe Recacewicz, Degraded soils, 2002, http://maps.grida.no/go/graphic/degraded-soils

United Nations, Matleena Kniivila, Land degradation and land use, 31 December 2004, http://unstats.un.org/unsd/ENVIRONMENT/envpdf/landdatafinal.pdf

UPI.com, Chile plans deepwater salmon farm to reverse poor yields, 2010, http://www.upi.com/Science_News/Resource-Wars/2010/01/12/Chile-plans-deepwater-salmon-farm-to-reverse-poor-yields/UPI-20481263313200/?utm_source=twitterfeed&utm_medium=twitter

US Environmental Protection Agency, Agriculture and Food Supply, Climate Change - Health and Environmental Effects, 15 October 2009, http://www.epa.gov/climatechange/effects/agriculture.html

US Environmental Protection Agency, Regulating Biopesticides, 4 December 2009, http://www.epa.gov/oppbppd1/biopesticides/index.htm

US Environmental Protection Agency, What are Biopesticides? 14 September 2009, http://www.epa.gov/oppbppd1/biopesticides/whatarebiopesticides.ht

m

USDA, Economic Research Center, Amber Waves, The Future of
Biofuels: A Global Perspective, November 2007,
http://www.ers.usda.gov/AmberWaves/november07/features/biofuels
.htm

USDA, Economic Research Service, Ethanol and a changing
agricultural landscape. November 2009,
http://www.ers.usda.gov/Publications/ERR86/ERR86.pdf

USDA, Natural Resources Conservation Services, World Soil
Resources Map Index, http://soils.usda.gov/use/worldsoils/mapindex/

USDA, PSD Online, http://www.fas.usda.gov/psdonline/psdHome.aspx

Vertal Ltd, Organic and food waste management,
http://www.vertal.co.uk/default.aspx?m=1&mi=41

VPRO Backlight, Here comes the sun, 21 October 2008, YouTube -
Here Comes the Sun (Rob van Hattum, VPRO Backlight)

Wal-Mart, Agriculture and Seafood, 2009,
http://walmartstores.com/Sustainability/9173.aspx

Wal-Mart, Supplier Sustainability Assessment, 2009,
http://walmartstores.com/download/4055.pdf

Wal-Mart, Sustainability Index Fact Sheet, 2009,
http://walmartstores.com/download/3879.pdf

Wal-Mart, Sustainability Index, 2009,
http://walmartstores.com/Sustainability/9292.aspx

Water Resources Research, Johan Rockström et al., Future water
availability for global food production: The potential of green water
for increasing resilience to global change, 14 February 2009,
http://www.agu.org/pubs/crossref/2009/2007WR006767.shtml

Wikipedia, Agriculture, http://en.wikipedia.org/wiki/Agriculture

References

Wikipedia, Arable Land, http://en.wikipedia.org/wiki/Arable_land

Wikipedia, Cod fishing in Newfoundland, http://en.wikipedia.org/wiki/Cod_fishing_in_Newfoundland

Wikipedia, Erosion, http://en.wikipedia.org/wiki/Erosion

Wikipedia, File:Median age.png, http://en.wikipedia.org/wiki/File:Median_age.png

Wikipedia, Hydroponics, http://en.wikipedia.org/wiki/Hydroponics

Wikipedia, Organoponicos, http://en.wikipedia.org/wiki/Organop%C3%B3nicos

Wikipedia, Overfishing, http://en.wikipedia.org/wiki/Overfishing#cite_note-2

World Future Society, 2009, http://www.wfs.org/forecasts/index.html

World Resource Institute, Grassland ecosystems: Food, forage and livestock, http://www.wri.org/publication/content/8270

World Resource Institute, Grassland ecosystems: Grassland extent and change, http://www.wri.org/publication/content/8269

World Resources Institute, Agriculture and genetic diversity, http://www.wri.org/publication/content/8213

World-Grain.com, Arvin Donley, Brazil's infrastructure challenge, 1 October 2009, http://www.world-grain.com/Feature_stories.asp?ArticleID=106545

World-Grain.com, Chris Lyddon, Black Sea has answer for future grain needs, 1 November 2009, http://www.world-grain.com/Feature_stories.asp?ArticleID=107216

World-Grain.com, David McKee, Feeding the world in 2050, 1 December 2009, http://www.world-grain.com/Feature_stories.asp?ArticleID=107755

World-Grain.com, Leo Quigley, Grain transportation's green alternatives, 1 October 2009, http://www.world-grain.com/Feature_stories.asp?ArticleID=106543

WorldGrain.com, Pakistan: Government decides to launch mechanised rice transplantation techniques, 24 March 2010, http://www.world-grain.com/news/newsfinder.asp?Action=UserDisplayFullDocument&orgId=586&docId=l:1149965439&topicId=14429&start=2&topics=single

WorldGrain.com, USDA experiments with grain harvesting device, 27 August 2009, http://www.world-grain.com/news/daily_enews.asp?ArticleID=105350

WorldPoultry.net, Breakthrough in antibiotic research, 1 April 2010, http://www.worldpoultry.net/news/breakthrough-in-antibiotic-research-7288.html

WorldPoultry.net, Israel: a new approach for layer farms, 1 December 2009, http://www.worldpoultry.net/news/israel-a-new-approach-for-layer-farms-4613.html

WorldPoultry.net, Phage therapy reduces Campylobacter in poultry, 13 October 2009, http://www.worldpoultry.net/news/phage-therapy-reduces-campylobacter-in-poultry-4419.html

WorldPoultry.net, World Nutrition Forum, The Future Starts Now, 8 July 2009, http://www.worldpoultry.net/article-database/world-nutrition-forum-the-future-starts-now-id2090.html

Yanko Design, Agricultural Urbanism by Greg Chun Whan Park, http://www.yankodesign.com/2010/03/16/massive-agricultural-urbanism/

About the Author

Born the son of a butcher and the grandson of a vintner, Christophe Pelletier was destined to food and agriculture. He obtained his Master of Science degree from the Institut National Agronomique Paris-Grignon in France, where he specialized in Economy and Development of Animal Productions. During his studies and versatile professional experience, he has been active in beef, dairy, animal feed and nutrition, pork, poultry and aquaculture. His functions have ranged from scientific and technical support to extension services, Sales & Marketing and senior executive management. Christophe has conducted business on four continents with farmers, traders, wholesalers, leading retailers, and food processors. He speaks English, French, Dutch, German and Spanish.

Christophe created The Food Futurist in 2009, first as a blog dedicated to the future of food production and food supply. The approach of the Food Futurist is to look at trends with a critical mind and without prejudice, nor bias. He is available to speak at industry, government, non-profit organizations and university conferences. He organizes and leads thought-provoking seminars to stimulate critical thinking about future trends, innovation and interactions between food production and demography, economy and environment. Christophe also offers strategic consulting on policy-making for food security, market-driven agricultural development and business organization.

He currently lives in Vancouver, British Columbia, Canada.

More information is available at www.hfgfoodfuturist.com

257

3551672R00152

Printed in Great Britain
by Amazon.co.uk, Ltd.,
Marston Gate.